POWER HUNGRY

POWER HUNGRY

WOMEN OF THE BLACK PANTHER PARTY AND FREEDOM SUMMER AND THEIR FIGHT TO FEED A MOVEMENT

SUZANNE COPE

Lawrence Hill Books
Chicago

Published by Lawrence Hill Books
An imprint of Chicago Review Press Incorporated
814 North Franklin Street
Chicago, Illinois 60610
ISBN 978-1-64160-452-9

Library of Congress Cataloging-in-Publication Data
Names: Cope, Suzanne, 1978– author.
Title: Power hungry : women of the Black Panther Party and Freedom Summer
    and their fight to feed a movement / Suzanne Cope.
Other titles: Women of the Black Panther Party and Freedom Summer and their
    fight to feed a movement
Description: Chicago : Lawrence Hill Books, [2021] | Includes
    bibliographical references and index. | Summary: "Two unsung Black
    women, Cleo Silvers and Aylene Quin, used food as a political weapon
    during the civil rights movement, generating influence and power so
    great that it brought the ire of government agents down on them"—
    Provided by publisher.
Identifiers: LCCN 2021021927 (print) | LCCN 2021021928 (ebook) | ISBN
    9781641604529 (cloth) | ISBN 9781641604550 (epub) | ISBN 9781641604536
    (pdf) | ISBN 9781641604543 (mobi)
Subjects: LCSH: African American women civil rights workers—Biography. |
    African American women political activists—Biography. | Quin, Aylene,
    1920–2001. | Silvers, Cleo. | Black Panther Party. Harlem Chapter. |
    Food—Political aspects—United States—History—20th century. | African
    Americans—Services for—New York State—New York—History—20th
    century. | Civil rights movements—United States—History—20th century.
    | McComb (Miss.)—Biography.
Classification: LCC E185.615 .C668 2021 (print) | LCC E185.615 (ebook) |
    DDC 323.092/2 [B]—dc23
LC record available at https://lccn.loc.gov/2021021927
LC ebook record available at https://lccn.loc.gov/2021021928

Typesetting: Nord Compo

Printed in the United States of America
5 4 3 2 1

To the women whose leadership and dedication to change continues to inspire my work, on the page and off. I hope to have done your stories justice.

To Mayone, Rocco, and Lu, who shared the writing of this book with me in many ways. Thank you for your love and support.

CONTENTS

AUTHOR'S NOTE ON SOURCES

Many of these books are also specifically cited in the text and in the endnotes of this book. But more so, they are texts that can provide additional context, greater detail, and different perspectives on the topics in this book and are adjacent to what is discussed here. These all have informed my work, and I owe gratitude to this work and lived experience.

Basgen, Brian. "The Black Panther Party." Marxists Internet Archive. 2002. https://www.marxists.org/history/usa/workers/black-panthers/.

Blakemore, Erin, "How the Black Panthers' Breakfast Program Both Inspired and Threatened the Government." A&E Television Networks. Last modified January 29, 2021. https://www.history.com/news/free-school-breakfast-black-panther-party.

Boyle, Robert J. "NYC Jericho Movement: Criminalization of the BPP." NYC Jericho Movement, n.d. https://jerichony.org/bobboyle.html.

Bynum, Thomas. *NAACP Youth and the Fight for Black Freedom, 1936–1965.* Knoxville: University of Tennessee Press, 2013.

Carson, Clayborne. *In Struggle: SNCC and the Black Awakening in the 1960s.* Cambridge, MA: Harvard University Press, 1981.

Cohen, Robert. *Howard Zinn's Southern Diary: Sit-ins, Civil Rights, and Black Women's Student Activism.* Athens: University of Georgia Press, 2018.

Collier-Thomas, Bettye, and V. P. Franklin. *Sisters in the Struggle: African American Women in the Civil Rights-Black Power Movement.* New York: New York University Press, 2001.

Collins, Patricia Hill. *Black Feminist Thought.* New York: Routledge, 2000.

Cooley, Angela Jill. *To Live and Dine in Dixie: The Evolution of Urban Food Culture in the Jim Crow South.* Athens: University of Georgia Press, 2015.

Crawford, Vicki L., Barbara Woods, and Jacqueline Anne Rouse, eds. *Women in the Civil Rights Movement: Trailblazers and Torchbearers, 1941–1965.* Bloomington: Indiana University Press, 1993.

Crenshaw, Kimberlé, "Demarginalizing the Intersection of Race and Sex: A Black Feminist Critique of Antidiscrimination Doctrine, Feminist Theory, and Antiracist Politics." *University of Chicago Legal Forum* 1989, no. 1. https://chicagounbound.uchicago.edu/uclf/vol1989/iss1/8.

Farmer, Ashley D. *Remaking Black Power: How Black Women Transformed an Era.* Chapel Hill: University of North Carolina Press, 2017.

Forman, James. *The Making of Black Revolutionaries.* Seattle: University of Washington Press, 1985.

Garth, Hanna, and Ashante M. Reese, eds. *Black Food Matters: Racial Justice in the Wake of Food Justice.* Minneapolis: University of Minnesota Press. 2020.

Hadden, Sally E. *Slave Patrols: Law and Violence in Virginia and the Carolinas.* Cambridge, MA: Harvard University Press, 2001.

Hamlin, Françoise, *Crossroads at Clarksdale: The Black Freedom Struggle in the Mississippi Delta After World War II.* Chapel Hill: University of North Carolina Press, 2012.

Harris, Jessica B. *High on the Hog: A Culinary Journey from Africa to America,* New York: Bloomsbury, 2012.

Harris-Perry, Melissa V. *Sister Citizen: Shame, Stereotypes, and Black Women in America.* New Haven, CT: Yale University Press, 2011.

Jeffries, Hasan Kwame. *Bloody Lowndes: Civil Rights and Black Power in Alabama's Black Belt.* New York: New York University Press, 2009.

Jones, Charles E., ed. *The Black Panther Party [Reconsidered].* Baltimore: Black Classic Press, 1998.

Jones, Martha S. *Vanguard: How Black Women Broke Barriers, Won the Vote, and Insisted on Equality for All.* New York: Basic Books, 2020.

Kwate, Naa Oyo A. *Burgers in Blackface: Anti-Black Restaurants Then and Now.* Minneapolis: University of Minnesota Press, 2019.

Ling, Peter John, and Sharon Monteith. *Gender in the Civil Rights Movement.* New York: Garland, 1999.

Martin, Toni Tipton, *The Jemima Code: Two Centuries of African American Cookbooks*, Austin: University of Texas Press, 2015.

Meister, Franziska. *Racism and Resistance: How the Black Panthers Challenged White Supremacy.* Bielefeld, Germany: Transcript, 2017.

Miller, Adrian. *Soul Food: The Surprising Story of an American Cuisine, One Plate at a Time.* Chapel Hill: University of North Carolina Press, 2017.

Moody, Anne. *Coming of Age in Mississippi.* New York: Bantam Dell, 1968.

Murch, Donna. *Living for the City: Migration, Education, and the Rise of the Black Panther Party in Oakland, California.* Chapel Hill: University of North Carolina Press, 2001.

Nelson, Alondra. *Body and Soul: The Black Panther Party and the Fight Against Medical Discrimination.* Minneapolis: University of Minnesota Press, 2011.

O'Brien, M. J. *We Shall Not Be Moved: The Jackson Woolworth's Sit-In and the Movement It Inspired.* Oxford: University Press of Mississippi, 2013.

Olson, Lynne. *Freedom's Daughters: The Unsung Heroines of the Civil Rights Movement from 1830 to 1970.* New York: Scribner, 2001.

Rhodes, Jane. *Framing the Black Panthers: The Spectacular Rise of a Black Power Icon.* Champaign: University of Illinois Press, 2017. https://muse.jhu.edu /book/49856.

Richardson, A. V. "Dismantling Respectability: The Rise of New Womanist Communication Models in the Era of Black Lives Matter." *Journal of Communication* 69, no. 2 (2019): 193–213. https://doi-org.proxy.library .nyu.edu/10.1093/joc/jqz005

Robnett, Belinda. *How Long? How Long?: African American Women in the Struggle for Civil Rights.* New York: Oxford University Press, 1997.

Seale, Bobby. *Seize the Time: The Story of The Black Panther Party and Huey P. Newton.* New York: Random House, 1970.

Social Justice. ". . . Because He Was Black and I Was White: Six Young Women Discuss Their Various Experiences in the Civil-Rights Movement." Vol. 39, no. 2/3 (1967/2013): 61–74.

Tompkins, Kyla Wazana. *Racial Indigestion: Eating Bodies in the 19th Century.* New York: NYU Press, 2012.

Travis, Brenda, John Obee, Robert Parris Moses, and J. Randall O'Brien. *Mississippi's Exiled Daughter: How My Civil Rights Baptism Under Fire Shaped My Life.* Montgomery, AL: NewSouth Books, 2018.

Twitty, Michael. *The Cooking Gene: A Journey Through African American Culinary History in the Old South*, New York: Amistad Press, 2018.

Umoja, Akinyele Omowale. *We Will Shoot Back: Armed Resistance in the Mississippi Freedom Movement*. New York: New York University Press, 2013.

White, Monica M. *Freedom Farmers: Agricultural Resistance and the Black Freedom Movement*. Chapel Hill: University of North Carolina Press, 2019.

Wilkerson, Isabel. *Caste: The Origins of Our Discontent*. New York: Random House, 2020.

Wolcott, Victoria. *Race, Riots, and Roller Coasters: The Struggle Over Segregated Recreation in America*. Philadelphia, University of Pennsylvania Press, 2012.

The Black Panther Party's Political Education Reading List

Franz Fanon, *The Wretched of the Earth*
Quotations from Chairman Mao Tse-tung
Malcolm X, *By Any Means Necessary*
W. E. B. Dubois, *Souls of Black Folk*
Paolo Friere, *Pedagogy of the Oppressed*

PROLOGUE

On a cool and gray January day in early 2020, I steered my rental car down Summit Street in McComb, Mississippi. I knew it was, during Aylene Quin's time in the 1950s, '60s, and beyond, one of the central streets for Black commerce and social life. But other than a historical plaque honoring this heyday, one would have only thought it another sleepy street in a quiet town. I had the address for her restaurant South of the Border, but only a few buildings had numbers posted on them. So I drove up and then back down the mile or so strip of low apartment buildings and single-story concrete block storefronts, most of which appeared no longer open for business. The most activity was at the car repair shop, where three men, middle aged and older, were out front, inspecting a car that had just pulled in. They had all watched me each time I had passed their garage. And now, as I pulled in and stepped out, they regarded me with curiosity.

"Hello," I said with a smile. "I'm in town researching Mrs. Aylene Quin. She owned a restaurant around here in the 1960s. Do you know where it was?" I pronounced her name A-leen, long *A*.

"Hey, L.D.," the first man, who appeared to be only a few years older than me, called to a gentleman who looked like he was about to get into his low pickup. "She here is looking for info on Mama Quin."

L.D. walked over. "Mrs. Aylene Quin, huh." He pronounced her name with a short *a*, like *apple*. "South of the Border was right there."

He pointed across the street to a two-story building set in the middle of an empty lot with scrubby grass and a gravel parking area. Then he smiled. "You know who you should talk to—my mother. She worked with Mrs. Quin when she was president of the NAACP back in the '60s. My mama was the secretary. She'd tell you stories all day."

"That would be amazing," I said.

"Follow me. I'm headed there now."

Ten minutes later, I was sitting in Mrs. Patsy Ruth Butler's living room. Converted from a garage, the walls were filled with framed certificates and diplomas and photos of family: her granddaughter's college graduation photos and grandson's elementary school picture were hung next to a letter of appreciation from the NAACP.

Before walking in, L.D. had reminded me to greet her with an honorific—"it's Mrs. Patsy Ruth Butler"—and then he opened the door and invited me to sit on her overstuffed couch while he went to find his mother. Mrs. Patsy Ruth greeted me with a hug and a wide smile, and talked to me for over an hour, jumping around a bit in time. "She's ninety, remember!" L.D. said from a hardback chair he sat in across the room, where he mostly listened, a few times adding his own memories of attending the Council of Federated Organizations (COFO) Freedom School or to remind his mom that I was asking about Mrs. Quin. Mrs. Patsy Ruth was generous with her stories—about the men who kept watch for KKK bombings from the roofs of houses and churches, signaling to each other with flashlights and whistles, and about visiting house by house with Mrs. Quin. By the time I got up to leave, she had invited me back to stay with her next time I was in town. Little did either of us know that the events of the year would not allow another trip.

———

I first heard of Aylene Quin when I saw her name in an account of the voting rights efforts in Mississippi, mentioned as a community leader who owned a restaurant that hosted civil rights workers. More research— listening to oral histories, searching books and articles and references— uncovered mentions of her in a sentence or two in many accounts of the work going on in McComb. Because Aylene died in 2001, there was no recording of her voice to be found on the Internet (except for one, eventually unearthed in a surprising place). I finally tracked down a single video recording of her, done by a couple who knew Mrs. Quin from their activism work in the 1960s. But as I spoke to people who knew her, I began to hear a remembered version of Aylene Quin in the stories folks told me. "She was very welcoming." "A force." " She could cook her butt off."

And in the Black History Gallery museum in McComb run by the elderly but spry retired teacher Hilda Casin out of a house on a residential street, there's a large, perhaps eleven-by-eighteen-inch, photo of Mrs. Quin. It's a bit grainy, and I might have thought of her as looking like a kindly grandmother—as she likely was when it was taken. In this photo she wears a blue dress and a long string of beads, metal-rimmed glasses, close-cropped hair, and a satisfied smile. Her daughter Jacqueline says she would pick out a dress pattern and have a seamstress make all her clothes. "Even at her size she was always dressed to the nines." In this photo I could perhaps begin to get a sense of the caretaker she was known for being—she'd never let anyone go hungry, and never accepted money from the activists who worked in McComb. Like so many matriarchs before her and since, ample meals of well-made food meant more than just nourishment, but love, a steadiness. And in the context of so many meals she made for others, it also showed those with a certain kind of power the power that she wielded as well.

Then there's the photo of her printed on a promotional fan for Quin's Motel and Restaurant—her hotel, and one of the few hotels around that allowed Black customers. A clever marketing tool for those who live in the Deep South, its copy offers "Let Us Serve Your Next Club Party" and notes "Mrs. Aylene Quin, Prop." Make no mistake of who was in charge. The photo on its front is of three women who are dressed in evening wear. The one in the middle smiles wide and offers a tray of food to the viewer. Aylene is on the right, in a long, dark, elegant dress with dramatic sleeves and a brooch. She holds an hors d'oeuvre in her hand and looks as though she just took a bite. It looks like a scene from a party, one with good food and laughs. One we'd want to go to.

There's another photo that I also think of often as I read these histories and consider Aylene Quin's outsized, but undersung role in the story of the fight for voting rights and civil rights. It's a picture of her as a member of the newly elected Parent Teacher Association. She's pictured with the other officers, and she's a head taller than anyone else. Her dress is prim, her expression is fierce. Perhaps the photographer caught her in the moment before she smiled. Or maybe she was thinking about what she was fighting for—in that role or any of the many others she undertook in her decades as a community activist. This is a similar expression to what she wears in perhaps the best-known photograph of her, sitting on the Mississippi governor's steps and holding a sign that says STOP POLICE BRUTALITY. Her mouth is set, jaw protruding in a look of defiance.

But how to turn these descriptors into a fully formed, and beloved, person for those who never knew her? These images show but snapshots of a woman who was well known and respected in her community and among those who fought alongside her, but not much more than a footnote in larger historical accounts of the time.

I wonder why there are no oral histories with Aylene Quin, when she's mentioned so often in so many others' stories. Were people not actively recording these histories when she was still alive? Was she resistant? I know she was open to interviewing, as she's featured in a documentary on race made by former Student Nonviolent Coordinating Committee (SNCC, pronounced "snick") workers Jane Adams and Doy ("D.") Gorton, and she gave researcher John Dittmer her time in the 1980s while he researched the voting rights efforts across McComb. Why was so little written about her? Why don't we know exactly what she cooked or have a recording of her own story in her own words asking her to recount more broadly her experiences? Especially because, as John Dittmer, the historian who has written the definitive history of this time, told me, "I could have said practically everything I wanted to say about the civil rights movement in Mississippi and the White response to it and all of that and stayed in McComb, yeah, because it was all there. The whole story was there."

———————

Better known than Aylene Quin's story is that of the Black Panther Party's Free Breakfast for Children Program that fed hungry kids and made them a target of the government while also influencing government policy. Were there ways that these stories might be related?

That same month, I was with Black Panther Party member Cleo Silvers in her Memphis apartment. Her kitchen was full from a recent shopping run—a few bottles of prosecco were on the table for future dinner parties or happy hours, boxes of crackers stacked near the crystal cocktail glasses. She had a variety of salts and spices overflowing from her cupboards. It was the kind of kitchen you knew was stocked and well used by a passionate and skilled cook. And Cleo does love to cook. Chopping vegetables and prepping ingredients was a gesture of love, she tells me. Over the days I spent with her, we cooked and talked—making soup and roasting veggies and putting out appetizers for a small dinner party she hosted when I visited. And she told me of times she cooked for others: for her in-laws nearby in Memphis, where she and her husband Ron had recently settled; for her friends in New York; for the Black Panther Party leaders who came to her tiny Bronx apartment in the late 1960s when she made them fancy French dishes because she could. Because they all worked hard and all loved hard and this was how she was showing her appreciation for the work they were all doing, this was her self-care.

There were magazines and books and CDs stacked near the plush sofa and chairs in the living room. At one point during our conversations that went on for hours during that first day, Cleo commented on how her apartments, from New York to Detroit to Los Angeles, had always had a circular seating arrangement, all the more to facilitate talking, glass of wine in hand, belly full of homemade food, as late as folks wanted to stay. Jazz or R&B or rock 'n' roll playing in the background, like we had as we talked and cooked.

I am eternally grateful to these women, and many other women and men who generously gave their time and energy to tell their stories or that of their family, as well as, of course, for the civil rights and justice work itself. My goal is to honor these stories and amplify them. To find the connections of action and outcome—of what they learned that I can also share with readers and activists today. Much happened during the yearlong research and writing of this book, although its seeds were planted years earlier. There were many echoes of the voter suppression, police brutality, racist attacks, and disenfranchisement of people of color that are written about here—both in the last few years, but also of course never having ceased. White supremacy did not end with the Voting Rights Act or the (supposed) dissolution of the Ku Klux Klan. It remains evidenced in the very fabric of the political and social system in which we live in America, and many of the systemic issues these women fought to correct are still in place.

This is not to say that their efforts in the 1960s were futile—not at all. These activists created much change—political and social—often using tools as common as a hot meal. This gave them power—and was a powerful act in and of itself. Food was a vital way to connect to the communities they helped, and this book will tell the story of their unsung work, so that people might use their model to embrace similar means of empowerment today.

But I will do more than just tell their stories, as civil rights activist Mr. Curtis (Hayes) Muhammad made me promise. He asked me to meet him at a café in a picturesque neighborhood of New Orleans in early 2020, where we sat under the lush foliage of the tree-lined street on a warm winter afternoon. He was impossible to miss in flowing white pants with long hair and a cane, and I waved to him from the outside table I had reserved.

The first thing he asked me was about my activism work. I told him of my efforts supporting my neighborhood schools in a historically Black and underserved neighborhood. I told him that I saw many people, especially after the 2016 election, become more activated around politics and social issues in a way they hadn't been before. I saw people wanting to do something, so they would host benefit dinners or go on marches. And of course I saw value in these things. But I also thought there were more, better ways to create change. And I wanted to find these ways in stories from the past that perhaps well-meaning White or middle-class folks, or those newly activated to work for change, hadn't yet heard. For these readers, I give as much of an overview of history here that isn't often taught in schools, with a focus on these unsung women and those they worked with. But there is no way that I can represent all the moments of the history that undergirds these stories within the space here, and that is one of the reasons I share a bibliography before the book begins, to point readers toward other resources that tell other and related stories in more detail and from different perspectives, adding to a broader understanding and perspective of this period.

But I also am writing this for the people I've interviewed and those they worked with. And for this audience I do hope to do their stories justice. My goal is to help share their message more broadly, honor their work and ideas in ways that haven't reached a larger audience, and also add a layer of understanding that connects these two narratives as complementary and building on each other in a way that has not been told widely before. And the common ingredient here is food—the preparation of it as an act of care, the selling of it as an act of independence, the serving of it as a means of community and communication, the elements on the plate a message of culture and strength.

Mr. Muhammad seemed satisfied with that answer, and he launched into his stories and shared his knowledge, the content of which brought me understanding of how these women's lives from across the country and the decade connected in ways I hadn't before realized. But he also, at the end of our conversation, told me that he was most successful as a civil rights activist and SNCC worker—and that the Black Panther Party was most successful as well—when they listened, really listened, to what those who were most vulnerable said. And so he made me promise to listen and truly open myself to what *the people* have to say. And I needed to do it from the humblest place possible.

So this book *is* to tell the story of the women who created such change and did so using what tools and access and knowledge they had. And their stories are meant to inspire others and honor their work, while also teaching us lessons from the past that might otherwise be lost. But this book is also the continuation of my own education and activism. I'm using the lessons I learned—from Curtis Muhammad, Cleo Silvers, and others—to make a difference beyond the page, as I hope you, dear reader, will as well.

A note on the research and writing:

Not everyone reading this book might know more than a rough sketch of the history of the civil rights movement, while others may have read many of the books on the "Sources" list. Those books certainly go into more detail, mention more moments and activists, and do more political analysis than I do here. But that is beyond my scope. Inspired by the womanist approach to research and storytelling, I am centering the women in this story while giving necessary historical context to understanding the larger story. Do go to these other extensively researched, beautifully written books for more on the important topics they cover in greater depth and with different perspectives.

Although I made the decision to use endnotes in lieu of footnotes to make a more fluid reading experience, I also want to be very clear about attributing the research I used and honor the intellectual and physical efforts of the scholars and activists whose extensive work informed and influenced my own, as well as the ideas and lived experiences of those I interviewed and read. That is one reason I foreground this book with a reading list, and I want to honor the scholars whose work greatly informed mine, especially Black female–identifying scholars.

My decision to emphasize the New York City Black Panther Party chapter was, in part, due to proximity. I live in New York City, and I wanted to research more about my own home, and I have access to local resources. But as I researched more, I came to believe that just as Dittmer said that the story of Mississippi civil rights efforts could be told through the story of McComb, the story of the impact of the Black Panther Party's survival programs could be told through the party's efforts in New York City—as could the story of the government's long and violent quest to stop their work. Some of these stories have been referenced to help add depth to the story I am focusing on here, and the assertions of fact are corroborated in ways I make clear in the endnotes.

Regarding the stories of FBI intimidation and outright violence, many have been recorded in various places among piles of reports and memos unclassified only in the 1970s and later—well after the aggression occurred. And there are some previously unpublished stories as well, in addition to allusions to even more surveillance and intimidation. I strove to honor the wishes of those telling me these stories by not prying for more salacious details when what was already being told should be egregious enough.

For those who have read a great deal about this period, you may note that some of my dates, perspectives, or memories conflict with what you may have read elsewhere, or that what you believe may be key details in the larger story of these people and places during this important time are missing or downplayed. I purposely made the commitment to center voices who have been less often interviewed, read, and memorialized, and it is true that some of these memories have conflicting dates or details than what is accepted as fact in other recountings. I have made every effort to note where there may be conflicting details across sources, but of course have not been able to flag them all. I will, however, say that every word written as dialogue and every scene re-created is based entirely on primary sources. Rare moments of conjecture are based on extensive research and clearly noted.

That being said, I am certain things have been left out—important details, names of meaningful individuals, and even major historical events. Some of these omissions are intentional to center the story on these characters; others are because of a lack of space or a decision not to tell a broader story than what I have here; others still may be an accidental omission—perhaps my research did not uncover those details, or I mistakenly did not believe them important to the story I was striving to tell. To those people, and those stories: I am sorry.

On archives and research in the time of COVID-19:

When I was weeks from finishing an early draft in fall 2020, I was in the (virtual) audience of an academic conference with a panel on silence, including the "silence" of what is *not* included when one researches subjects through various means. This had great resonance with my own research and writing of this project—what I could find in my research, whose voices are centered, how accessible they are to various people and during this unique time, and ultimately what I had to choose to focus on in a single book. My limited access to sources was compounded by lack of archive access and certainly shaped the scope and perspectives represented here, but that narrowing was also probably necessary as I already had to trim from what I had initially wanted to share here because of lack of space.

But one silence I would like to highlight is regarding archives. I was lucky enough to visit some early in my research, which began in earnest in early 2020, but many others remained closed throughout almost all of my time writing, and some that opened near the end were far enough away that travel was unsafe or impractical. I wish I could tell you what I *couldn't* include from not being able to view these archives, but the act of archival research is more of an uncharted journey. I don't know—can't know—what I couldn't find. And it is hard to characterize what details, aspects, or voices are lost from the lack of archive accessibility. I may have just added a few descriptive details from what I found, changing just a handful of sentences in this book, or I might have had a completely different understanding of a major event or claim that I make here. Unfortunately, these silences will persist until the next researcher comes along, and I hope they do.

1

ON A HOT SEPTEMBER NIGHT IN 1964, a bomb exploded under the bedroom of five-year-old Anthony Quin, youngest child of Mrs. Aylene Quin. Aylene was a single mother of four, restaurant owner, and voting rights activist in the small town of McComb, in southern Mississippi, deep in Klan country. It was her daughter Jacqueline's ninth birthday, and after the bomb collapsed the front of the house where she and her brother were sleeping, you could see party streamers and birthday cake through the gaping hole.

This act by the KKs, as they were locally known, would be the reason Aylene Quin was often mentioned in histories of the voting rights efforts in Mississippi in the 1960s: she was active in the movement, fed workers in her restaurant, and her house was bombed. Rarely do we learn more, often less. For anyone who knew Mama Quin, as she was called by the young activists she fed, the idea that she would be remembered for an act of violence committed against her and her family, and not for her many brave actions of community organizing and service to the movement, is a disservice to her lifetime of work.

But the story of why Mama Quin's house was bombed—why she was considered such a threat that her life and those of her children were in grave danger from White men—is the story of Black women's activism. It is the story of persistence in the face of great violence, and of individual civilians wielding what tools were available to fight for Black

Freedom, despite a coordinated and insidious effort by the state and federal government to stop women like Aylene Quin. To tell her whole story, or as much of it as those who knew her remember, is to represent how Mrs. Quin was "fierce" and "generous" and "one of a kind," as her daughter Jacqueline describes her. Her story also shows the power of community organizing (or "activist mothering," as Dr. Françoise Hamlin coined it), of the "bridge leadership" of Black women (which Dr. Belinda Robnett describes), and of the ways she used what roles she had available to her—owning a restaurant and the cooking and serving of food—as a tool for social and political change. But telling her story is also to show the bigger picture of how the many intersectional forces that limited the roles for women, and compounded the discrimination against them, has had a lasting effect on the experiences and perceptions of Black women—and Black women leaders—today. It is only by learning from the past, and not just acknowledging it, that we can begin to move beyond these stereotypes and the social, cultural, and political structures that caused them.

Aylene Quin was known to quote her grandmother and say, "The 4th of July wasn't for Black people . . . in May, that's when we was free." She was likely referring to the month when news of the Emancipation Proclamation reached different areas of the South, May being when the document's resulting legal freedom reached her grandmother, who was living, enslaved, in Mississippi. Born in Walthall County, Mississippi, Aylene gained her own understanding of history from her grandparents, which was likely much different from the propaganda that the White-run schools insisted be taught, and from her own lived experiences. In particular, her politics were shaped early on by conversations about her lineage, which included White (her grandfather's father was his enslaver) as well as American Indian and African ancestry, and by her memories of walking to school in the mud while White kids in school buses passed by. She was struck early on by the blatant inequities: not being allowed to eat in the same restaurants, having to attend different schools with many fewer resources—"I didn't have no books," she said. "I had to study out of my brother's"—and she only completed the seventh grade. Since she was young, Aylene would have conversations with her grand-mother, prompted by watching the relationship between her grandfather and White half sister, who acknowledged their kinship, but whose lives were marked by very different privilege.

In 1943, near the end of World War II, she moved to Biloxi for her first job at the Keesler Army Airfield, where she met other Black people more openly questioning why they were treated as second-class citizens and what they could do about it. There she joined the NAACP and first registered to vote, convinced that a path to creating change meant first changing who held political power. Aylene was just one of many who led the NAACP in rapid growth during the 1940s: membership increased tenfold during the war, and the number of branches in the South tripled. The NAACP's goals at this time were straightforward: they would work within the system to change laws to support Black civil rights and to enforce what laws were already there. They would put pressure on school systems for funding and encourage Black people to register to vote, all to help make the government work in the way it, in theory, was supposed to: liberty and justice for all. Wasn't that what Americans—Black and White—were fighting for across the globe in World War II, after all?

Aylene Quin moved to McComb in 1953 to help her brother with his restaurant, and with her arrival she became one of the only Black registered voters in town, although she was not registered locally. At six feet three, and always impeccably dressed, she stood out among McComb's new neighbors, and folks in her new community took note when she became active in the local NAACP. Not long after she arrived, she took over her brother's restaurant and tavern named South of the Border, after it became too much for him to run both the business and his family farm. She would be the main cook and proprietor, serving gumbo and plate lunches and southern fare, with legal beer (and extra-legal liquor) to help solidify her place in the local Black middle class. These roles would come to define her influence in her new hometown.

In the article titled "South of Freedom" in the August 1971 issue of *Ebony* magazine, there's an image of a young Father Earl Neil standing with another Black Anglican priest and three White priests, all five with black frocks and white collars, in front of a bombed-out church in McComb, Mississippi, in the first days of autumn in 1964. He would spend that week—taken as vacation time from his parish in Chicago—volunteering in McComb in support of voting rights, and he was assigned to sleep at Aylene Quin's bombed house, destroyed the same night as the church. He had arrived the day after the bombing, the cloyingly sweet smell of the nitroglycerin in the dynamite still lingering in the humid air. Why didn't he stay at a home that didn't have the front blown off? The town was running out of folks whose houses weren't firebombed and who were also willing to house volunteers.

Three years after that photo was taken and four before it was published, Father Neil would befriend the founders of the newly formed Black Panther Party in Oakland, California, offer them meeting space, and work closely with them to start their Free Breakfast for Children Program. He knew that the violence Mama Quin and Bobby Seale and Huey Newton were all working against was inflicted by White supremacists—in power through their own manipulation of the ballot or the bullet—on the Black community. He also knew the power of a hot meal: it fed the hungry, yes, but also an ideology. Who provided the food, what food was on the plate, and who it was shared with all represented a political stance and a worldview. Members of the Black Panther Party knew this—especially the women who would come to be leaders in Free Breakfast for Children programs around the country—and before them so did Mama Quin and many other activists. This was, in part, why so many restaurants became both meeting places and sites for protests, why food helped raise both money and awareness for social and political causes, and why the government and others with influence destroyed or withheld food as a means of taking back or hoarding this power.

The bombing of Mama Quin's house, in part as punishment for feeding both White and Black activists, can be seen as the moment when momentum shifted in the fight for Black voting rights in McComb and around the state, although there would be plenty of fighting left to do. How did the bombing of the home of a single mother and restaurant owner become such an important moment that spurred political and social change? Let's start by clarifying the story of what would become the land on which these bombed houses—of worship and of living—fell to the ground.

———————

Mississippi's state capital of Jackson, about an hour north of McComb, was so named in honor of the man who brutally altered the state to serve White landowners, at the great expense of enslaved people and Native Americans. Andrew Jackson was beloved by the White establishment for his role in the Battle of New Orleans in 1815, and both before and after he flexed his military prowess he was elected to Congress and became a wealthy plantation holder and enslaver, before being elected president of the United States in 1829. His presidency, considered rather favorably by most mainstream (White) historians, was noted for creating the "spoils system," which gave plum jobs to supporters after winning an election, and for the Indian Removal Act, which forcefully took land from Indigenous people and banished them to unfamiliar reservations farther west. Ironically Jackson's presidency ushered in what has been called the "Age of the Common Man," as he was seen as the first "self-made" man to become president. Of course it is rarely examined how much of his alleged successes were stolen from efforts and resources of enslaved and Indigenous people. He was the first American politician to have widespread support despite bankruptcy and rumors of bigamy, not to mention slave ownership and wartime murder. Apparently the "common men" liked a lawbreaker if it meant that he promised to make laws that benefited them—no matter that Jackson would also profit handsomely.

That land that is now the state of Mississippi still homed Native Americans until 1828, with European colonizers staying near the Gulf Coast until the newly created state and federal government conspired to push these First Nations from their land. This theft was legalized with two State Law Extension Acts that extended state power over tribal land and made it illegal for Indigenous tribes to practice their own culture, while also striving to use this eradication of culture to manipulate them into giving up their land.

In 1830 Jackson signed the Indian Removal Act that forced the Chickasaw and Choctaw from lands within the colonizer-determined

borders of the state of Mississippi and the Cherokee, Creek, and Semi-
nole Native American tribes, from elsewhere around the South, to cede
their land east of the Mississippi River, ostensibly for "suitable" land
farther west. This land was never found or agreed on, and any supposed
agreement between Native nations and the American government was
not honored as settlers from the East quickly occupied Native land.
Starting in 1831 the forced relocation of Native nations along the Trail
of Tears killed thousands who were made to travel from their ancestral
land to land set aside in present-day Oklahoma. Treacherous weather,
disease, and poor living conditions contributed to the death toll. Like
so much of the history of European colonization of Native land and
the enslavement of Africans, not only are few details of these stories
taught to kids in history class, but also they are often whitewashed, and
false narratives of peaceful coexistence or of the noble White settler or
"master" are told in place of the truth.

In 1832 Mississippi adopted a new state constitution, with changes
made, in part, to pressure resisting Native tribes to leave the state. It
also eliminated property requirements as a prerequisite for voting or
running for office and allowed for almost all state officials to be decided
by popular vote. But of course, the vote wasn't "popular" at all. Only
White men were eligible, and this new voting requirement brought more
together under a shared goal of hoarding political power. Any sense of
the "democracy" that was fought for in the American Revolution was
a farce.

By the end of 1833, most members of Native tribes in what is now
considered Mississippi were forced to cede their land to the government
to make way for the state to become the highest-grossing cotton pro-
ducer in the country, an industry built primarily by enslaved Africans,
whose numbers grew by nearly 200 percent during the next decade. One
figure counts one hundred thousand enslaved people entering the state
that decade, many coming from the Natchez slave market in the southwest of the state, which made the city of Natchez at that time the fourth
wealthiest in the country behind New York, Boston, and Philadelphia.
Much of the great wealth that would establish the southern aristoc-
racy from which social, political, and economic power would spring
was taken in the form of land and labor and life from Indigenous and

Black people, which has continued to dictate the wealth gap today and affects access to opportunities and resources.

The government was not by the "people's consent," nor were its inhabitants "equal" as the United States Constitution declares, and as Mississippi demonstrates perhaps more starkly than any other state. Rather, White men with guns used that firepower to steal land and enslave people and then wrote laws that solidified that ill-begotten power, despite the fact that for much of this time they were outnumbered by Native Americans and Black people who were denied political or social agency. The state of Mississippi was built by and for relatively wealthy White men, who grudgingly gave up some rights to less wealthy White men in the mid-1830s to solidify their nexus of power. This political jockeying established the mentality that political power was both scarce and finite—people should hoard what they can, for as long as they can, and use it to advance their own interests as egregiously and forcefully as possible.

In 1861 Mississippi was the second state to secede from the United States and join the Confederacy, clearly stating that the defense of slavery was a primary reason. This wasn't a surprise—enslaved people outnumbered Whites in the state: 437,000 to 354,000. On many plantations in the Deep South, those in power deliberately kept national news and Civil War updates from enslaved people as much as possible, which was often slow to reach the South regardless. Most Confederate fighters were poor, young, and rural, and despite a draft system implemented, the wealthy were often either exempt or could pay someone to take their place, prompting the Civil War to be called "a rich man's battle but a poor man's war."

There was also a prevailing belief among many Confederate soldiers, especially as the end of the war grew near, that the North was their "oppressor," and they rued returning to their hometowns "without support," as a letter from a soldier lamented. He went on to bemoan that "no monuments will be erected" for the fallen Confederate soldiers, whom he called "martyrs of liberty." If only his fears had been founded. Before the war was even over, what would become the enduring narrative of White supremacy was being sown into revisionist history and hypocritical victimhood, at the continued expense of Black Americans.

Of course, we know that monuments were erected, and the need to continue to oppress to feel "free" would pervade both social norms and official policy making for the next century and beyond.

The Reconstruction era in Mississippi that followed the Civil War, with its majority Black population and previous heavy reliance on the unpaid labor of enslaved people, shaped the unfolding events. While the United States Congress established a Freedmen's Bureau to help ensure that the civil rights of formerly enslaved people were upheld, their task was easily and frequently undermined. The assistant commissioner of the Freedmen's Bureau himself noted the defiant attitude among White Mississippians in the months after the war. He wrote, "Wherever I go— the street, the shop, the house, or the steamboat—I hear the people talk in such a way as to indicate that they are yet unable to conceive of the Negro as possessing any rights at all. . . . [They] will cheat a Negro without feeling a single twinge of their honor. To kill a Negro they do not deem murder." In her powerfully argued book *Caste*, Isabel Wilkerson explains this as the solidification of an American caste system, in which Black people are given the lowest possible status in our country's society, deliberately seen as less human than higher-caste White people, to ensure their continued dominance. This social force, she argues, had scarcely changed a century later.

Despite this White defiance in the years immediately following the Civil War, Black Americans became active in local and national politics. Beginning in 1867, branches of the Union League, which encouraged Black political activism, spread from the North and through the South. Black and White Americans stood side by side for the first time in state constitutional conventions, and during this time sixteen Black men were elected to Congress and many hundreds more to state and local offices. In Mississippi—while there was federal oversight of the new voting and citizenship laws for Black Americans—the state elected two Black senators, and there were high levels of political involvement among the newly free Black populace.

However in 1877 when Reconstruction ended (which was part of a political compromise to keep the relatively liberal ruling party in the White House) and federal troops (and thus oversight) left the South, White supremacy was quick to grasp control again through violence, intimidation, and economic sanctions. The latter form of manipulation was through threats by White employers—who still controlled most wealth and land in the South—to fire, evict, or refuse to hire or adequately remunerate Black people who didn't adhere to White supremacist social norms. It was during this time as well that many White supremacists would practice their tactics from beneath a pointy white hood as members of the rising numbers in the terrorist group the Ku Klux Klan.

The White men who still controlled most government offices instituted various legal measures to suppress Black voters, and thus Black legislative power: poll taxes that had to be paid for two years prior to being allowed to vote, literacy tests, and other measures quickly diminished the percentage of Black men able to vote from 90 percent during Reconstruction to less than 6 percent by 1892. Along with these draconian voting laws came Jim Crow laws that restricted nearly all areas of life for Black people in the South. Mississippi enacted twenty-two such laws, the last in 1958, that ranged from mandating segregation to disallowing Black jurors to criminalizing marriage between people of different races. The oppression of Black people persisted legally and under the threat of violence, with little recourse. Mass media reinforced the perception of Black people as lower social status or caste, notes rhetoric scholar Jane Rhodes. She references a study done in the 1940s that calls southern newspapers the "greatest single force in perpetuating" stereotypes of Black people, which also served to dehumanize and segregate them on the page while reinforcing these perceptions and actions in real life.

Those who ascribe to the people's history, as Howard Zinn has called it, will acknowledge that the stories recorded and elevated are primarily those of men, and especially White men, even as efforts more recently have been made to find and tell the stories of people of color and women. It would be easy to dismiss patriarchal influence as the reason women's contributions, even among new retellings of history, are still often overlooked. It's true that women were less likely to hold official positions of power or leadership, and for many decades, they were banned from holding elected office and ostensibly shut out from accumulating wealth, although some women—particularly White women of higher status—found ways around this.

But it is also important to reframe what we think of as power and influence to understand the role of women as leaders—especially in the Black community. Dr. Martha Jones notes that "slave society did not mirror the gender conventions of the white world" and that during slavery Black women had long been "spiritual leaders" until Emancipation. But when formerly enslaved people were integrating into the dominant White culture, gender roles became more pronounced, particularly in the church, where women continued to be seen as "spiritual guides" but were often shut out of formal leadership. Further, the Civil War reinforced gender stereotypes as combat would help to define manhood for Black males, while Black women "reconstructed their identities as wives and mothers."

Black feminist scholar Patricia Hill Collins further notes the forces that robbed Black women of formal and informal social, political, and intellectual power. During enslavement and beyond, they were relegated to domestic work like cooking and child-rearing to serve the dominant caste and perpetuated stereotypes of Black women as "mammy" or "jezebel" while being denied literacy and education. Yet Black women have long been leaders within their community without having to hold jobs with community status, and without formal schooling, while breaking free of the stereotypes that pervade mainstream—White—media. Maria W. Stewart, who was Black, was the first American woman to lecture on politics in the 1830s—and even then encouraged Black women to use their role as mothers for political activism, as well as in communities of women. Thus, Collins and others have argued, what may not look like leadership or "power" from the dominant patriarchal and capitalist perspective actually holds much sway within communities that do not necessarily accept this way of thinking as the default. The power of community organizing, which requires skillful leadership but is at its heart putting power into the hands of the people, is starting to take a more central role in understanding how history was shaped—and who helped shape it. And Black women were often leading this change, as they are today in the current reframing of these roles.

When Aylene Quin arrived in McComb, she wanted to register to vote. While she had been registered in Biloxi, she had to pay her poll tax again for two years and wait to take the new, more onerous poll test that was put into law in the mid-1950s in Mississippi. "So I started paying my poll tax, I talked to some of the ladies about it . . . and some of them wasn't interested in it . . . but I kept talking to people," Aylene said. She would even take other community members' taxes to pay as well, bringing back a receipt, until she was finally eligible to take the test. "And they gave me an application to register, so when I filled it out, they told me they would notify me in thirty days, and they said I didn't pass. And then I went back again and I didn't pass again. So I didn't give up."

The poll test had as many had as many as twenty-six questions to answer, with questions given at the whim and discretion of the poll registrar. One infamous section gave the registrar the choice in assigning the hopeful voter what section of the state constitution to "copy and interpret," and the registrar alone could determine if the response was satisfactory. Notoriously an easy section would be given to White applicants—such as "ARTICLE 12 Section 240. All elections by the people shall be by ballot"—and judging done with great leniency. However, a Black applicant would be given a difficult section, perhaps even one on which even legal scholars disagree:

> ARTICLE 7 Section 182. The power to tax corporations and their property shall never be surrendered or abridged by any contract or grant to which the state or any political subdivision thereof may be a party, except that the Legislature may grant exemption from taxation in the encouragement of manufactures and other new enterprises of public utility extending for a period of not exceeding ten (10) years on each such enterprise hereafter constructed, and may grant exemptions not exceeding ten (10) years on each addition thereto or expansion thereof, and may grant exemptions not exceeding ten (10) years on future additions to or expansions of existing manufactures and other enterprises of public utility.

Often, no amount of preparation or studying could help a Black prospective voter pass the test. Incensed at these discriminatory practices that she hadn't faced in Biloxi, Aylene Quin soon befriended local movement leaders like Webb Owens and C. C. Bryant and helped to increase local NAACP membership by over 50 percent in the mid-1950s.

Aylene was inspired to join the Pike County NAACP not long after she arrived in town, in part because, she said, "I was tired that the children couldn't go to certain places, and I knew that wasn't right." When her older daughter was six she remembered "that she would want to go into the restaurant, and get a Coca-Cola. But if I wanted to go in I had to go in the back door. So I never did go in this restaurant. . . . And she wanted to ride the horse outside . . . and she couldn't ride the horse. Different things like that." Aylene wanted to fight for a better world for her children.

But this work was dangerous, she noted years later. "If you were a member of the NAACP you kept it kind of a secret. If you had any kind of a job or anything you couldn't let it be known." Yet this didn't daunt her. Aylene's restaurant soon became a hub of social and political activity. Black business owners had a specific kind of power in the community, something that didn't escape Mrs. Quin. They were much less affected by financial sanctions from the White community—they wouldn't lose their jobs, for example, because of their activism—and could more readily create wealth and offer opportunities to others in the community. While often enough these businesses paid rent to White landlords, some were generally satisfied to allow a successful financial relationship to continue, like Aylene Quin's. But there were also numerous examples of White property owners kicking out paying tenants as retribution for attempting to register to vote, known activist activity, or for any reason—or no reason—at all. There was generally the same tenuous financial relationship with businesses like beer distributors or other industries that required Black entrepreneurs to engage with overwhelmingly White owners or managers. Black business owners like Aylene Quin would anchor a burgeoning Black middle class and would bring and keep economic power in their communities, including the means to support those in need and influence social activism—but there were still financial pressure points that could be exploited by White authority if they wanted to punish or subjugate a successful Black business.

Owning a restaurant was among the businesses most accessible to Black women (beauty shops being another, and Aylene Quin would open one of those too). Feeding people was a historically acceptable role for a woman, and owning a restaurant allowed a woman proprietor to be seen as an expert and boss more readily within her community and beyond, although there were still many barriers to women owning and running any business. Further, restaurants were among the few places where Black people could convene without scrutiny (church was another, although many sought to both stay apolitical and preserve their property as threats and violence increased), and that is why so many became meeting places for activists and hubs of the Black Freedom Movement. But it also made these business owners particularly vulnerable to the ire of Whites who were incensed by examples of Black success. McComb was well positioned to support a number of Black businesses, despite its relatively small size and location in the bull's-eye of where some of the most virulent White supremacist terrorism had historically taken place.

The town of McComb was born, apocryphally, because railroad baron Colonel Henry Simpson McComb wanted to house his workers on the southern end of the Illinois Central line as far away from the sin and vice of New Orleans as he could. Established in the late 1870s, the town itself lies almost exactly one hundred miles directly north of the Big Easy and coincides with the maximum distance allowed by union regulations for train crew relief. So crew could reside in McComb but work out of New Orleans. While a Main Street of McComb housing city hall and White businesses was created early on, many Black residents lived in the neighborhoods of Baertown or Burglund on opposite ends of town, and Summit Street in Burglund became a hub of businesses largely owned by, and catering to, Black residents. Besides South of the Border, there were juke joints and pool halls along Summit, and famous blues musicians would regularly come through. Bo Diddley was born in McComb in 1928 and was no doubt influenced by the town's spot on the "chitlin circuit," hosting many legends, including Muddy Waters, Louis Armstrong, and B. B. King, among others, at clubs within blocks of South of the Border.

Summit Street and the surrounding neighborhood had almost everything the community needed, including a supermarket and butcher shop, various restaurants, beauty parlors, shoe repair, and a cleaner, with the high school nearby. With many Black residents working for the railroad for union wages, which were higher than what was offered by many other White bosses, there was more money to support local Black-owned businesses, as well as capital to open their own. Houses were mostly low-slung and close together, and much was within walking distance. While McComb didn't differ greatly from other similarly sized towns in many ways, it was not a town built around growing cotton and housed relatively more Black residents who were less beholden to the whims of individual White bosses, although Whites certainly did control much of the local land and wealth, and all the elected offices and police force. None of this was lost on Aylene Quin, and she used her role as restaurant owner to further her work in the NAACP to support voter registration, seeing these facets of her community involvement as intimately connected.

––––––––

McComb wasn't the only town around the state seeing increased activism in the 1950s. In the Delta, in the northwest corner of the state, there was greater poverty, with a majority of Black residents working as sharecroppers on plantations. Their numbers had been dwindling in the previous decade, however, due to increased mechanization in farming and migration north and west after returning World War II soldiers saw opportunity elsewhere—and an escape from the deep racial oppression of their youth. But not everyone could leave, or wanted to. In Clarksdale, Black business owners again took the lead in local activism, and a local chapter of the NAACP was active in voter registration despite fierce opposition from local Whites. Beauty shop owner Vera Pigee, born to sharecropper parents, would be among the local leaders during that decade and beyond who would also use her position as a local entrepreneur to support community activism—feeding and housing people at her salon and heading the local youth chapter of the NAACP. Scholar Françoise Hamlin examines Vera's approach to activism as "activist mothering—in which mothering became an organizing tool, harnessing youthful energies and shepherding them (hopefully safely, down constructive paths)." This is one framework that helps illuminate why so many women doing traditionally gendered caretaking work have been unsung for their contributions to what is often called, simply, "the movement."

Of course Mississippi was far from the only place around the country where activism was brewing—and more often than we read in history books, women were on the forefront and often wielding power through roles that were traditionally seen as feminine and that extended their influence well beyond the dining table or beauty chair. Many people have been taught that the Montgomery bus boycott in 1955–56—the first major desegregation action in the country—was started by Rosa Parks, with much of the planning and organization credit given to Dr. Martin Luther King Jr. However, the boycott was largely planned and supported by a group of female activists prior to Dr. King's involvement, and a majority of those who enacted the boycott were women. It was they who regularly took the bus to their jobs around the city, often as domestic workers and cooks—that is, to perform women's work.

And it was women who did much of the work to provide the necessary resources to sustain the boycott. Only recently have the women who made food to both feed activists and financially support them begun to get their due. Their efforts in the kitchen were about so much more— it was women's organizational and financial support and sacrifice and fortitude that were instrumental in ensuring the boycott was successful. And successful it was. They achieved their immediate goals of desegregating public transport but more so inspired a nation of activists. It is easy to blame the perspective of those recording it as the reason so many Black women were overlooked in histories of the civil rights movement, but the reality is that these omissions are also deeply rooted in racist stereotypes and the ways that patriarchal White dominant culture imposed its own values and hierarchies on Black culture.

Yet while civil rights activism in Alabama and other states received more national attention, Mississippi rarely made headlines in the same way, in part because of the historically tight grasp of White supremacy in power. Up through the 1950s, larger-scale, effective Black Freedom actions had been largely absent from Mississippi, partially because of the state's effort to uphold White supremacy through laws, yes, but even more so through violence and intimidation. In essence, it was especially dangerous to be an activist in Mississippi.

Furthermore, at the moments when public policy and opinion were turning in favor of desegregation—such as with the ruling of *Brown v. Board of Education* in 1954, which ostensibly desegregated schools around the country—the Mississippi state government passed laws to undermine federal laws in anticipation of future federal policy toward civil rights. This ruling had a ripple effect around the South—and the country. In many places White leaders and citizens notably ratcheted up efforts to oppress the local Black population through new laws meant to reinforce segregation or through economic or violent intimidation. And the mainstream media coverage reflected this racist anxiety as well: through op-eds and articles in the White section of newspapers, once-segregated newspapers were dealing with the first major legal challenge to their White supremacist way of life. White public sentiment can be tracked through editorials around the region that expressed outrage, mixed in with some calls for acceptance. But in Mississippi, the vitriol around this court decision was used as an excuse to double down on racist rhetoric and practices. Rhodes writes, "A study of Mississippi newspapers found that while their editorial responses ranged from 'outright defiance to cautious acceptance, the latter usually followed by a quick reversal.' . . . The tensions—and violence—playing out in the towns and cities would be echoed in the press."

Local laws and elected and appointed officials in Mississippi were also heavily influenced by the creation of White Citizens' Councils (also known simply as Citizens' Councils), which were created as a more publicly palatable organization of White supremacists who convened initially to oppose school desegregation. Stocked with many former Ku Klux Klan members who often also held professional and influential roles in the community (the Klan had effectively disbanded in the state more than a decade earlier), these councils had an outsized effect on local policy and affected laws up to the level of the statehouse. They exercised their power in myriad ways, including passing a bill requiring that the state library buy books on White supremacy and passing a statute that made "nonconformance with established traditions [and] customs" of the state an arrestable offense, leaving interpretation open to local White leadership.

The McComb Citizens' Council included the town's mayor among its members, along with local attorneys and business owners who met at the local White high school and Pike County courthouse. It was the kind of role that men boasted about in reelection campaigns and obituaries. It was no secret to Aylene and the Black activists in McComb how the local government officials and law enforcement upheld the White supremacist views of the council since many of them were active members.

In May 1956 newly elected governor James Coleman signed a bill that created the Mississippi State Sovereignty Commission (MSSC), whose noted charge was to "do and perform any and all acts and things deemed necessary and proper to protect the sovereignty of the state of Mississippi, and her sister states" from "encroachment . . . by the Federal government." While ostensibly this was about states' rights, written with purposely racially neutral language, the commission's goals were clear: to use what power it had to halt desegregation, voting rights reform, and other efforts to uphold basic civil rights for Black Mississippians.

The formation of the MSSC was supported by the political power of White Citizens' Councils around the state, and its members were appointed by current state legislators with the governor as the de facto head. The MSSC consisted of three branches: executive, public relations, and investigative, and how these were used changed with each governor. Its purview through Governor Coleman was initially focused on creating a public narrative of Mississippi as happy segregationists with little racial strife, but by the next governor's term in 1960, it would realize the power of its investigative arm.

By 1960, most Black activists around Mississippi were persisting in small, local actions, primarily around voter registration. While it is quite likely that the fiery Aylene Quin might have galvanized almost any neighborhood in which she lived, that she had come to McComb meant that she met other dedicated leaders like C. C. Bryant and she would become a part of a dedicated group of local activists. In the coming years she would show herself stalwart in the face of some of the worst White supremacist terrorists in the state, in arguably the most violently racist state in the country. She would come to lead against the violence and intimidation aimed at her, her family, and her community—often from across the dinner table.

2

AT 4:30 PM ON MONDAY, February 1, 1960, four Black college students dressed in coats and ties walked into the Woolworth's in Greensboro, North Carolina, purchased some essentials at the store's single checkout, and then sat down at the stainless steel counter in the restaurant a few feet away. As a White waitress approached from behind the counter, one of the four politely ordered a coffee.

"I'm sorry," the waitress replied, "we don't serve Negroes here."

The young man replied, "I beg to disagree with you. You just finished serving me at the counter only two feet away from here."

The waitress became angry and demanded the four order from the segregated stand-up counter. "You won't get any service here!" she said. But still they sat, occupying just four seats among the sixty-six spread out along the L-shaped counter.

Once she walked away, a young Black woman who worked there came by and hissed, "You're acting stupid, ignorant. That's why we can't get anywhere today." But still the men stayed seated. They sat until Woolworth's closed, only about an hour later at 5:30 PM. The store manager told his employees to just ignore them—that was official policy from the Woolworth's franchise, which had anticipated this day. Police and local journalists were called, but nothing was done and the four left out of the side door.

The next day more than thirty college students arrived at 10:00 AM and took seats along the counter. The waitress ignored their occasional requests for service, while serving White patrons seated next to them. Reporters were on hand as well, taking photos and interviewing students who declared they were ready to come every day for years until they were served. The students sat for hours, and then left.

The next day there were more activists than seats, taking up as many as sixty-three of the sixty-six chairs at one point, with a line quietly waiting to sit down if someone were to get up. White students came by to express solidarity—and local Ku Klux Klan showed up, spouting threats.

By Friday, White students from a nearby women's college sat with the growing number of Black students in solidarity—and local Whites also sat down in a counterprotest. Police and reporters were on hand—this had become a national story—and the presence of the White college students incensed the counterprotesters. One was arrested for trying to light a Black student's coat on fire, and others were removed for yelling insults and epithets, prompting a White observer to comment that the activists "would take things nobody would take."

The students called a stalemate by Saturday, with negotiations promised, but soon they inspired demonstrations and sit-ins in cities like Nashville that bordered northern states. It would take months—until July—for Greensboro's lunch counters to desegregate, with other cities desegregating over the course of 1960 as well. The sit-ins worked. The effect may not have been immediate, but they ignited activism among young people, who saw this kind of direct action as something they could take part in and as something with more immediate effects than allowing lawsuits to meander through a White supremacist system.

That it happened at lunch counters seemed appropriate as well. A relatively new innovation, lunch counters made dining out more accessible to working-class White people, many of whom relished what they saw was an elevated status over the excluded Black population, no matter their ability to pay. And while segregation was ostensibly established to keep races separated, at restaurants where Black chefs cooked the food and Black waiters served it, there was no actual separation. Also, as scholars Angela Jill Cooley and Grace Elizabeth Hale argue, the fact that Black customers could walk through the restaurant to spend their money at the register, or eat the same food from the stand-up window, further demonstrated that this outrage at desegregated eating was really about reinforcing the caste system, especially around an act as seemingly "intimate" as touching food to one's lips. Many parents, like Aylene Quin had said, wanted to shield their children from this dehumanization. But its prevalence at a store selling necessities made it impossible.

That spring of 1960, the venerable civil rights leader Ella Baker brought a room of eager young Black activists—many of whom were inspired by the sit-ins of the previous few months—to quiet. "Ladies and gentlemen," she intoned. "What's the worst state for Black people in the whole United States?"

"Mississippi!" was the resounding chorus, as civil rights activist Curtis Muhammad tells the story. It was the state that had long held a well-earned reputation for White brutality and violence, because of its relatively spread-out smaller towns, economic strife, and swaths of land that left many folks geographically isolated.

Ella said, "Now you gotta realize we've been here for almost four hundred years. And we done had a movement ever since we've been here." She knew these students were hungry for dramatic actions, and she wanted to pull them back from what she knew were their ideas of dramatic direct action. "I know many of you are from some of the quote-unquote best schools in the country. So when you do go into rural areas, don't go in there thinking you are going to lead the people. Find out what the people want."

Ella Baker—who some say had oratory skills that could rival Dr. King's—was helming the first meeting of the Student Nonviolent Coordinating Committee (SNCC), a group she founded to help focus this passion for change. There was murmuring and excitement—many recognized the authority and experience of Ms. Baker: she had been the director of branches of the NAACP and had, essentially, invited them here to make plans on how to support the movement that they could feel growing in intensity and breadth. She famously said this fight was "bigger than a hamburger!" The sit-ins were about being able to eat at the lunch counter but also, of course, about so much more. This was also about breaking down the caste system.

Ella Baker was also looking for her next big project. At age fifty-six she had established herself, believing that everyone had a skill or idea to offer and focusing on community organizing through interpersonal relationships. In her previous decades of quiet leadership, she had had a hand in motivating key court cases, such as *Brown v. Board of Education*, and she had helped to plan and support actions like the Montgomery bus boycott. Ms. Baker had traveled around the Deep South in the 1940s through her work in the NAACP, shaking hands at beauty parlors and holding meetings at churches, all to help organize local communities to work together to fight for civil rights. It was in this work that Ms. Baker learned the power of connecting with individuals, noting how a quiet woman commenting on the similarities in their dresses after a meeting demonstrated a moment where they could relate to each other, and Ella could perhaps help this woman find her own agency. And although she was one of many Black women leaders working in the civil rights movement who brought a mix of nurturing and community-organizing experience to help create real change, she was among the relative few in formal leadership roles that have been recognized by history.

Ella Baker had created SNCC initially as a temporary coordinating group of other student activist groups, and had gathered them, as was her leadership style, to allow the students to come to their own decision about what they should focus on next in the ongoing fight for civil rights. But it is with SNCC where we see Ella Baker wanting to do more than what she had done with the NAACP. She wanted to support the local efforts of folks like Aylene Quin, for she believed that there would be lasting change only if these eager students involved and deferred to the local leaders. And while she did not know Aylene Quin personally, the two women shared a philosophy. Both were ready to move beyond local efforts, valiantly pioneered by the stretched-thin NAACP members, whose numbers were dwindling as a result of the increasing violence and intimidation around the state since *Brown*. Ms. Baker would set the plan in motion from her director's role with an army of student activists ready to act, and Mrs. Quin readily supported the crew that would come to her in McComb in one of SNCC's first major campaigns.

Robert Parris Moses was also activated by the Greensboro sit-ins and would soon come to be a leader within SNCC. He grew up in Harlem, in New York City, and attended the prestigious Stuyvesant High School, Hamilton College, and then graduate school at Harvard—all places where he felt like he was treated as an exception as a high-achieving Black student. He has noted that he felt accepted by his mostly White classmates and instructors—he was even elected class president in high school—but for the most part he wasn't engaged in broader civil rights efforts in the 1950s. Bob dropped out of Harvard to help support his family, and returned to the Bronx to teach at the selective and private Horace Mann School. There he began to more deeply consider the struggles of Black America beyond his own experience. In one pivotal moment in 1959, recounted in his biography, Horace Mann alumnus and activist Allard Lowenstein spoke at the school of the need to establish the right to vote in communist Europe. Bob discussed with a colleague how Black Americans should be afforded the same rights. His colleague responded, "That's different." This response—and its implications in the lack of willingness of even seemingly liberal White Americans to support civil rights efforts—began to change Bob Moses's thinking.

Soon after, in early 1960, Bob read a *New York Times* article about the four college students staging daily sit-ins in Greensboro, North Carolina, and felt drawn to their work, which married the local and the national. He felt that they were making a real difference. That summer he headed south to join the Southern Christian Leadership Conference (SCLC), helmed by a young Dr. Martin Luther King Jr.

At the SCLC offices in Atlanta, Bob was tasked with office work, and it was there that he met Ella Baker and found that she was similarly inspired and planning a new group to harness this passion for change. They connected over their shared belief that this form of direct action was inevitable and necessary. The NAACP had helped usher in legal changes outlawing some segregation, but many businesses openly ignored the law, and there was no willing institution that would take on enforcement. Young people, particularly in southern cities farther north, were ready to act. The actions in Greensboro—and then Nashville and other cities soon after—directed the movement away from the SCLC and

NAACP's law-focused efforts, which appeared to many to be stalled in the face of White resistance in towns and cities across the South.

Dissatisfied with his initial charge to lick envelopes, Bob Moses left the SCLC not long after leader Ella Baker did and followed her to SNCC. She found him willing to travel around the South on his own dime, tasked with finding out what the people wanted SNCC to help them with. She gave him a handful of names of local community leaders from around the South whom she had met from her previous work with the NAACP. She said, "You tell them who you are and what you've been doing. And ask them what can you do to help their movement," emphasizing that he would be taking the lead from what had already been happening, not bringing in his own ideas before they were asked for.

That summer of 1960, Bob Moses traveled as SNCC's first field coordinator around the Deep South—primarily Alabama, Mississippi, and Louisiana—with a goal to plan future actions there. On Bob's travels through Mississippi in particular, he was struck by the realities facing Black people in the state. Community leaders often slept with guns by their sides, aware of the present threat posed by White supremacists angry at their work. Few of the realities of the violence against Black people in the South were widely reported in the North, and what Bob heard from local activists was sobering. White police regularly harassed Black people and were known to arrest and beat community members of almost any age or gender for any perceived misstep of local racist, dehumanizing mores. White terrorists—who were just as likely professionals from town as good old boys from the rural outskirts—made harassing phone calls, shot at houses in nighttime drive-bys, or fired or evicted Black citizens for known civil rights work. There was a constant fear of physical or economic retribution for, as Wilkerson labels it, daring to defy the caste expectations of being Black in America, particularly in the Deep South. Police ignored reports of illegal activity and were as likely to be involved as merely complicit through their inaction.

While most White people have been brought up to believe that the police force works to protect them, the history of police departments is actually rooted in White supremacy and based on slave patrols and night watches that were created to control the actions of Black, Indigenous, and other people of color. Sally Hadden details this history in *Slave Patrols* and notes that police departments in the South evolved from "early fascination, by white patrollers, with what African American slaves were doing. Most law enforcement was, by definition, white patrolmen watching, catching, or beating [B]lack slaves." After Emancipation the police force would continue to be staffed primarily by poor, White men who relished the authority that came with this role after feeling left out of other economic and social power structures—and this pattern of harassment, violence, and racial profiling persisted. This dynamic has continued to the modern day, coupled with the enduring stereotypes perpetuated by media and propaganda, of Black people as lawless and in need of keeping "in line," as Hadden writes.

As he traveled across the Deep South, Bob Moses met with various leaders, asking how he and SNCC could support their existing home-grown efforts. Again and again, voting rights was the response. Bob Moses also learned that only 5 percent of Black Mississippians were registered to vote, and fewer than half of that group were able to exercise that right because of fear of violence or retribution. One leader he connected with was Amzie Moore, who owned a service station and restaurant in the Delta and served as president of the local NAACP chapter. He had long been engaged in working for voting rights and desegregation locally and had deep connections among other people in the state doing the same. Mr. Moore shared Ella Baker's philosophy of change making: he had already been focused on increasing voter registration and even tried to start his own "citizenship school." He and Mr. Moses discussed Mr. Moses's return the following summer of 1961 to help him continue this work.

Bob Moses brought his research back to SNCC and returned to finish the last year of his teaching contract at Horace Mann. But he knew he wanted to continue his work in the South when his contract was over. He had asked local leaders like Amzie Moore and the people they served what they had been doing that they wanted his help with, just like Ms. Baker had asked. Locals around the South had told him about the brutality at the hands of the locally elected White sheriff, and their frustration with the state's unwillingness to take any steps toward federally mandated school integration. These issues, and many others that affected their daily lives, were created by officials who were elected to office and had been working for nearly a decade to suppress the power of Black voters. These local Black people believed they were not fully citizens unless they were able to exercise their right to vote.

As SNCC sought to determine its priorities between the fall of 1960 and summer of 1961, some SNCC members advocated for voting rights efforts, believing this was the path to change and a will of the local people, while others wanted to continue direct action campaigns. Ella Baker shared the findings with the gathered group of young student activists: that the people of Mississippi wanted the activists' help fighting to exercise their legal right to vote. A fight ensued. Some said that it didn't make any sense. Curtis Muhammad remembers decades later, "It was obvious that we were gonna have to start with literacy. It just seemed to be too painstaking."

Other student activists wanted SNCC to focus on direct action, like the sit-ins some of them had been doing in other parts of the South and the planning of the Freedom Rides. "Miss Baker finally, with her little sweet self, she listened," as Curtis tells the story. "Then finally she said, 'Well, why don't you have two arms—one for direct action and one for voter registration.'" She would later say it was one of the very few times she would make any special effort to influence, truly believing these efforts should be student initiated and run.

By the summer of 1961, most SNCC members were well underway planning and supporting the 1961 Freedom Rides across the South, which were direct actions testing the new outlawing of segregation on interstate travel. But Bob Moses was among the few who wanted to head back to Mississippi. He was originally going to return to the Delta, but Amzie Moore wasn't ready for him and sent Moses the contact information for Pike County NAACP president C. C. Bryant instead. And when Bob arrived in McComb in July, he sat down for the first time with Aylene Quin.

Bob Moses was the first SNCC worker to arrive in McComb on July 10, 1961, with a goal to start meeting the community and set up voter registration classes, with a few more volunteers to join him after the Freedom Rides concluded. C. C. Bryant was happy to welcome Bob to help with the efforts he and Aylene Quin and other local NAACP members had been engaged in to help increase voter registration numbers around Pike County.

C. C. Bryant was a longtime NAACP officer in McComb, a Sunday school teacher at Society Hill Baptist Church, and a one-time union president. Working for the railroad as a crane operator during the day, he was also a licensed barber and operated a shop next to his house on Friday evenings and weekends. His barbershop was a social hub, as well as a central port of information and organization around voting rights efforts.

Whenever the shop was open, it was filled with people talking about issues from the day, sharing information, and creating a sense of community. It was well stocked with important Black and mainstream publications like *Ebony*; *Jet*; the NAACP's magazine, the *Crisis*; the *Chicago Defender*; and *Time*. Mr. Bryant received many of these magazines through his work on the railroad: Black railroad workers had an informal system of passing magazines among themselves as they moved through the country, sharing information and news from state to state. And C.C. was an avid reader, sharing what he read with those who stopped by, as well as with his children around the dinner table.

While the barbershops were typically a place for the men to gather, at C. C. Bryant's place, women and children were frequent visitors as well. His daughter Gladys remembers that the kids would play in the Bryants' yard, or someone would be sent to buy fried fish from a favorite local spot like Mama Johnnie's on a Friday night. And the more people who came by, the more who had access to what was often referred to as a "library" of reading material on Black culture and civil rights. Teenagers and adults alike would come for a haircut and receive an education at the same time, through the reading in the waiting area or the conversation with Mr. Bryant himself. He recruited teens for the NAACP Youth Council and spread the word of citizenship schools.

Joe Martin, who was around the same age as C.C.'s daughter and son, Curtis, remembers reading the books and magazines even as a young teenager while waiting for his hair to be cut. "So I got involved with the NAACP Youth Council at a very early age, around ninth or tenth grade," he says. "I was informed about the struggle long before it got here through books and local people." As Ms. Baker had warned the student activists, there was much happening in these small towns. It was their job to listen and honor local leaders, and Bob Moses spent plenty of time in C.C.'s barbershop doing just that.

The Pike County NAACP branch, operated out of McComb, had been active for decades, but White intimidation had recently forced it underground. Ella Baker herself, when working with the NAACP, had authorized Pike County's charter when interest surged after World War II. McComb only had about twenty-four interested members, and a charter required fifty. But in 1944 Carsie Hall, president of the Jackson branch, wrote to Ms. Baker requesting that she make an exception for Pike County because of their passion for change. Sixty-three people would eventually form the charter membership later that year. C. C. Bryant would be elected president in 1954, a role that, he told his granddaughter Judith, was "very, very dangerous." He would later describe a scene to his family that inspired him to take on that treacherous role when no one else would. One evening while walking home from church, he saw a young Black man, who appeared drunk, being beaten by two law-enforcement officers. It then became clear that the man was disabled and couldn't stand up straight.

C.C. intervened and told the policemen to "stop beating him like that!"

"Shut up, or we'll beat you too," they replied.

"No, you won't," he retorted in a fit of bravery. Despite the threat, the officers left the man alone, and C.C. made up his mind to continue to fight such abuses, in part through his work in the NAACP.

———

Much of the NAACP's work was already focused on voter registration, and women like Mrs. Quin were an important part of their strategy.

Mrs. Quin and other local women like Patsy Ruth Butler would go door to door during the day, when many women were home and the men were working, to invite them to the NAACP's voter registration classes and encourage them to try to register. They weren't always well received. Folks expressed fear of what their White employers or other White townspeople would do to them when they found out they tried to register. Scholar Belinda Robnett warns against thinking about the Black community as a monolithic bloc, as they weren't all "eager to join the movement or even knew about the movement. Particularly in rural pockets of the South, any media coverage portrayed the movement as Communist backed" propaganda perpetuated to suppress civil rights efforts. Others, like the Black waitress at Woolworth's in Greensboro, thought that aggressive action was just inciting White backlash and delaying progress.

But people remember Aylene using her big personality and visibility as a local proprietor to her advantage. She knew a lot of local people through her restaurant, and others through the school her children attended. Scholars Robnett, Hamlin, and Collins all provide perspective on how to view her leadership—she was seen as a leader by others within her community, but her strengths and contributions were not fully recognized beyond it. People trusted her, and she became a "bridge leader," as Dr. Robnett defines women with informal but important and influential roles in making the movement accessible to their communities. But she also exerted leadership through her own reclaiming of—and expansion beyond—the roles Black women were long relegated to in dominant society. She knew the fears and desires of the mothers and the financial challenges of supporting a family— and could use these mutual interests in her favor, perhaps convincing other women to at least check out a meeting. She was a person where "if anybody was running for office they had to get her endorsement." At the same time, she would be the one to feed and support someone who was ill or in need, telling her daughter, Jacqueline, "to go take Mrs. so-and-so a plate."

With Mrs. Quin as a periodic officer, the Pike County NAACP did other community work in addition to their voter registration efforts. It used its leverage to support causes that were important to the community, such as increased funding for schools (one statistic has Pike County spending less than a dollar per Black student versus more than thirty dollars for each White student), buying new playground equipment, or making sure broken streetlights were replaced. C. C. Bryant was close with Medgar Evers, the Mississippi state field secretary for the NAACP, and both were also connected with the organization at a federal level, doing work like putting pressure on the federal government to enforce new desegregation laws. Strategies for change were discussed and organized among NAACP members at the local, state, and national levels, and Mr. Bryant was calculating in using appropriate legal actions to fight for change.

When Bob Moses arrived, he drew on the advice of Ella Baker, and planned to embed himself in the town, helping to support what was already happening. Something was bubbling, he knew, since McComb had 250 registered Black voters at that time. This seemed inconsequential in electing antisegregationist candidates, considering that the town of more than twelve thousand was around one-third Black, but seeing that in five of thirteen nearby Mississippi counties that were over 50 percent Black there were no Black registered voters, this felt like a groundswell of activism. C. C. Bryant had invited Bob Moses to McComb, hoping his presence and organizational efforts would help feed their existing efforts. Bob Moses would stay with the Bryant family, and he used much of his small stipend from SNCC to print informational material that they often prepared and disseminated at Mr. Bryant's barbershop. Within a few days of Bob Moses's arrival, Mr. Bryant took him around McComb, introducing him to the local community leadership, including a stop at South of the Border. In order for this work to be successful, Moses needed the support—financial and otherwise—of the local community.

They could probably smell what Aylene Quin was cooking before they reached the restaurant's front door. C. C. Bryant introduced Bob Moses and explained that he was there to help their collective mission of increasing voter registration. Aylene would have offered them food—perhaps her black-eyed peas that she slow-cooked for days, or her renowned macaroni and cheese or gumbo. She was known for her homestyle plate lunches and dinners and seafood, and since Mr. Bryant didn't drink, they likely sat at a table in the restaurant section of South of the Border, rather than at the bar that ran much of the length of one wall. Mississippi was a dry state, even in the 1960s, where only beer was legally available, although where to find bootlegged liquor was well known—and South of the Border was just one of a number of such spots.

Bob Moses explained that he would be there for a few weeks and then a few more SNCC workers would be joining him. They would set up citizenship schools to go over the voter registration process and practice the questions on the poll test. He was about to start going door to door to invite folks to come to the classes and encourage them to try to register. When C.C. was at work, Bob Moses would go out with Doc Owens to knock on doors. Aylene and C.C. and other NAACP members had been doing similar work for years, but she was excited at the new energy and resources, and said she was pleased he was "starting to get things going—that's just what I wanted to do."

Bob Moses assured her that he wasn't there to tell folks what to do: he wanted to work with Aylene and C.C. and other local community leaders to support their ongoing work in whatever way he could. He didn't have his own agenda.

"Whenever any of these SNCC workers come by," C. C. Bryant told her, "you feed 'em, you feed 'em whether they got money or not." Of course Aylene would feed them—that's what she did. And then she went back to work.

———

Moses began working with Doc Owens, who was known as Super Cool Daddy. Doc was an older man who walked with a cane, and he was never seen wearing anything other than a dapper suit. He had a weak eyelid and wore glasses with a hook that held the eye open, creating what Bob described as "a kind of a fish-eye that looked out at you." Financially independent from business conducted in Illinois, he was the NAACP treasurer and was deeply trusted with financials and other matters in the community.

When Bob Moses first arrived, Super Cool Daddy would pick him up from the Bryants' house each morning in a taxi, and they would visit community members "of substance," as Moses recalled, to solicit donations. "I described it—voting, and what we were doing, and talked to them about SNCC." Owens would ask them for a five- or ten-dollar donation, which would be used to house and feed Bob and a few more SNCC workers who would be arriving shortly. Moses acknowledged the importance of building on the work community leaders had already begun: "You couldn't have gotten a project like that off the ground . . . if you didn't have someone in the community that the people could trust."

The presence of Bob Moses and the specter of the Freedom Riders across the state made a difference in the town, as he and local activists canvassed McComb, drumming up interest in the voter registration classes that would begin on August 7. Young people in particular were interested, Bob recalled, remembering them looking at him in awe saying, "There goes a Freedom Rider." The SNCC workers who had chosen the direct action arm in the meeting the previous fall had worked with the Congress of Racial Equality (CORE) to organize and plan the Freedom Rides, sending groups of White and Black activists on bus rides around the South starting in May 1961, sitting together in the front seats that were still often illegally reserved for White riders only, refusing to move. Often they were met by angry mobs, police conspicuously absent, who would demand that they move, beating many of them. When police did arrive, they often arrested riders for breaking laws like disturbing the peace, disobeying an officer, or trespassing if Black riders tried to use "White" facilities—developments all covered by local and national news. Although the Freedom Riders only totaled a few dozen volunteers—many would leave wills and letters for loved ones, truly believing they might not return alive—they created a nation-wide crisis as federal and state officials conflicted over how to keep the peace. This ultimately taught SNCC the power of how a few can truly upend the status quo, if they are willing, and was a critique of the federal government for hypocrisy, as Clayborne Carson writes, "for failing to act forcefully to achieve civil rights goals at home while proclaiming democratic values abroad."

Within a few weeks John Hardy (recently released from notoriously treacherous Parchman prison along with other arrested Freedom Riders) and SNCC worker Reginald Robinson joined Bob in McComb. More SNCC workers—Chuck McDew, Marion Barry, and Charles Sherrod—arrived a few weeks later. They set up voter registration classes at the local Masonic Hall at night and went door to door during the day, encouraging people to attend classes and explaining how to register. At each receptive house, they would detail the process of going to the registrar, who would give them the poll test and a form to fill out. The registrar would then let them know if they had passed. The classes they were offering would show them examples to help them feel comfortable.

While the SNCC workers were in town, they did as they had been taught by Ms. Baker—they integrated themselves into daily life in the town as well as they could. D. Gorton was a White SNCC worker who grew up in northern Mississippi but was sent to Americus, Georgia, before he arrived in McComb, because of fears that White supremacists would "decide to blow my mother's house up." Gorton explains that when SNCC workers first arrived at a new place they would start to "open up the town." The first place they would go would be the local restaurants—a barbecue joint, maybe, or a restaurant like South of the Border—"because there was only two kinds of folks that had money there that were entrepreneurs. One was undertakers, and the other one was the cafés and restaurants." Once the local restaurant owner knew the Freedom Riders were in town, word spread fast. And if you had the support of these social connectors and community leaders, then you could move with much more ease. In McComb, Aylene Quin's assistance was not hard won. She welcomed the SNCC workers with open arms, never charging them for food and offering what other resources she could.

But the danger from local White supremacists was visceral. Bob had been harassed since his first day in town, and the calls to the Bryant household, threatening the work C.C. had been doing with the NAACP, only increased with Bob under his roof. It became so treacherous, particularly for the local activists, that Mr. Bryant wrote a letter to friend and NAACP colleague Medgar Evers on August 7 explaining the difficult position they were in. In it, he assured Mr. Evers that the local chapter was supporting the project, "however we feel that it would be injurious and unwise to say so publicly. We are telling the public that the Student Nonviolent Coordinating Committee and the Southern Christian Leadership Conference is sponsoring the project. The students are supplying the manpower and SCLC is helping some with the finances." Violence and threats had driven many NAACP chapters to close, and Bryant didn't want that to happen in McComb.

But this hesitancy to fully align with SNCC came from other tensions as well. SNCC was considered radical and willing to work outside the law. The NAACP fully understood that President John F. Kennedy's administration didn't approve of the Freedom Riders, thinking that these actions angered White southern leaders and distracted from Kennedy's priorities on civil rights efforts, and they wanted to keep working relations positive with the president. It was the NAACP's desire to keep gears moving at the federal level that led them to a relatively conservative stance on direct action on the ground, which also created tension between the NAACP establishment and the SNCC revolutionaries. The relative few who could bridge these divides were local people, like Aylene Quin, who had long been—and continued to be—active in their local NAACP chapter while still supporting the more ambitious actions of the young activists.

The voter classes the SNCC workers began were ostensibly to familiarize folks with the voter registration test and help them study for it. They went through copies of the state constitution, sent by SNCC, and practiced filling in answers. But they also discussed the psychological aspects of attempting to register: to go directly to the registrar with a neutral expression, not to react to slurs or attempts to provoke. Of the twelve local residents who attended the first class, ranging in age from youth to elders, four traveled to the county seat in Magnolia and took the test on August 8, and three passed. Two days later another three took the test and two passed. It was a small victory, but a win nonetheless. And one that White residents began to notice. On the third day, nine people went to Magnolia to register. Only one passed, and the McComb *Enterprise-Journal* published a story about the sudden interest of Black residents trying to register.

Brenda Travis, a high school student whom Bryant had recruited to be the president of the NAACP Youth Committee and who had been helping Bob Moses canvass for voting rights, believed that what was likely meant as a warning to the White people in and around McComb became an inspiration to the Black population. They continued to attend classes and express interest in expanding efforts beyond McComb in Pike County to neighboring Amite and Walthall Counties where there were zero Black registered voters.

Brenda Travis, at sixteen years old, was too young to vote but would become a pivotal figure in McComb's fight for Black independence. Her home was a stone's throw from C. C. Bryant's, and one of her first memories of local civil rights activities was of Mr. Bryant talking about voting rights at their church. She was brought up as the middle of seven children by her mother and grandmother—her father had to leave the state because "even years after his original outspokenness it was still too dangerous for him in Mississippi" (presumably because he angered dangerous local White supremacists)—and occasionally extended family members, in a household that didn't much discuss civil rights in the 1950s. Until *Jet* magazine's story on the lynching of Emmett Till, when Brenda was ten. In her memoir Brenda remembers her family talking about his death and her mother gazing at his picture and saying, "He was just a boy, just a boy."

Some friends were traumatized by the story and the accompanying photos of Till's open casket; others had parents who used it as a moment to teach the fraught lesson not "to step out of line [or] you might be the next person whose death photo would appear" in *Jet*.

Brenda remembers that she and her friends "could see ourselves and our siblings in those pictures." She knew then that she would do something with her life to work to fight these forces. It wasn't until the summer of 1961 that she had an idea of what that might be.

Brenda remembers spending "every waking hour that summer at the Masonic Temple or canvassing the community" with the SNCC workers who had come to join Bob Moses to support voter registration in McComb, as one of their first initiatives of this kind. They trained Brenda and the other mostly young volunteers to "talk to the people about the importance of registering to vote, how the vote could liberate them, and the steps necessary to go about registering, including the oppressively burdensome constitutional interpretation requirement." Brenda recruited some of her friends to join as well, and she would canvass the Black neighborhoods, sometimes alone, so hopeful about change that she continued despite the number of people who would "turn away or retreat into their homes, or just plain tell us they didn't want to fool with this registration business. We knew these reactions were because fear reigned supreme."

In addition to voter registration classes, SNCC volunteer Marion Barry also taught nonviolent resistance and direct action techniques at the Masonic Hall. In these classes, Brenda and other young activists did a lot of role-playing, putting attendees into situations where they might expect violence, such as at a bus station or a sit-in at a lunch counter. They were taught to walk in with their head held high, and not to react to the expected jeers or physical retaliation.

"We were instructed not to react in a self-defensive manner but to accept as a given a violent attack for the audacity of us trying to break down what belonged only to Whites," Brenda Travis recalls. Class leaders would role-play angry White bystanders while Brenda and others learned to curl themselves into a ball to attempt to protect their head and vital organs. Brenda and other youth from the town, including Curtis Muhammad and Hollis Watkins, studiously attended the classes, and they steeled themselves for another lesson Marion taught them: that they had to be prepared to go to jail if they engaged in direct action.

Among the now-released documents from the Mississippi State Sovereignty Commission are comprehensive reports of SNCC's time in McComb in 1961. The five-page report identifies Bob Moses and other SNCC workers, lists some of the locals in McComb who attended the voter registration classes, and gives details about the local meetings hosted by SNCC and the NAACP, noting that "Aylene Quin attends every NAACP meeting there and always sits in the front row." The report even cited the presence of the FBI at some of these events. While some planning meetings were in secret because of the fear of retribution, "mass meetings" that were designed to be inclusive of the larger community couldn't be. And numerous reports noted the many police, FBI, or White supremacists who stationed themselves outside the meeting place, or perhaps even stood close enough to listen in, generally with a goal to gather information to report to others and intimidate.

The author of one such report, A. L. Hopkins, writes in his cover letter to attorney and MSSC member Aubrey Bell from the Mississippi Delta, "I sincerely hope this information will be beneficial to you." Aubrey Bell was known for wearing French cuffs, quoting Shakespeare, and throwing lavish parties in Greenwood, notably the state headquarters of the White Citizens' Councils, which also held a contest for high school students, offering a $1,000 cash prize for the best essay on the "moral necessity of segregation." It was clear that Mr. Bell and the rest of the MSSC were keeping tabs on the work in McComb and elsewhere in the state with the help of local informants and were in contact with local police and the KKK. These groups were known to share information and likely assured local police that the governor wouldn't interfere with their campaign of intimidation and violence.

Clearly the MSSC knew that Bob Moses was in contact with John Doar from the Justice Department, who was sympathetic to civil rights efforts and was in frequent contact with the NAACP and Black leaders to help fight back against illegal retribution from White supremacists around the South in what ways he could. In a letter, Mr. Doar emphasized, "In the event there are any economic or other reprisals against citizens of Mississippi who attempt to register to vote or against citizens who peacefully aid or encourage others to register to vote, you should immediately report this to the nearest Federal Bureau of Investigation Office and call me at my office in Washington."

Mr. Doar wouldn't know for years that the FBI would have been of little use to Bob Moses even if he had called them.

3

ON REPORT CARD DAY IN McCOMB, students from the local school would walk down the street knowing they were expected to proffer their grades to whoever asked.

"Girl, let me see that report card," a friend's parent or elder might ask, "'cause I know you did us good." The Burglund neighborhood, home of the Black high school, was a close-knit one. On the south side of the railroad tracks, kids might play jacks or jump hopscotch for a while, but when they got together, they would mostly just talk about the world around them. Their social life revolved around the church, school, and each other's houses—and because of segregation, all the teachers, pastors, and community elders lived nearby, strengthening the support system of elders who had a vested interest in these teens' success. If one family had food, so did their neighbor. And despite the many obstacles that Black teenagers of the late 1950s and early 1960s faced in the American South, Jackie Byrd, who was among these teens, felt that she and her friends were taught to hope that change would come and that they might be a part of it.

This optimism existed in spite of, and even because of, the injustice and violence of the day. Many of these parents also didn't shy away from talking about the issues, discussing even the most painful and gruesome headlines around the dinner table. In 1955, when Emmett Till was murdered and his mother insisted on an open casket, most parents did the same as Brenda's mother: they shared the newspaper stories and images, seeing this as a moment to help their children learn what they needed for their freedom and safety. Jackie Byrd, who was a classmate of Brenda's, says it was a defining moment for her understanding of the realities of race in America. For many folks leaning toward activism, the murder of Emmett Till became a turning point.

It was a moment when the White media began to take notice of what Black people had long known—that it was dangerous, even deadly, to be a Black person in America—and especially in Mississippi. This kind of senseless and racially motivated violence was not new, but the media coverage was—and it affected Black and White audiences across the nation in varying ways. Many Black activists remember this as the moment of their childhood when they became more fully aware of the violence and White oppression that affected Black communities, especially in the South. For White people, this was a wake-up call to violence and oppression they had long been able to ignore. And major newspapers like the *New York Times* began to realize the importance of telling stories from the South and around the realities of segregation and race-related violence, sending a group of reporters in 1956 to "Report on the South," an effort that resulted in the highest sales of a single weekday issue in the paper's history. But with a cadre of almost entirely White (and male) reporters, there was still a great lack of stories about Black people that weren't about race or law enforcement.

Because of this expanding media coverage, after Emmett Till's murder, momentum toward larger-scale activism grew as people around the country who weren't affected by racial violence finally began to grasp that Black people could hardly move through the world without fearing that the wrong sidelong glance, or merely everyday actions, could result in the torture and murder of a child.

That was what the kids talked about with each other. They talked about world events, and how to achieve the professional successes they wanted in their lives. When a parent went out to buy books—and buying books was necessary since Black children were banned from the town library, and many had read everything in their school collection—they bought different books from what their neighbors had, sharing all the titles. And the kids read. They read everything on the shelves—even the set of encyclopedias that two teachers on their block owned and offered to anyone in the neighborhood. And these teenagers, including Jackie Byrd, her brother Jerome, Aylene's daughter Carolyn, C. C. Bryant's daughter Gladys, Brenda Travis, and others, felt confident about community support and had an optimism—even an expectation—that they would be the generation that would create change.

So when Bob Moses came to town in the summer of 1961, they were already primed to see themselves as agents of change. They had also heard of the sit-ins in Greensboro that had so activated Bob Moses and the venerable Ella Baker. They were also inspired by an action closer to home. On March 27, 1961, a group of Black students at Tougaloo College outside of Jackson, known as the Tougaloo Nine, walked into the White library and read books that weren't available to Black students in their segregated library, before being forcibly removed and arrested.

Inspired by these stories—and the direct action classes at the Masonic Lodge—on August 26, 1961, Curtis Muhammad and Hollis Watkins, both a few years past graduation, decided to stage the first direct action in McComb and the first restaurant sit-in in the state of Mississippi. They went to the Woolworth's downtown and sat at the counter. But unlike the students in North Carolina a year earlier, who sat there day after day and were simply not served, in Mississippi the local police arrived quickly to brutishly haul the peaceful activists to the county jail in Magnolia and charge them with disturbing the peace.

Brenda attended a meeting a day or two later at the Masonic Temple with around two hundred people in attendance, including many young people. James Bevel, "a fiery SNCC orator," came down from Jackson and "exhorted the crowd not to let Hollis and Curtis sit alone in jail, but to follow up and take additional direct action," Brenda recalled. Bob Moses said that the activists had to show that a little adversity wasn't going to stop them. A follow-up to the Woolworth's sit-in was planned at the Greyhound station the next day and they asked for volunteers. Brenda was one of the three to raise her hand—the only female, and the only minor.

After the meeting, Brenda, Ike Lewis, and Bobby Talbert were coached by SNCC volunteers about what they would do the next day. The three were to enter the station and go directly to the White counter to purchase tickets. They were given money, and the Freedom Riders reviewed the lessons for nonviolent resistance that they taught in class. Brenda went home and packed the few items she would take with her. She kissed her mother goodnight without breathing a word of what she would do the next day and then went to bed and prayed.

The next day, Bobby, Ike, and Brenda met at the Masonic Temple, where they received encouragement from the SNCC workers, and then walked to the bus station. Brenda remembers that no one paid any attention to them as they entered until they walked to the Whites-only counter. A murmur of disgust rose up from the White people in the station, and they began jeering and shouting what Brenda called "the no-word." The police were quickly called and the three of them arrested, eventually taken to the county jail in Magnolia where Curtis and Hollis were held.

Brenda was at peace with her decision and its inevitable outcome of jail, believing that it was "a necessary part of the process of bringing about change." While in jail she and Curtis, Hollis, Bobby, and Ike would sometimes sing spirituals or freedom songs like "This Little Light of Mine" and "Oh Freedom," Brenda joining their chorus from the women's cell a floor away. But she soon would find out how dangerous it could be. Early in her stay Brenda was held with one other woman who said that the guards attempted to coerce her to harm Brenda in exchange for a shortened sentence. The other woman declined, saying she knew Brenda's family and was afraid of her uncle, but the ways that the police worked were becoming apparent.

While Brenda was being threatened in jail, the situation beyond the cell walls was even more dangerous. Bob Moses was beaten and arrested, and other SNCC workers were also injured and intimidated by White supremacists angered at the workers' encouragement of these direct actions. Throughout the country, SNCC's direct actions were seen as radical despite the fact that they also espoused nonviolence like Dr. King. And as SNCC began to gain both media attention and broader influence among young people, the MSSC began its disinformation campaigns to undermine their work.

———————

Brenda's mother visited her in jail as often as she could, and one day early on she reported that there were rumors circulating that Brenda was promiscuous, likely started by the MSSC, although Brenda and her family didn't know that at the time. And in another visit her mother told her of the murder of a young local father, Herbert Lee, who had driven Bob Moses around nearby Amite County when he had first arrived. It would take years for the real story to come to light: on September 25, 1961, state representative and local farmer E. H. Hurst approached Herbert Lee waving a pistol, later telling the police the confrontation was about an alleged debt. Mr. Lee responded that he wasn't going to talk to Mr. Hurst as long as he had his gun out. E. H. Hurst then shot Mr. Lee in the head, unprovoked. Mr. Hurst intimidated the only eyewitness, an impoverished Black farmer named Louis Allen, to get him to agree to his story: that Herbert Lee had attacked him with a tire iron and he responded in self-defense, and that he must have "pulled the trigger unconsciously." An all-White jury ruled the murder a justifiable homicide. Only later did Louis Allen risk his life to tell Bob Moses and the Justice Department the truth.

It would be twenty-eight days before the five young people would be released, bailed out of jail with a check signed by Dr. Martin Luther King Jr.

———————

On October 4, 1961, Brenda returned to school for her sophomore year. She was excited to see her friends on the bus and eager to get back to her schoolwork. But when she went to the school office to register, she was told by Principal Higgins that she was expelled. Brenda was stunned. Principal Higgins had seemed willing to go to great lengths for the students in Brenda's underfunded high school, such as pressuring the White school board for more supplies. Brenda couldn't understand how he could betray her like this.

"I don't know how you can let white folks run a colored school," she retorted. And then she up and left.

Brenda walked down the hall, not knowing where she would go or what she would do when she reached the school doors—she was only sixteen years old, and she had imagined her days being structured by school and perhaps SNCC meetings or work in the afternoons and evenings. On that long walk down the hallway some of her friends saw her and asked what was wrong, her face betraying her emotions. She told them what had happened and word spread among her classmates, while one friend encouraged her to come to the assembly that was about to start. Her friends created a plan to question the principal about his support for them—and the movement they had been learning about all summer.

As the students took their seats in the auditorium, there was murmuring as the story of what happened to Brenda made its way among the students, along with the plan to test Principal Higgins's standing on Brenda's enrollment. Soon after settling in, classmate Joe Lewis raised his hand and asked why Brenda Travis would not be allowed to return to school. Senior class president Jerome Byrd, Jackie's brother, demanded an explanation. The principal wouldn't give the students a straight answer, and even seemed angry, ordering Joe to see him after the assembly.

"Hey, y'all," Jerome yelled to his classmates, "let's walk out of here!" Students stood, grabbed their things, and started walking toward the front door.

Fearing the inevitable retribution, some students returned to class, including Brenda's older brother, who was in his senior year, and C. C. Bryant's son Curtis, who knew his father would not approve. But more than a hundred students walked out and marched down the street, many singing freedom songs they had learned at the Masonic Temple: *Woke up this morning with my mind stayed on freedom.*

The students left school with the initial idea that they would march the nine miles to the county seat in Magnolia, but realizing that was too far, they went to the Masonic Temple above the nearby Burglund Supermarket instead, where a SNCC meeting was being held. There they told the SNCC workers what had happened, and Bob Moses and

Chuck McDew both tried to temper their excitement. Bob could imagine what his friend C. C. Bryant would say about the walkout: that it would anger local White people and make life difficult for many of the students' parents, not to mention the complications with their months of voter registration work. C.C. liked his activism as rule abiding as possible, and a mass student walkout during the school day did not fit that description.

However, Charles Sherrod and Marion Barry were both in town fresh off the Freedom Rides, and direct action was their preferred approach. They wanted to harness the student enthusiasm and encouraged them to keep marching. Ultimately, they devised a plan to make signs and continue to McComb city hall. Most of the SNCC workers agreed to go with them, including Curtis Muhammad and Hollis Watkins. Robert Zellner, who was the first White SNCC secretary, was initially going to stay behind because he knew that the sight of a White person standing in solidarity with Black activists would further enrage McComb's White leadership.

The students finished their signs, some saying FREEDOM NOW!, LEE COULD BE ME (referring to the murder of Herbert Lee), and WILL YOU BE AN UNCLE TOM, OR WILL YOU BE A MAN?, while others expressed outrage over Brenda's expulsion. None had poles, so the students couldn't be accused of bringing weapons. Placards hoisted aloft, they continued their walk to city hall. And then Robert Zellner changed his mind and ran after them.

By then some students had gone home instead of to the Masonic Temple, fearing retribution against their parents or themselves, and word traveled quickly of what was to come. Their route took them down Summit Street, where Aylene was at the restaurant. She could probably hear the freedom songs through her open windows and stepped outside to see where they were coming from. "I didn't even know they was going to walk out that day," she said, "and when they started coming down the street they had to pass by the side of the bar." She stepped out of South of the Border to watch them, her sixteen-year-old daughter Carolyn among the group who would carry out the first high school direct action in Mississippi.

Perhaps Mama Quin asked where they were heading and then ducked right back inside to take off her apron, make a few calls to other parents and allies, and then head downtown to do what she could to support the students when they reached the inevitable angry mob. While word of the walkout spread among the Black community in McComb, so did it spread among the White people.

Some parents confronted their children as they marched, begging them to come home or even threatening them. But Mama Quin would be among the few parents who vocally supported the students. Mrs. Quin knew that she wouldn't face the same economic sanctions as some parents for their children's actions. "So she did not have to answer to anybody or worry about losing a job," Jacqueline Quin says—an independence Aylene would fight to preserve her entire life. More so, she saw Carolyn doing exactly what she herself had been modeling through her own work since they got to McComb.

————————

As the protesters neared city hall, they could see the mob of irate White townspeople and police awaiting them. Still they marched toward the steps, ignoring a policeman's order to disperse. One person tried to run his truck into the crowd and narrowly missed Chuck McDew. The driver then jumped out and began swinging a large wrench like a club, calling McDew a "black nappy-headed son of a bitch." Others in the mob, which was swelling to well over a hundred, brought chains and pipes as weapons, while news reporters sought to document the melee and FBI agents stood idly at a gas station nearby, taking notes.

Hollis Watkins was the first to walk up the steps of city hall and say, "I've come to offer prayers for this peaceful assemblage." And then he knelt down to pray. An officer grabbed him and arrested him immediately. Brenda ascended the steps next and knelt to pray as well, and was pulled up by a policeman so violently she lost her shoes.

The piercing rebel yells increased, while Robert Zellner clung to a Bible he had received in McComb, and the students dropped to their knees, reciting verses: "Our Father, who art in heaven . . ."

The police proceeded to arrest a number of students before turning on the remaining SNCC activists and beginning to beat them. As expected, they attacked Robert Zellner with special force. He represented what the White supremacists hated most: what they called a "race traitor." They feared that once White people began supporting Black civil liberties in greater numbers, their stranglehold on power would end. One man tried to gouge out Mr. Zellner's eyes, while another went for his throat. Robert Zellner remembers seeing a surreptitious nod from a local official, approving of the escalating violence against him, while other officers attacked him as well. Bob Moses and Chuck McDew tried to shield Mr. Zellner with their bodies.

Mr. Zellner's Bible fell to the ground, and he remembers hearing the cries of evil, of the mob yelling, "Bring him here, we'll kill him." From the blows to his head and body he fell unconscious.

Finally the police blew their whistles for the beatings to stop.

The police herded more than a hundred Black protesters into the small and dank cells below city hall, while squad cars sped to the neighborhoods of Baertown and Burglund, armed with an excuse to find any reason to terrorize activists and ratchet up charges. Their goal was to try to stop the rising momentum that SNCC's presence had brought. As they rounded up as many SNCC workers and other activists that they perceived as threats, SNCC member Charles Jones escaped detection by donning a butcher's apron and making phone calls from the butcher's phone at the supermarket below the Masonic Hall. He called news outlets to tell them about the first "mass arrests" for civil rights actions in the state of Mississippi, and even called the singer and supporter Harry Belafonte, who then called John Doar at the Justice Department, hoping their awareness would stop the local police from allowing vigilante "justice."

Most of the underage activists were released to their parents later that day, many of whom came in groups to claim their children, fearing retribution. Carolyn wasn't old enough to be held in jail. "So they called us in to go get the children," Aylene said of that day. When the children were released, some parents berated or hit them on the steps, perhaps in part to exaggerate their disapproval to the local Whites in an effort to mitigate their inevitable economic and social sanctions. A number of parents still lost their jobs or received other forms of retribution by some of the White establishment, as C. C. Bryant had feared. But Aylene Quin refused to buckle to White expectations of acquiescence. "When we came home, I didn't say anything," she said. "A lot of parents were saying something to the children for walking out but I didn't say anything because I was for it."

Those who were eighteen and older remained in jail, and the young men and women were again separated, so most of the recollections of the next month they spent behind bars are from the point of view of the young men, who were arrested in greater numbers and whose stories have been better preserved. Curtis Muhammad remembers that Mama Quin, or one of the handful of women who worked closely with her, would bring hearty, hot meals every day and would usually be allowed to stay for a half hour or so, catching them up on what was happening outside the jail cell walls.

"By now, this is about the third time I'm in that jail," Curtis remembers. "So the jailer has been trained. They know they can't handle us. They know we gonna do what we want to do. And the FBI showed up; the Justice Department showed up. They don't do nothing to them. But it makes them nervous. So they don't want to mess with us too much."

Mama Quin would unwrap the plated meals—every day something different. Maybe steak or chicken, with a side of rice or potatoes and vegetables, the smell and warmth filling up the cell and reminding both the jailed activists and the jailers that there were many people invested in these young people's well-being and political mission. The jailed youth were eating better dinners than the jailers themselves, most likely. "I mean, it was like we were outside almost," Curtis says. "Like, we got to keep educating the children. We got to keep them moving. . . . That was enough for us."

Bob Moses wrote of eating rice and gravy, with bread for sopping up the extras, and big town cake—a snack cake like a moon pie—for dessert. Bobby Talbert said he gained more than twenty pounds from these feasts while jailed. The frequent visits and the time spent slow-cooking beans and meat—days, in many cases—were a signal to everyone in the jailhouse that there was an entire community there to support these young people and take care of them. And often enough they might secretly exchange correspondence, such as letters from Bob Moses that made their way to the SNCC office in Atlanta, describing their time in jail. Of course mother figures would be seen as much less threatening delivering food, and this gave them access that males would never be allowed. As Dr. Hamlin explains, not only has Black women's activism been overlooked "because strategies of nurturing are oftentimes confused with notions of 'naturalness' or the ordinary activities of women in their communities," but also this underestimation is what "permits many women to engage in subversive activities." She notes that "they are not suspected, their activities are not prone to arrest for inciting lawlessness or civil disobedience because of the protected space they inhabit, safe from violence." It is perhaps why Mama Quin often sent women who worked with her, whose names have been lost to history, to be the necessary link between the jailed activists and the work done outside the prison, using food as the ruse. Yet at the same time, these expectations are what kept women from formal leadership roles and women's stories from being better collected as representations of the movement.

Between food drop-offs, Moses writes, the twelve of them "sprawled out along the concrete bunker" and talked into the night, often about girls. Moses sat in the corner writing and thinking. The young women Myrtis Bennett and Janie Campbell were "across the way wedded to a different icy cubicle. Later on Hollis will lead out with a clear tenor into a freedom song, Talbert and Lewis will supply the jokes, and McDew will discourse of the black man and the Jew. McDew, a black by birth, a Jew by choice, and a revolutionary by necessity, has taken the deep hates and deep loves of America, and the world, reserved for those who dare to stand in a strong sun and cast a sharp shadow."

Hot meals were one of the only reasons someone from the outside could enter a jail cell full of activists, and a woman might be the only one allowed to linger because of her perceived lack of threat. And what did it say to the jailers who begrudgingly allowed Mama Quin to enter? Here was a community that didn't forget about its people, no matter how long they were locked up. Here were people so revered, so beloved, that a community would cook all day to make sure they were kept strong and healthy. Yet, at the same time, the White establishment, because of its sexism and racism, failed to see the power of a Black woman with a

plate of food beyond nurturing and the way that the food—and all that
these meetings accomplished—made sure the songs didn't end and the
hope didn't die.

———————————

Meanwhile, the students who had been released were allowed to reenroll
in school only if they signed a pledge that they would not participate in
further civil rights demonstrations. More than half refused to sign. Curtis Muhammad emphasizes that it was the kids who refused, sometimes
against their parents' wishes, that prompted Medgar Evers to promise
the NAACP's support. For days, school officials pressured the students
and their families to come to the principal's office to sign the slip, under
increasing scrutiny from White townspeople who insisted on being present. The local White Citizens' Council had already compiled and shared a
list of the students who had walked out, and some parents were fired or
threatened with retaliation by their White employers. But still, sixty-four
children refused to sign. They were expelled—and forbidden to enroll in
any public school in the state.

The students continued to lead, holding demonstrations protesting the jailing of the SNCC workers and their older classmates. At the
same time, Mama Quin and her crew of women also began organizing
schooling for the teens through their communication at mealtimes at the
jailhouse. "They were the leadership," Curtis Muhammad says. "They
had two churches that we could meet in and they had had all kinds of
stuff put together." When the SNCC workers and adult students were
released, SNCC started their own Nonviolent High School to continue
their education. Bob Moses taught them math and other subjects, and
Chuck McDew introduced Harriet Tubman and Frederick Douglass. The
workers were astounded that the students knew little Black history—and
that the entirety of what had transpired between 1860 and 1875 had been
erased from state textbooks, in part as a tactic of oppression to deny
the humanity and self-worth of Black people. The school would eventually be shut down by local fire officials, and the students would soon
be welcomed at Campbell College in Jackson to finish their education.

Meanwhile Brenda Travis was sent to a juvenile detention center more than an hour north and cut off from communicating with her family and community until the following spring. She would later speak of a woman, Mama Turner, who would do for her what Mama Quin did for the SNCC workers. Mama Turner would wake Brenda from her dormitory and bring her quietly into the kitchen at night, offering her home-cooked meals and reassuring her that someone cared. Brenda was released in the spring of 1962 and forced to leave the state to ensure her safety, Ella Baker herself taking care of her and eventually helping her enroll in a private Black college in North Carolina.

Others were also unhappy about this new direct action approach. C. C. Bryant feared this could undermine the NAACP's voting rights efforts. And while he believed that Bob Moses, with whom he had developed a close friendship, was not responsible for planning the walkout, the fallout was clear. Mr. Bryant could foresee the ripple effect of the walkout, how the expelled students would reduce the student population, which could affect funding and parent involvement in the PTA, in addition to the immediate retribution of economic sanctions and increased violence and threats. As much as he loved Bob Moses, he was worried the SNCC workers had overstayed their welcome in McComb. SNCC had already halted much of its community work after the murder of Herbert Lee, and this youthful insurgence put much of the Black community even more on edge.

Mama Quin, however, believed that the children needed to be involved to grow the movement and provide hope for its longevity. She welcomed the energy the SNCC workers had brought and the way they inspired action among the teens, including her daughter. That was one of the reasons she made sure the young people knew that she and other community members supported them. By the end of 1961, the jailed SNCC workers were released, and they left McComb, some to help with voter registration and other activist work in the Mississippi Delta. The numbers were damning: months of work resulted in $15,000 in fines and just eighteen newly registered voters of the thousands of Black residents who were eligible—not to mention the beatings, arrests, and economic fallout. Bob Moses would call this time in McComb "a tremor in the middle of the iceberg." The lessons learned would be valuable to both SNCC and local activists like Aylene Quin and C. C. Bryant, who wouldn't stop their movement efforts. It took the SNCC activists a few months to learn the realities of White violence and resistance to change—something the local people had long known. Yet it also seemed clear that true progress couldn't come without the two groups working together.

4

CLEO SILVERS REMEMBERS THAT when she was five years old she found a bag of green leaves while digging through her dad's drawer. She dumped those out. Beneath them was his construction worker union book, which she pulled out next, finding inside a pink card that said COMMUNIST PARTY. Cleo had learned to read when she was four, and in a moment those words on the card and the conversations she had been hearing from around her house's long, and often packed, dining room table came together in a new moment of understanding. The bag of dried green leaves, well, that she would figure out later.

Cleo's childhood home in Philadelphia was the hub of her Elmwood neighborhood in the 1950s. She lived with her parents and extended family, including her grandmother, who kept a thriving garden in the backyard. With their house situated across the street from the church, everyone was angling to get an invite to her grandma's Sunday meal. The pastor had locked down that invite, but there was always room for a few more around the table that, even on a quiet weekday, usually sat seven or eight family members and neighbors. That garden provided food for neighbors as well, her grandmother making sure nothing was wasted and no neighbor went without a meal.

Her grandma was known for her fried chicken and fixings. She'd head out back where they had a chicken coop and wring the chickens' necks herself and then clean and pluck and butcher and dredge the chicken in between making collards and mac and cheese and blackberry cobbler and peach ice cream, using fruit off their tree.

While her grandma was known for cooking, Cleo's parents were known for the conversation they brought to the table. They were both voracious readers who always had copies of mainstream Black magazines like *Jet* and *Ebony* and the NAACP's *Crisis,* in addition to the *Crusader,* stacked around the house—a library similar to as the one in C. C. Bryant's barbershop. The *Crusader,* considered particularly radical, was published by Robert Williams, an antisegregation activist for Black freedom in the 1950s who spoke out for the need for armed self-defense against White supremacist terrorists. It was this stance, in great part, that forced him to seek asylum in Cuba in 1961, then later in China, and whose work was considered among the first defining Black Power. Cleo's parents would read all of these cover to cover, and they kept her aunts and uncles, cousins, and neighbors up to date with everything that was happening with Black people in America. They didn't protest or march—"good church people didn't do that," Cleo says—but they knew what was happening and were progressive in their politics.

From a distance of many decades, Cleo can see what that Communist Party card meant to her family at the time. Until the Red Scare in the late 1940s, the Communist Party and organized labor were closely aligned. While later propaganda aligned communist philosophy with despotic and totalitarian governments, the Communist Party's ideals promoted a socialist economic vision alongside the United States' democratic government structure. They were antisegregationist and illuminated the class struggle, supporting workers' rights, safe conditions, fair pay, and reasonable hours from the employers who were getting rich off their labor. Particularly in working-class and middle-class Black neighborhoods in Philadelphia, what might be considered socialist principles already reigned: if one neighbor had food, no one went hungry. It was the kind of neighborhood where if someone was out of work, the neighbors might show up with a few dollars or hand-me-downs, no questions asked. For someone like Cleo who had spent her childhood in the embrace of this community but also was acutely aware from her family's conversations about civil rights, she knew she was luckier than many and also less privileged than others. But like her grandmother's overflowing dinner table taught her, like her father's outspoken support of his union demonstrated, she had a deep sense of fairness and was brought up to work hard and fight for what she, and her community, rightfully deserved.

When Cleo graduated high school, she was working the overnight wait-ressing shift at Linton's, an all-night local diner chain that boasted of its "Biggest Breakfast in North America." One day after her shift ended at 7:00 AM, she was watching television when a commercial for the new federal VISTA program came on. "Join VISTA and see the world!" it promised. So Cleo sent in her application and was soon accepted to the second cohort of volunteers. During her training in Washington, D.C., a few months later, she found out that she was the first Black woman to participate. It would soon dawn on her that the program was intended for well-off White kids from the suburbs: in her cohort was Jay Rockefeller, who was placed in West Virginia, where he would later become governor, his brief volunteering stint providing someone from his privileged background enough bona fides for locals to vote for him. After her training, Cleo was assigned to the Bronx with her partner Paula Bowers, where they were sponsored by St. Anselm's Church and tasked with community initiatives.

The VISTA program, today better known as part of AmeriCorps, began in the early 1960s from an initiative begun by President Kennedy. He had commissioned a task force to examine creating a national organization like the Peace Corps, the goal of which would be to assist Americans affected by both rural and urban poverty. This wasn't realized until 1964 when President Lyndon B. Johnson created Volunteers in Service to America (VISTA) as an element of his War on Poverty efforts. The first cohort of volunteers went into the field in 1965 to live among the communities with which they were working. Cleo began later the same year.

As part of her training with VISTA, she learned the basic tenets of community organizing. Among them was to serve those most in need first, to ask the community how she could help, and to not arrive with preconceived ideas of what she wanted to offer. She also began to think more critically about the nuances of the power structures that created the systems of inequality in the communities she served and to work to organize people to help themselves. Even as a teen, Cleo and other VISTA volunteers were considering how they might empower those who felt the most desperate. And so she and her partner Paula jumped into one of their first missions: providing after-school programming for one of the most underresourced schools in the South Bronx.

Cleo and Paula weren't that much older than the students they were tasked to help when they walked into the office of a crumbling South Bronx middle school clutching their VISTA program qualifications and asked to speak with the principal about volunteering.

"That's lovely, girls," he said with condescension, "but these kids are the worst. They'll only be garbage pickers."

Cleo persisted. "It won't cost you anything," she said with her characteristic smile. "What's the harm?" So he relented, telling them that they needed to get the parents' approval first.

───────────

The school population was about 60 percent Black and 40 percent Puerto Rican, and it was in a neighborhood that had horrible health conditions, which were exacerbated by the inequities that came hand in hand with White flight. The neighborhood's majority non-Hispanic White population had all but disappeared in the previous fifteen years, taking its relative wealth and resources with it. Remaining landlords all but abandoned many buildings, and because of racist budgetary practices, schools, health care, and other community supports were radically underfunded. In the mid-1960s one in four people was addicted to heroin, and there was rampant hunger. The school itself had low attendance and often received rotted, moldy, or other poor-quality food to serve for lunch. The students Cleo and Paula would be working with were reading at a second-grade level and were known for their unruliness. But the young women were undaunted, with the positive attitude of teenagers who were newly inspired to use community organizing to create real change. They made their way to the run-down apartment buildings where many of the students lived, prepared to make their case to the kids' parents that they should be allowed to help tutor their kids, and maybe take them on some field trips around the city.

It was there that Cleo saw the apartments with plaster ceilings falling in from plumbing leaks, opening up huge holes allowing rats to roam. The last warm days of that fall sometimes sent the temperature skyrocketing, but she would later feel frigid in the winter from broken heat. Most parents agreed to allow her to teach their kids, asking few questions. Two eager teens who wanted to spend time with their children—what could be the harm when there were so many other things to worry about?

The South Bronx's challenges were also fueled in part by the construction of the Cross Bronx Expressway that was completed in 1963. This project displaced thousands of people and many businesses, devalued property that was now close to the highway, and was a deciding factor for many families who had the means to move out of the borough. Many who were left, especially in the pocket where Cleo and Paula's students mostly lived, were in a now-isolated corner of the borough bordered by the Bronx River, the new expressway, and the longstanding Bronx River Parkway. Built on the now ironically named Evergreen Avenue, the school was nestled less than a block from the newest transportation project: the Bruckner Expressway, on which construction began in the mid-1960s, all so those with cars and more money could drive past a place like the South Bronx on their way elsewhere without having to view its reality from street level.

Changes in housing laws had also designated that many of the buildings in the South Bronx be rent controlled, which disincentivized landlords from maintaining the buildings, while redlining further devalued housing in this, and nearby, neighborhoods. One of the results of this devalued neighborhood was the lack of local jobs—Bronx residents had much greater need to leave the borough to find sustainable employment, which added to their financial stress and childcare needs. Likewise there were few businesses in the surrounding neighborhoods; most lacking were proper grocery stores, making the South Bronx a bone-dry food desert. With all these stressors—and the dismissive attitude of the school administration—it was little surprise that so many of these students were struggling.

Having been brought up within a supportive community and fully educated on the systemic oppression that created economic and social situations like in the South Bronx, Cleo brought her recent training and youthful optimism to her first group of students. If they threw paper airplanes, she and Paula found a college professor to teach them about aerodynamics. After they got permission from parents to take them on field trips, they took the kids to a comic book store and taught them all to read at grade level.

———————

Another charge through the VISTA program was for Cleo and Paula to do code enforcement in local housing. Cleo recounts how she and Paula were trained by two New York City Housing Authority employees to visit apartment buildings and note code violations. Cleo explains, "Conditions would be so horrible that they would say to us, we can't do this but you can. . . . They wanted us to help people to have organized rent strikes. So they taught us how to do it." And so the duo, neither yet twenty years old, invited people in the buildings to meetings to tell them about escrow accounts and explain how to put their money in the bank to legally withhold rent or make repairs necessary for health and safety. Many of these buildings would be taken over by the people within the next few years, and they were then able to improve them and start to build some wealth and stability.

———————

For Cleo, this first year in the Bronx was transformative. The small apartment she shared with Paula was furnished with finds from the street. They knew to go to Fifth Avenue on trash night, from which they would lug home beautiful pieces on the subway, like a handcrafted rocking chair that held a place of honor in their small living room. They had room for few other furnishings besides Cleo's sewing machine, which she used to make dresses out of locally purchased African prints.

Soon their apartment became a hub of dinner parties where Cleo would spend her last dollars on ingredients for cosmopolitan dishes like coq au vin, one of many French recipes that represented, to a teenager brought up on her grandmother's southern-inflected dishes made from ingredients plucked from the backyard, the sophistication and worldliness of her new life in New York City. While she had been taught to cook growing up, she had mostly learned to make the fried chicken and collards and macaroni and cheese of her youth. But in her first small apartment she relished learning French technique from a secondhand cookbook, spending hours making elaborate meals for her new friends on the weekends after her long days with her various VISTA projects. It would be decades before scholars and chefs would begin to examine and counteract the ways that White supremacy affected the perception of White and European food as fine dining, and the cuisine of Black Americans, which is by no means monolithic, as simple or less desirable. What was clear at the time was that French technique, and European dishes, were all the rage for dinner parties or in fancy restaurants. Knowing how to cook a lobster or make a béarnaise sauce was the defining skill of a good cook.

In the evenings Cleo and Paula hosted Father Philip—the young, White priest of St. Anselm's—some of his more progressive church colleagues, and other musicians and friends Cleo had met through work or when she went out to see live music at clubs like Slugs', where she would later meet Lee Morgan and other famous jazz musicians. They drank wine late into the night. Often someone picked up a guitar, or they would just talk—about politics and revolution. For the holy men, this was a refuge from the often-conservative roles they had to play at their churches. And through these elaborate dinner parties, Cleo began to learn how powerful the act of feeding people was—it was a representation of the life she wanted for herself: full of debate and hopeful ideas, of the worldliness and connectedness she saw among the diverse people she was meeting, and a way to honor her friends with delicious food made by her hands, with love. Little did she know that she would be using food to show her care, to provide a window into other cultures and people, and as a way to connect communities in various ways for the rest of her life.

After their year's commitment to VISTA, Cleo and Paula parted ways. But not long afterward Cleo acquired a new roommate: she and Father Philip, twelve years her senior, fell in love and got married, settling into a different Bronx apartment. He left the priesthood for her and supported her next role as a community advocate, working at a nearby hospital. She was now committed in a different way to helping the families she had befriended through the school and housing work. There was no way she'd leave—she was just beginning to make a difference.

5

Across the country in Oakland, California, two young men were having a revelation similar to Cleo Silvers about serving the people. In October 1966 Bobby Seale and Huey Newton were meeting to formalize a new organization they called the Black Panther Party for Self Defense. Both were in their twenties and had worked with Merritt College's Black Studies movement, but they saw this group more as galvanizing Black youth whose families had moved from the South to the Bay Area over the last few decades in hopes of job opportunities and to distance themselves from the Jim Crow South. What they and so many others had found instead was dwindling job prospects, poor living conditions, and a different kind of oppression that shared only some characteristics with what they or their parents had experienced in places like Louisiana, where Newton was born and spent his early childhood. In contrast to the segregated and underfunded, but supportive, school districts of many towns in the South, Oakland city schools were hostile and dismissive of their Black students, as Cleo had found.

Also like in the South Bronx, there was inadequate health care, poor housing conditions, and food deserts that had worsened over the previous few decades as White people had fled the city during the second wave of the Great Migration. Midcentury had brought three hundred thousand Black people moved to the Bay Area to work jobs in the shipyards and manufacturing. But postwar job instability and White flight displaced Black families while leeching resources from the cities. Many Black people were thrown into poverty after jobs disappeared or changed after the war. Despite the lack of resources, the Black population continued to grow in Oakland in particular. By the mid-1960s, local youth like Newton and Seale were subject to inadequate education and few nearby job prospects—as well as the routine harassment by law enforcement. For many of the young people's parents, who had been brought up in the South and had moved to a city to escape racism, they found the change of scenery did not provide much relief from police intimidation and brutality.

Huey Newton and Bobby Seale's plans to start the Black Panther Party for Self Defense were ignited by this injustice in and around Oakland, but they borrowed their imagery—the black panther—from other groups similarly fighting for Black rights and liberation in the South at the same time. They had come across a pamphlet for the Lowndes County Freedom Organization (LCFO) in Alabama, which used on its third-party ballots the imagery of a large, crouching black cat. The LCFO was begun by SNCC leader Stokely Carmichael in 1965 to support Black candidates and was dubbed the Black Panther Party by the White media.

The black panther symbol was adopted by various organizations around the country that felt that the animal represented their stance: one that would retreat until cornered and then fight back for self-preservation. Many Black supporters believed that this was the moment they would, collectively, be fighting for their rights after years of oppression. And this idea spoke to Huey and Bobby as well. They had both recently taken part in—and found fault with—various established social action groups in the Bay Area and so had decided to start their own. Using Huey Newton's familiarity with penal codes from his time in law school, they discovered that it was legal to openly carry firearms, and they decided to recruit local community members to make a statement about self-defense in the face of rampant police brutality. But the men also wanted to present potential members with a thought-out program to support involvement, with a balance between theory and practice. So on October 15, 1966, they sat down and in less than twenty minutes drafted their Ten-Point Program, dividing the points into "What We Want" and "What We Believe." Bobby Seale would later say this represented "concisely all the physical needs and all the philosophical principles" that undergirded their activism. Drawing from similar missions espoused by the NAACP, Nation of Islam, and even the United States' Bill of Rights, the ten points that would guide future Black Panthers emphasized a right to employment, education, housing, and adequate food, as well as safety from harassment and equal treatment under the law.

With their Ten-Point Program in hand, Bobby Seale and Huey Newton began recruiting young people from Oakland and around the Bay Area, with one initial goal to set up patrols to monitor police activity. While there had been numerous previous community efforts to hold police accountable for harassment and violent acts against the Black community, up until this point these community watchdogs had carried notebooks and recording devices to document these illegal actions. But now, with the penal code on their side, the Black Panther Party for Self Defense would make their presence known all around the Bay Area. If they saw a Black resident being questioned, they would stand the legal distance away, ask if the person was being mistreated, and sometimes quote the penal code if the police were committing an obvious infraction. With their legal open-carry rifles slung over their shoulder, they also purposely strove to invert the power dynamic of intimidation between residents and cops, who, they asserted, did more to injure and harm local residents than keep them safe.

Most of the Black Panther Party recruits were also transplanted southerners themselves and had grown up with a comfort around guns for hunting. Yet their early actions also did more than focus on armed patrol. They actively looked to the community to ask what they could do to help and would perform visible public actions, like free food giveaways or directing traffic at a dangerous intersection, that worked to shame the government for not providing social services for their residents and to bolster community respect. This did spur some government action—the city of Oakland installed a light after Black Panthers directed traffic, for example—and it also angered many officials.

The media, of course, were drawn to the sensational image of beret-wearing, gun-toting inner-city Black men and perpetuated the narrative of young Black people as violent and thuggish, through nationally circulated images and articles that crafted a biased account of their patrols and other actions. The Black Panther Party for Self Defense was just one of many groups organizing to fight poverty and assert Black Freedom at this time, including another group locally that had also adopted the Black Panther name. But none were as visible and mediagenic as the party of Huey Newton and Bobby Seale. Jane Rhodes writes that "the press customarily framed stories about the civil rights movement within binary oppositions . . . good versus evil, justice versus lawlessness, and North versus South." The Bay Area mainstream media had written about Freedom Summer and nonviolent Black protest with sympathy. But by spring 1967 when local press finally took notice of the Black Panther Party for Self Defense, the group's early adoption of a kind of uniform of leather jackets and visible weaponry played into the media narrative of Black men as violent and aggressive, and their message was incompatible with the White press's understanding of Black protest. They didn't look or act like the media's version of a "good" protester.

There were other elements that contributed to the media's biased reporting, including the vastly White newsrooms being "largely ignorant" of the issues, realities, and growing "resentment" in Black communities, Rhodes adds. "Reporters relied almost exclusively on official government sources, paying little or no attention to the concerns of minority communities," with seemingly little motivation to engage more deeply or question their biases. This would also leave a vacuum of critical thinking that allowed the FBI and MSSC to feed their own propaganda to major news outlets, which was reported with minimal examination. It was little surprise that those creating the national narrative on race and civil rights were often neither Black nor especially critically engaged on the variety of issues affecting Black communities. Nor was it a surprise that activists had to look to nonmainstream publications for news and engagement that felt authentic to their lived experience.

And while Huey Newton and Bobby Seale courted the media to help communicate their message through what they knew would be shocking and inflammatory imagery to the White establishment, it wouldn't be until their first audacious action that they became nationally known. In early May 1967, a group of Panthers, in leather jackets and with guns slung across their backs, calmly marched into the California statehouse to protest a new proposed gun law they believed was intended to curb their community patrols. This action, and subsequent arrests, made national news headlines for the first time. And the Panthers quickly became a target for local police and the FBI.

The MSSC initially considered public relations as their primary tool in upholding White power: their investigation into Black activists was, at first, intended to support this propaganda arm. It was only with the changing of the governors in the early 1960s that investigation and infiltration into Black Freedom groups became more prevalent. And the MSSC's success in creating what numerous scholars would later describe as "a police state" inspired some of the most nefarious actions of a shadowy FBI initiative that had started around the same time.

J. Edgar Hoover, the director of the Federal Bureau of Investigation from its inception in 1924, was instrumental in dictating the scope of the organization as well as continually proving the need for "America's police force." As FBI historians Churchill and Vander Wall write, from as early as the 1930s, Hoover perpetuated the fiction of a "crime wave" and a fear of dangerous criminals to build his early reputation, in part by focusing on various small-time criminals he designated as "Public Enemy Number One" in a "brilliant public relations gimmick." He continued to seek positive press, manufacturing high-profile arrests, even supplying agents as actors for films glorifying the FBI. And Hoover created a direct line of communication with journalists who would receive "exclusive and privileged information for reporting purposes"—a violation of federal guidelines on the dissemination of information—also ensuring that the press reported as fact assertions or beliefs by the FBI, all while denying less ingratiating reporters information.

Prior to the First World War, the Bureau of Investigation (BOI), the FBI's precursor, collected information on hundreds of thousands of "radicals," including suspected draft dodgers, labor organizers, Black activists, anarchists, socialists, and communists. There are also numerous reports of intimidation of many of these same radicals by illegal wire-tapping, search and seizure, mail tampering, arresting on false pretenses, blackmail, beatings, and even murder. These actions continued under Hoover's newly formed FBI, as he acted as an even more powerful central leader, closely directing the organization's priorities. The rhetoric around the United States' "communist" foes in World War II gave him even more leeway to investigate and stop organizations considered supportive of, or even "sympathetic . . . with . . . totalitarian, fascist, communist, or subversive" people as allowed in an executive order by President Truman in 1947. At the same time, however, he ignored the actions of United States–based industrialists and businessmen who had actively done business with the Nazis, while undermining innocent citizens whom he considered unsavory. For example, Hoover investigated the personal life of, and launched a smear campaign against, a highly regarded State Department official because he disapproved of the official's homosexual activities.

By the late 1940s Senator Joseph McCarthy was touring the country espousing his Communist witch hunt, using supposed documents that named, as he cited at various times, citizens who were defined as "communist," "liberal" or "communistically inclined," among other changing terms, calling them "Un-American" and "dangerous." His outspokenness and resulting propaganda during the Red Scare, as this campaign became known, coupled with the residual fear from the recent end of World War II, turned *communism* into a dirty word—and gave the FBI the opening to investigate anyone who might fit into this category, including anyone this supposed impartial organization considered "too radical" or liberal. In the late 1940s and early 1950s anticommunist rhetoric permeated popular culture from movies to books to articles in popular print media, like the *New York Times*' editorial in 1956 that asserted, "We would not knowingly employ a Communist party member in the news or editorial departments . . . because we could not trust his ability to report the news objectively."

Churchill and Vander Wall go on to report that as early as 1940 Hoover began equating criticism of the FBI as "Un-American," putting the institution at odds with "Communists" and "goose-stepping bundsman" alike. While the story of the ramp-up of McCarthyism is relatively well known, less known is that of McCarthy's downfall. In the early 1950s, Senator McCarthy turned his eye toward military brass, accusing some members of being soft on suspected enlisted Communists. This went too far in the eyes of President Dwight D. Eisenhower, who came to the presidency through his lauded military accomplishments during World War II. McCarthy was officially sanctioned by the Senate, ending his specific attacks. But the damage was done. According to Churchill and Vander Wall, Hoover's FBI had engaged in some 6.6 million "security investigations" of Americans between 1947 and 1952, placing hundreds of informers within "the entire spectrum of the social and labor movements of the country, actualizing in real life Orwell's fiction that 'Big Brother is watching.'" By 1957—just a few years after Cleo first noticed her father's Communist Party membership card—the FBI and federal pressure had reduced party membership from two hundred thousand at its height decades prior to less than ten thousand. And as many as 1,500 of this number were FBI informants. For decades Hoover directed campaigns against any critics, keeping files on them and sending unflattering and perhaps even false information to employers, media, and the like to discredit them and their work. The FBI even had an entire division devoted to public relations and propaganda.

What is generally referred to as COINTELPRO, which stands for counterintelligence program, is actually a bureau term for a single (often illegal) counterintelligence operation; however it has come to represent all the actions the FBI took under this mantle of opposing domestic "dissident groups" starting in 1956. COINTELPRO's initial aims were to combat groups and individuals seen by government officials as a threat to national security, namely those believed to be communist or "Un-American."

By the early 1960s Hoover had used his seeming mandate to operate outside the law to expand his surveillance and intimidation of any groups he considered a threat to his own power and that of his conservative political allies. The bureau used extensive surveillance such as illegal wiretaps, tails, and breaking and entering to gather information about targets and create a sense of paranoia—a term the bureau would use themselves—about being watched. They would also tamper with mail and create fake correspondence, disseminate propaganda, falsely arrest and intimidate and coerce through the legal system, recruit spies and agents provocateurs, and resort to outright violence and murder.

Among the better-known COINTELPRO initiatives was the campaign against Dr. Martin Luther King Jr. A once-classified FBI file notes that from 1963 until his assassination in 1968 he was under constant physical surveillance and was known to have had his phones tapped and been blackmailed, in addition to a broader propaganda campaign waged against his activist efforts and personal character. At one point the FBI sent him a fake letter threatening to go public with infidelities and encouraging him to commit suicide. In 1999 Dr. King's family filed a civil suit in Memphis, where he was assassinated, that ruled that the local, state, and federal government were liable for his death, but there has been no official admission of guilt from the FBI.

By the spring of 1968 the FBI was already actively monitoring and undermining any groups organizing to work toward Black Freedom around the country, and it had a playbook for gaining information and threatening their efforts and credibility. And this playbook, some scholars note, was influenced by the MSSC's years of success in thwarting Black Freedom efforts in their state of Mississippi. By the end of 1968, the Black Panther Party would officially be on the FBI's list and would become a prime target. Using the protocol it had established the previous fall for discrediting the groups and individuals fighting for racial and class justice, Special Agent Francis Haberek sent a now-declassified memo to the special agent in charge in the New York FBI office, listing ways to subvert "Black Nationalist—Hate Groups." Suggestions include using some of the FBI's many, well-positioned informants to let opposing groups know about appearances, having informants "heckle the speaker" or ask challenging questions that "the office could prepare," using "trick photography" to insinuate false alliances, circulating leaflets from "non-existing (racial) organizations" with false and inflammatory statements, and using various means to invite group leaders to events as "entrapment appearances" with press present to manipulate the media to create a false narrative of their work and associations. These tactics—and many more nefarious others—would soon be put into play to secretly sow discord, affect public opinion, and otherwise hinder the efforts of Black activist groups in New York City and around the country in the 1960s.

Mae Jackson was one of the handful of New York City–based workers at the local SNCC office, located at 100 Fifth Avenue, on the eighth floor. Mae tells the story of being a young SNCC office worker, mostly doing fundraising for SNCC's continuing southern efforts with a few other "young sisters," including her good friend Janet Cyril and Harry Belafonte's sister Shirley. The East Village was abuzz on May 20, 1968, with the news that the West Coast–based Black Panther Party was holding a benefit at the Fillmore East music club for jailed members. Amiri Baraka (then known as LeRoi Jones) was a headliner, along with Panther leaders giving speeches and Black theater troupes performing socially conscious skits.

Mae and her office mates were among the crowd of more than 2,500 people, including, as the New York Times reported, Black youth, and "hippies and conservatively dressed middle aged persons." The performances were an homage to Black pride, with poet Baraka repeating the word Black so many times the New York Times critic noted that he finally realized that he had to stop using the term "negro." He continued, "[Baraka] uses words like a weapon, if he stirs up an audience he has done what he is trying to do, and he did exactly that."

But what Mae remembers best are the Panthers who spoke. Bobby Seale, standing on the stage surrounded by five or six other members, likely all in their black leather jackets, wearing berets or with bullets in a bandolier across their chests. "It was very impressive to see them stand at command, but disciplined," she remembers. "And they were handsome. And they were strong." Bobby Seale put a cigarette in his mouth and another brother lit it for him. It was like a scene from a movie for teenaged Mae and her friends. The Black Panthers were just as edgy and beguilingly provocative as their photographs in the papers. And while these same images may have been seen as threatening to many White people, the Panthers were heroes to these teenaged young women who were already working in the Black Freedom Movement. They giggled and whispered among themselves at Bobby Seale's speech, hissing along with the rest of the audience at J. Edgar Hoover's name. Mae had a feeling that what she was seeing was going to change the world.

Mae lived in Brooklyn and had to leave to head home—the event was going on past midnight—and she left Janet and the others there. The next morning back at the SNCC offices, she was the first to arrive—a rarity, especially because Janet and the others were so dedicated. Finally the young women drifted in, enraptured with the night before. They had stayed afterward and hung out with the Black Panthers, telling them they worked for SNCC.

"We're Black Panthers now," Janet told her. James Forman, an MC at the event and a leader of SNCC, would forge an alliance: Mae's New York SNCC office would do work for both SNCC and the Black Panther Party—and they considered themselves the beginning of the New York City chapter. Janet Cyril would become the Harlem officer of the day—what they called the office manager—when they expanded and got their own office space—and she remained close friends with Mae afterward and throughout her life.

Mae had been drawn to activism after fifteen-year-old James Powell was murdered by an off-duty cop who believed he pulled out a knife after a man sprayed him with a water hose in Harlem. Witnessed by more than dozen people in July 1964, this murder sparked a week of protests against police brutality and poor living conditions, primarily in Harlem and Brooklyn. Mae was around the same age as James and had been working for the Brooklyn chapter of the Congress of Racial Equality (CORE), and she was also part of Freedom Summer. "And that is what really captivated a whole group of young people. . . . Although Malcolm used to stand on the corner in front of the bookstore there, it wasn't until that riot that we listened to him." Mae notes that the community organizing by multiple groups in the wake of the protests of James Powell's murder focused on jobs for young people, among other issues like antipoverty, and it was at this time that Mae was recruited to join SNCC by Stokely Carmichael (who later renamed himself Kwame Ture). In the mid-1960s, Mae, Janet, Shirley Belafonte, and their other colleagues were focused on SNCC fundraising to keep programs like the Lowndes voter registration project going. She says it "made better sense" to raise money from their Manhattan office "because you had more money, more people, more resources here." And then in 1966 "when Kwame said 'Black power,' then we became more of an activist organization." After that, she says, "young people who had never looked at anything before . . . it caught their attention, their imagination." In the second half of the 1960s, she saw activism and interest among young Black people rise across New York City.

The summer in 1968 was also tumultuous for its presidential campaign pitting Republican Richard Nixon against Democratic nominee Hubert Humphrey (who became the front-runner after Robert Kennedy's assassination) and Independent candidate George Wallace, who ran on a segregationist platform. The Republican candidates are remembered for their rhetorical contribution of the "silent majority" of those who propelled them to victory as conservative populists who were anticounterculture and pro "law and order"—thinly veiled racist dog whistles against continued civil rights protests and in favor of heavy policing in urban areas and elsewhere, rhetoric that would periodically resurface over the next five decades. Candidate Wallace, who was never expected to win, was also quoted as saying to a group of (presumably White) police officers in Oklahoma, "There's nothing wrong in this country that we couldn't cure by turning it over to the police for a couple of years. You fellows would straighten it out."

———

In fall 1968 the FBI's campaign against the Panthers intensified. Black Panther Party founder Huey Newton was arrested after the death of an Oakland police officer who had pulled Newton over while he was driving. While the accounts of what happened next are disputed, one officer ended up dead and another injured, as was Newton. The only bullets found at the scene were from the officer's firearms. The *New York Times* headline ANGRY MEN "AT WAR" WITH SOCIETY didn't mince words about the paper's point of view as it detailed Huey's sentencing after being found guilty on charges that the Panthers and their supporters had declared unjust from the beginning. (The courts would agree in 1971, finally exonerating Mr. Newton, who had been incarcerated for nearly three years.) Many agree that his arrest and initial conviction were politically motivated, and there are allegations that the FBI was involved.

Even liberal-leaning *Time* magazine perpetuated this narrative of the Panthers: "They have guns, determination, discipline and the makings of a nationwide organization. In a dozen black ghettos, Panthers prowl in uniform: black jackets, black berets, tight black trousers. They proclaim their right to bear arms, and they have an affinity for violence. Committed to revolution . . . they are gathering notoriety as an American Mao-Mao." The article goes on to accuse party members of taking part in burglaries, coercion, and planning armed offenses. Interestingly, no author is noted, and it isn't a jump to consider how much of this language was provided by members of COINTELPRO.

The New York City chapter of the Black Panther Party largely formed in the wake of the party's evolving focus, during meetings that took place after Mae and other SNCC workers began supporting the party. Sekou Odinga, widely considered, with Lumumba Shakur, a founding member of the New York City chapter, remembers that the first meeting to gauge interest in starting a Black Panther chapter in New York City took place at a SNCC member's apartment in the East Village. After that, a larger initial meeting was held at Long Island University in Brooklyn, which Bobby Seale and other central leadership attended along with a full and enthusiastic crowd of interested young New Yorkers. Sekou Odinga took on a leadership role and helped move the meetings to a storefront on Nostrand Avenue in Bedford-Stuyvesant, Brooklyn. Soon after that, the New York City chapter of the Black Panther Party would expand to include chapter offices across the city, with the main office in Harlem organizing offices in other boroughs. Across the city, early members noted the presence of many female volunteers and many who were already active community workers, as well as the early and consistent focus in New York on serving local communities.

From the beginning, the New York chapter of the Black Panther Party included those who were already active in community organizing. While a number of people who showed up to the early large meetings at LIU were drawn to the aggressive image promoted in the media, there were many others who came with the desire to help revolutionize their Black communities. And in fact, by mid-1968 nationally the party was already shifting its focus from armed patrols to what would be called survival programs. Huey Newton was convicted (wrongly, the Panthers and many others believed) of voluntary manslaughter in September 1968, and from prison he directed the party to focus more on "community development. . . . We should turn away from the arms because too much had been made of them." He added, as quoted in the *Los Angeles Times*, "The gun itself does not symbolize a revolutionary. . . . Fascists also carry guns."

Newton would perhaps reflect on the Black Panther Party's true goals during this summer while watching these rhetorical and physical battles play out from his jail cell. For it is against the backdrop of this campaign year that the Panthers would refocus the party on community programming, even as the media continued the narrative of the Panthers as armed and violent. They dropped the phrase "self defense" from their name, and their rhetoric shifted to define this term as that which supports public health and well-being.

––––––––––––

Cleo's post–high school desire to see the world ended just a short bus ride north to the Bronx, but she had no desire to leave. Her immersion into community issues during her time in VISTA connected to so many of the conversations she had grown up hearing—starting with her father's Communist Party card and the ways that the government was failing so many, in particular Black and Brown communities. She wanted to be part of what she saw was an imminent need for change: fighting for better nutrition, better housing, and better community health. Their interconnectedness was starting to become apparent. And at the same time, she relished discussing these ideas with her new community of like-minded young activists, preferably over a home-cooked meal, drinking wine.

In early 1969 Cleo heard that Lincoln Hospital was hiring community mental health workers. She interviewed and was hired on the spot. She continued to work with local tenants and school groups she was still connected to from her time at VISTA, and living with her husband in the Bronx, she often walked around the neighborhood organizing or headed a few dozen blocks south to Harlem for socializing. If she wasn't working or volunteering, she was going to a jazz club or hosting a dinner party, often with conversations turning to the needs of the community and how she and her friends were trying to make a difference.

She had seen Panther brothers selling newspapers on local street corners, and she sometimes even bought a copy. But she had also seen the press "saying really horrible things about them" and heard what the local community had to say about them as well. Local Bronx residents with whom she was friendly said, "Watch them because they nuts. They wanna shoot up everybody." Older Black community members were especially wary. They'd say, "No, don't bother with them, because they're really crazy."

While the Panthers had become more involved in community work, mainstream media continued to fit them "into narrow, unidimensional frames that told the public little about why the organization existed, its appeal to black youth across the nation, or its relationship to the nation's racial crisis," explains Jane Rhodes. "Nowhere was the problem defined as racism, discrimination, poverty, unemployment, the decay of urban landscapes, or other social ills. Rather, the cause was identified as a 'spirit of lawlessness' and a 'hatred of whites' that was gripping black America."

Cleo had noticed the office on Adam Clayton Powell Jr. Boulevard not long after they had first started playing recorded speeches from speakers out front—who could miss them? The Panthers had also started a karate dojo with free classes for the community, which Cleo sometimes joined, invited by a new colleague, Panther Doc Dawkins, who was one of the union leaders at her job. And she started seeing brothers and sisters around the apartment buildings where she was also doing community work. But she didn't give much thought to joining. They seemed to be working for similar efforts, and she admired their work from a distance.

But within a few weeks of Cleo's starting her new job at Lincoln Hospital, workers began organizing to take over the hospital to protest their horrendous treatment and overmedication of patients. Black Panther members started attending the planning meetings, offering ways they could help. It took until they were sitting around the same table for their efforts to finally collide.

6

THE MEETING ROOM AT LINCOLN HOSPITAL was packed on an early spring afternoon in 1969. Cleo sat around a table with members of the Local 1199 Hospital Workers Union—who were known by other unions as "renegades"—along with members of the Black Panther Party, members of the Puerto Rican community organization the Young Lords, and others who were helping to organize to spur the hospital into action to better serve the local population. Lincoln Hospital was the only hospital serving the South Bronx and was known locally as the Butcher Shop for its high instances of malpractice, long wait times, and lack of interpreting services for the large Spanish-speaking population, among other lack of services. Only twenty-one years old, Cleo was eager to demonstrate her commitment to the cause and willingness to put in the time to get the work done.

Thinking back on that day, Cleo says, "I was putting my two cents in," responding to proposed assignments by more experienced folks in the room. "I was telling them: this is what I'm going to do, this is how much time it will take me, this is when I'll be back, and this is the result."

Brother Rashid Grisby and Dr. Curtis Powell were at the table representing the Black Panther Party. Brother Ray was a party section leader in Harlem and Dr. Curtis Powell had a PhD in chemistry and would go on to develop a vaccine for African sleeping sickness. The Panthers and the Young Lords had been working together in and around the neighborhood, and the men were there to give ideas and lend support. After all, the issues affecting Black residents in the South Bronx and around the city were largely affecting Puerto Rican residents as well. They had watched the spirited Cleo give her opinion, volunteer for even the most arduous tasks, and show little hesitation in becoming a vital part of this action, despite her relative youth. As soon as the meeting adjourned, they called her aside.

"Hey, sister," Rashid said to Cleo, "we've been watching you. We want you to join the Panthers." Cleo was flattered—it hadn't really occurred to her to join. She couldn't believe that now they were recruiting her.

"Yes," she replied without hesitation. "What do I do?"

"Just go down to the office and tell them we sent you," Dr. Powell told her. She thanked them, her characteristic wide smile tugging the corners of her mouth, betraying her excitement, as she turned and ran out the door.

———

"I was a runner in those days," Cleo says. "I ran everywhere." That day was no different, and in her home-sewn African-print halter minidress, she ran the two miles, over the Harlem River, to the Black Panther Party headquarters at the intersection of Adam Clayton Boulevard and 122nd Street in Harlem. As she was approaching, she could hear the Malcolm X record playing, with speakers connected to make it audible on the sidewalk:

> Lyndon B. Johnson is the head of the Democratic Party. If he's for civil rights, let him go into the Senate next week and declare himself. Let him go in there right now and declare himself. Let him go in there and denounce the southern branch of his party. Let him go in there right now and take a moral stand—right now, not later. Tell him, don't wait until election time. If he waits too long, brothers and sisters, he will be responsible for letting a condition develop in this country which will create a climate that will bring seeds up out of the ground with vegetation on the

end of them looking like something these people never dreamed of. In 1964, it's the ballot or the bullet.

Damn, Cleo thought. *The neighborhood is going to be so politically developed.* She had heard records playing most days she had walked by the office—the karate dojo was next door. But today she considered this constant soundtrack in a new way: she would be part of this group whose every action was to help the people.

Out front two women, just a year or so older than her, were sitting on the stoop. She knew them from their work with tenants at some of the same buildings where her students and patients lived. But this time she would be doing more than smiling and walking past.

"Hi," Cleo said. "Dr. Powell and Brother Rashid told me to come down here and sign up. I'm Cleo." The women regarded her for a moment, taking in her short dress and uncovered hair and friendly, open face.

"Do you know how to tie a gele?" the first woman, perhaps wearing a dashiki and bell bottoms, asked her in greeting.

"A what?" Cleo asked, her smile fading a watt or two.

"Odafonda, will you please get our sister here a gele?" The second woman ran upstairs and returned with a brightly patterned African cloth.

"Panther sisters need to know how to wrap their hair," the first woman said, draping the yards of brilliant fabric around Cleo's head at the hairline like a crown, and then wrapping it around in dramatic pleats before tying the excess fabric near the nape of her neck with a practiced hand.

"There," she said a moment later. She gave one firm tug to tighten the knot and then stepped back to admire her work. Then she reached back toward Cleo's nape and untied the wrap. "Now you do it."

Cleo took the limp fabric in her hands and paused. Then she took a breath and wrapped the gele in movements she trusted were similar to what she had just been shown. "How'd I do?" she asked as she tightened the final knot and tipped her head from side to side to check the weight and tightness of the gele.

Finally the first woman smiled and nodded. "I'm Afeni," she said, reaching out her hand.

"Odafonda," said the other woman.

"Now let's get this little thing signed up," Afeni said, leading Cleo inside.

Afeni Shakur, whom Cleo thought of as her big sister in the Panthers, has written about her own path to joining. She says she remembers seeing Bobby Seale in Harlem in 1967. "I was walking down 125th Street and got to Seventh Avenue and saw the same old crowd, a lot of people standing around listening to somebody on the box. Now 125th Street and Seventh Avenue is the corner where everybody and his brother has to make at least one speech in his lifetime. Marcus Garvey, Malcolm, Kenyatta, all of them have used that corner as a meeting hall. There is never a Saturday that doesn't find at least a small crowd gathered there."

But that day, she writes, "was different. The people listening were a mixture of people, it wasn't just cultural nationalists, the people dressed in dashikis." Bobby Seale's message seemed to speak across the Harlem demographics: "everybody was standing listening." Afeni doesn't remember details of what was said, but rather that the Black Panther Party felt more inclusive than any other group she had come across. "I knew he was right, because even though I didn't know anything about the Black Panther Party, I knew I had more respect for them than I had for all the organizations in the world. I knew they had heart. And everybody standing there listening seemed to love Brother Bobby." There wasn't yet a chapter in New York City, but Bobby had said that there would be one soon. "I just knew from the beginning that it would branch out into something beautiful—it had to," Afeni says. She knew there were Black people "all over the place that felt like I did." She would join not long after, near the end of 1968. When Cleo arrived, it was only a few months after that—but in that short time the New York Panthers had already done so much to work with and integrate themselves into the community.

Upstairs in the main office of the Black Panther Party headquarters, Cleo met with Janet Cyril, who was office manager of the Harlem branch of the New York City Black Panther Party. In her early twenties, she was "a genius," according to Mae Jackson, one of her best friends. There may have been a few young brothers and sisters sitting in chairs, reading the Panther paper. Everyone was expected to sell papers, and for many who dedicated all their time to the Panthers, the nickel commission they got from each twenty-five-cent paper sale was their only income. Cleo had seen plenty of Panthers selling papers on corners around the city. Most Panthers had their beat—some stayed in Harlem or the Bronx, others went to Washington Square or down to the West Village. And every Panther knew the stories they were selling and would call out the headlines—the best, Panthers said, could really "blow." The term was borrowed from jazz solos with a modern anticapitalist twist. "Not only were you selling papers, you were giving a show," Cleo recalls. There was an art to it—one that Cleo would quickly pick up with her friendly and chatty nature. She would be expected to sell papers too, despite her full-time job and additional Panther duties. But unlike the others who relied on the commission for money, she would donate all her proceeds to the party.

"Here's your Red Book," Janet said, handing Cleo a copy of Chairman Mao Tse-tung's Little Red Book, one of hundreds that were gifted to the Black Panthers by the Chinese government. Cleo knew a Panther was never without their Red Book—the telltale red cover could be seen peeking out of back pockets and purses around the city wherever there were political actions or demonstrations taking place, identifying sisters and brothers in the party. Cleo recalls, "One of the things the Panthers did immediately was to inform you that this is not no gun problem that we're dealing with. This is an education problem, and we have Political Education every night of the week, and your job is to show up at Political Education, have read all the books that were assigned to you for that particular day, and be prepared to have a discussion with the rest of the folks."

"Here's tonight's reading," Janet said, noting the passages that evening's PE class would be discussing, adding, "You'll need to know the Ten-Point Program for the meeting as well. Don't think you won't get called on."

Cleo checked the clock on the wall. She still had a few hours to get back to the hospital and then do her homework.

———————

That evening Cleo climbed back up the stairs to the Panther headquarters for her first PE class. These nightly meetings were required of all Panthers and were the core of their philosophy to educate members so they could know what they were fighting for, not just against. The room was already packed by the time she arrived, but because she was a new recruit, there was a seat saved for her near the front. Since her visit a few hours earlier, the room had been transformed. All the chairs were lined up, and most were filled. Other Panthers stood leaning against walls or desks, or sitting on the floor, filling the space. The Malcolm X record that had been playing all day was turned off—other than the murmur of voices, the room was quiet, waiting for the PE lesson to begin.

As at every meeting, they began with the Ten-Point Program. First the room recited it together, and then the leader of the night's lesson—perhaps it was Brother Dhoruba—was certain to call on a newer recruit to recite part of the platform. Cleo had made sure she studied before she arrived.

"You, brother," he pointed at a recruit in the front row. "Recite point nine."

The young brother paused, the room silent, and then spoke in a clear, loud voice: "Point nine is 'end to the use of police brutality in the community.'"

"Explain, young brother," Dhoruba said.

"The police historically have been beating Black people and killing Black people, and our demand is that they stop coming into our community and that the Black Panther Party is going to make sure that this ends because we are going to follow the police around and watch them to make sure they don't beat up or hurt anybody in the community." When the young man in the front row finished, he waited for Brother Dhoruba to nod his head in approval and then he sat down.

Cleo could barely suppress a smile. *That is so cool,* she thought. While she was already familiar with the work they were doing, she was amazed at the time and care they took with educating all members on the philosophy that informed their actions. It reminded her of the conversations she and her husband had had with their friends when she first moved to the Bronx.

"Now take out the Red Book!" Brother Dhoruba called. Everyone in the room pulled their books out and shook them in the air, like so many flags waving. "OK, now we're going to start our reading. Anyone who can't really read, sit next to someone who can." There was minor shuffling of bodies and riffling of pages, and the room quieted again. A few of these teens and twentysomethings, like Afeni Shakur, may have placed highly on school tests, enough to be admitted to more prestigious high schools. But Afeni ended up dropping out, never feeling like she belonged. Others, like Cleo, may have grown up reading newspapers and magazines emphasizing Black excellence and asking for critical thinking of the supremacist political policies around them. Still others had maybe dropped out of a high school that had done little to encourage them to stay. But Brother Dhoruba, or Afeni Shakur, or the other Panthers who helped lead the PE classes, all had the goal of helping folks feel empowered. They were all expected to work with others to understand the readings of the day—that day it might have been from Mao's Red Book, but they also read psychiatrist Frantz Fanon's *The Wretched of the Earth*, Brazilian educator Paulo Freire's *Pedagogy of the Oppressed*, and writings by Malcolm X.

After a few more minutes of quiet reading, Brother Dhoruba called the group to attention again.

"What's the name, sister?" Brother Dhoruba called on Cleo, who was sitting in the second row.

"Cleo!" she responded, sitting up straighter as all eyes turned to the new recruit.

"Yeah, Sister Cleo, tell us what you think this is saying!" And so she did.

The PE class continued for well over an hour. New recruits and old were called on to read aloud, analyze, or answer questions. As Cleo recalls, it was never with the goal to shame people for not reading or understanding, but rather to illustrate an expectation of excellence, of intellectual rigor, and to help all Panthers understand the Panthers' mission that they were fighting for. They were there to serve those who needed their help the most. To ask the people what they needed, and address that need—not come in with their own ideas of how to help. "Being a Panther is about serving the people, mind, body, and soul," Jamal Joseph, who was a high schooler when he joined the Panthers, wrote about what he learned when Afeni taught PE class: "If you're here because you hate the oppressor and you don't have a deep love for the people, then you are a flawed revolutionary."

Even Cleo, who was friendly with a number of Panthers from their paths crossing through their community-organizing work around the city, was surprised at the welcome, rigor, and selflessness of her first PE meeting. She realized that the media's narrative of the Panthers had influenced her opinion of them too. Yet what she found when she started working with them on the hospital takeover, then here at PE class, and for every day thereafter, was that Panthers were anything but self-serving or violent. They were generous and kind, firm in their convictions and convinced that through hard work they would accomplish their goal of empowering the people they served. Everything they did was for the community. She left that night excited at the debates and conversations she had, and with her first orders to report to her shift at the Free Breakfast for Children Program in the South Bronx at five thirty the next morning to help cook.

7

AT PANTHER PADS AND SHARED APARTMENTS around the city, Panthers woke up before dawn to arrive at their assigned breakfast place by 5:30 AM. Some lived near the breakfast programs where they were assigned. Others who worked a day or two a week in between other assignments doled out by the officer of the day might crash at a nearby Panther pad to make the morning commute quick. But without fail a group of Panthers would be at each of the breakfast programs spread across the city by dawn to start preparing.

It was a well-choreographed system in the South Bronx community center where Cleo was assigned. Posters with images of Black leaders and FREE HUEY were taped to the walls, and long tables ran the length of the room. The Panthers started by setting the table, placing a paper plate, napkin, and a plastic fork and knife at each seat. It was important that the kids felt like they were sitting down to a real family meal, and the Panthers would teach them how to properly use their utensils if they didn't know how.

Then the team would start cooking—the bacon would be sizzling, someone would be scrambling eggs, someone else would be boiling water for grits, another person would be pouring orange juice. "It was never chaotic," Cleo remembers. The five-person teams might have changed their exact makeup daily, but each breakfast location had a consistent leader. It was expected that everyone did their time in the breakfast program, and on the rare occasion that someone didn't show up, they usually got a talking-to—Janet Cyril was known for her lectures. They went something like this: the breakfast program was integral to the Panther's ideals of serving the people and was created in a direct response to a need from the communities they supported.

"What's wrong with you?" she'd say. "Don't you know how important it is to feed hungry children?"

———————

Around seven the kids started arriving, some greeting the Panthers with their own chant: "All power to the people!" The Panthers would then respond, "All power to the people!"

If one of the kids asked what they meant, a Panther would use that as an opportunity for a mini-PE lesson: "Well first of all, we need to fight against the avaricious businessman who is doing terrible things to the people, keeping them poor."

The kids were mostly elementary-school aged, and some wore berets or had Black Panther pins tacked to their lapels like the young Panther role models they looked up to. Most of the children were Black, but there were also Puerto Rican and White kids too—upward of fifty or more every morning, all from the neighborhood, and no one was ever turned away. The kids clamored into their seats, still wiggling and bouncing, calling to their friends down the table or playing silly games until the food was served. One of the young Panther men started serving the bacon, eggs, toast, and grits. Cartons of milk were passed out, and the kids tucked in, with only occasional reminders to use their utensils properly, or eat over their plate. Over the next hour kids continued to trickle in—even those who had breakfast at home wanted to come to hang out with their friends and the cool, young Panthers who taught them songs and told them they were powerful and gave them ready hugs.

"Who has homework?" Cleo would ask as the kids were finishing breakfast.

"I do, I do!" some of the kids yelled, pulling sheets of paper and books out of their backpacks.

Cleo cocked her head and asked, "Well, did you do it?" If the answer was no, she sidled up next to them and started to help.

After the homework check, the Panthers taught them songs like "Revolution Has Come," and the often-cavernous church basements and community centers became a cacophony of singing and yelling and foot stomping.

By then the kids were fully awake and energized.

"Do you know who's responsible for the traffic lights?" another Panther asked the kids. They all chanted back, "A Black man!" There were lessons about the history of Black people in America and reminders of all that Black people had accomplished despite their centuries of oppression—lessons reminiscent of those taught at SNCC's Nonviolent High in 1961, which Panthers would later refine into their Freedom Schools in the years afterward.

And finally they took the kids to school. "Pack up your bags—it's time to go to school!" There'd be groans and resistance. "They always wanted hugs," Cleo remembers. Before they left the breakfast program, Cleo lined up for hugs, and then watched them head out the door, behind a Panther who walked the snaking line of wiggling kids to school, in time for the first bell.

"The kids never wanted to leave. But we had to go to work!" Those who were left at the kitchen finished the cleanup: scrubbing the pots and pans, washing the tables, tossing the paper plates and cups, and bringing out the trash. And then they left for their next assignment, the Panther office, or work, like Cleo.

———————

Cleo joined not long after the start of the New York City chapter breakfast programs, but they were already in full swing. The first breakfast for kids was served at St. Augustine Church in Oakland, California, in January 1969, serving eleven kids grits and eggs and bacon. The need was so great that by the end of the week they were serving 135 children a day, a feat accomplished by working closely with Father Earl Neil. Father Neil, who had recently been transferred from his church in Chicago to St. Augustine in Oakland, met Black Panther Party leader Bobby Seale, and they became friendly, with Father Neil recognizing many of the same goals as stated in the Panthers' Ten-Point Program.

After that the Black Panther Party would meet regularly at St. Augustine, for PE class and occasional workshops. In more than one workshop, Father Neil recalls, leaders emphasized the importance of asking the people what they needed and responding to that need. This was basic community-organizing theory—what Cleo had been taught in VISTA. And Father Neil was in a position where he was acutely aware of his congregants' many needs as well.

Father Neil remembers that Bobby Seale approached him after members of the party had canvassed the community as community organizers had taught them. "What were they concerned about? What could the party do for them?" the canvassers asked.

"Sometimes my kids go to school hungry. I can't always help them with their homework because I work late," they heard. Seale came to Father Neil with their findings. He wanted Father Neil's help to start a breakfast program from local kids.

Father Neil says he was tasked with the logistics: making sure the space was inspected and approved for food service by the health and fire departments. His parishioner Ruth Beckford made nutritional recommendations and helped connect to local mothers. By spring the Oakland Free Breakfast for Children Program had become so popular—both in numbers of kids fed and in positive response from the community—that the party mandated that all local chapters start their own Free Breakfast Programs. The New York City branch had robust chapters across the city when this mandate came down, and they readily implemented breakfast programs into their regular community organizing. And what they found as well was that the breakfast programs provided a connection with the neighborhood that opened lines of communication and eased mistrust in ways other community work didn't.

At the start of the Free Breakfast Program, Bobby Seale noted that there was some dissension within the party about this shift away from an armed neighborhood presence. He writes that early in the fall of 1968 Eldridge Cleaver, the Panthers' minister of information, came to the office, a gun under his khaki bush jacket, and declared in front of more than a dozen other members that the Free Breakfast Program, which was in its planning phase, was a "sissy program."

In his book *Power to the People*, Bobby Seale recounts how he pulled Eldridge aside and said, "That's some one-dimension thinking, man. Voter registration and community programs unify the people, Eldridge. I'm here trying to organize people in opposition to the racist power structure fuckin' over everybody and you're here trying to be some macho dude with these kids, these young women, and these men out there because you've been in a shootout." Bobby writes that Eldridge acquiesced after that and was on board with the shift in resources and focus.

The few photos that are most often shared of the breakfast program usually show beret-wearing young men in leather jackets or turtleneck sweaters serving grits to kids. These photos were often taken by progressive news agencies or local photographers who considered themselves aligned with the Panthers' politics, and were used in news articles reporting on their growing survival programs. The striking juxtaposition of the tough and the tender made it easy for detractors to claim that the photos of tough guys serving kids was a well-planned photo op. Sowing doubt about the Panthers' intentions became a way for the FBI and other law enforcement agencies to undermine what had become a popular program and was making powerful gains in the community.

But what few outside the party and the communities they served recognized was that in the New York City chapter nearly two-thirds of members were women (other chapters had similar gender ratios) and the men were the ones being photographed because the women sent them out front to serve. Meanwhile the women coordinated the cooking and the cleaning, managed the donations to make sure enough was cooked but not too much, and oversaw that the room was returned to its original condition.

"There's so few pictures," Cleo explains, because "we never did anything for recognition. Everything we did was for the community."

And despite the FBI's painting these programs as a way to manipulate the public sentiment, Panther historians and scholars don't believe
that this was calculated as a response to media coverage or a manipulation of public sentiment. Rather, party leadership recognized that true
revolution—an overthrow of the existing power structure—was not
going to happen on the swift timetable they originally, and ideally, had
believed. So they shifted even more resources to connect to the community to find out how they could serve, while also using these interactions to teach their core message: the ways in which the established
system was oppressing them and their call to rise up and fight for true
revolution. These various efforts to support residents' day-to-day needs,
including health care, housing, food, and education, would become what
the neighborhoods they served knew them by and would become the
ways that the Panthers were influential in their communities as they
responded to the needs of the people—and why the FBI would find
them so threatening to the existing power structure.

———————

A few years later Huey Newton would write an eloquent justification of
the survival programs, stating:

> We recognize that in order to bring the people to the level of
> consciousness where they would seize the time, it would be nec-
> essary to serve their interests in survival by developing programs
> which would help them to meet their daily needs. . . . All these
> programs satisfy the deep needs of the community, but they are
> not solutions to our problems. That is why we call them survival
> programs, meaning survival pending revolution.

But the New York chapter, partially because of when it was established as well as the interests of those who began the chapter and who
joined early on, had been focused on survival programs from its beginning. This was in part because of the city's extreme needs—and those
who joined the New York City Black Panthers early on knew, and were
often from, these neighborhoods and wanted to serve them. Also, the

large number of women who were drawn to the Panthers in New York used their passions, resources, and community-organizing skills to push the Panthers toward these initiatives as well. Women were soon the majority of the rank-and-file party members not just in New York but also around the country. In the Bay Area, Newsreel interviews note that "the Panther women basically ran the headquarters," while New York chapter members remember similar contributions of female members, both in the office and in the growing number of projects around the city.

While these women were younger than Mama Quin, in many ways their work can also be seen through the lens of activist mothering, the term coined by Dr. Hamlin. Though many were in their late teens or early twenties, it's no logical leap to see how they might find their power through nurturing children, cooking, cleaning, or administrative work, as these were the same roles socially modeled and considered acceptable for them to embrace within society at large, through dominant cultural stereotypes, even within a relatively progressive organization. As multiple female Panthers note, despite their rhetoric around gender equality, the Panther males (and females) were still influenced by the patriarchal stereotypes of the dominant society in which they lived. But it was through these perhaps traditional skills of care, domesticity, and interpersonal strengths that many Panther women were empowered as they advocated for a more community-based nexus of feeding, health care, and education, providing necessities for the—often—women and children in need.

Complicating this is Patricia Hill Collins's work, which views communities of Black women in the United States, such as the female Panthers, as "refashion[ing] African-influenced conceptions of self and community . . . to resist the negative controlling images of Black womanhood advanced by Whites as well as the discriminatory social practices that these controlling images supported." Tied up in these stereotypes and resistant identities is a critique of the capitalist power structure that the Panthers explicitly engaged in, specifically through the readings and discussions in their Political Education classes. The breakfast program—and other survival programs, the realms of which were often also seen traditionally as women's work—became locations for this challenging and remaking of identity.

Afeni Shakur's work exemplified the way traditionally feminine qualities and roles like nurturing and feeding and clothing were turned into leadership roles within this reimagined social construct. She was an early leader in the party, not just through the time and commitment she gave to the party from early on but also through her kindness and her concern for people. Cleo remembers Afeni as being someone who had the concerns of the community in the forefront of her mind, and people knew if they needed something they could come to their local Black Panther Party office and ask. "If she was in that office, it was going to get taken care of. Which made the Black Panther Party that much more personable and that much more connected . . . to the community, and which made the community love us that much more."

It was this concern that prompted Afeni to ask a dry cleaner in Harlem near the office to donate the clothes that folks never picked up. "Any old clothes that you have, just give them to us," she told them. And so the cleaner went to the warehouse and brought a truckload of clothing donations to the party office on Adam Clayton Boulevard. Afeni took it upon herself to organize the clothes and distribution to those who needed it—fellow Panthers remember racks out in front of the office, with Afeni helping people choose items in a way that felt dignified.

Afeni also convinced a local shoe company to donate pairs of shoes that she distributed around the neighborhood and kept in the office for emergencies. More than once she saw people without shoes on the street and ran after them to ask them their size, instructing them to wait while she fetched them a pair from the office.

———

New York City, with a large number of student and community activists, was already home to a large FBI presence, even before the Panthers were officially on the COINTELPRO list of groups to watch. When the New York Panther chapter officially emerged, and with it great interest from local youth, the FBI was poised to immediately begin a campaign to undermine their organizing work. In a highly redacted April 1968 memo from the "Director, FBI," the New York office is directed to use "ridicule" to discredit party leaders and make them "ludicrous to ghetto youth." Four paragraphs of details are then blacked out. By July, the New York office submitted a plan to the director: they suggested creating five thousand copies of a propaganda pamphlet and paying boys from the community ages ten to thirteen to distribute them in sections of Harlem and Bedford-Stuyvesant.

"Perhaps $2–$3 to each boy would do the trick," the memo notes. One such propaganda pamphlet that was disseminated was photocopied and handwritten in script, with the headline STRANGLE THE BLACK PANTHER and a drawing of two hands around a panther cat's throat. "Brother, we're telling you like it is—SNCC and Black Panther is uptight with the MAN. . . . Don't be fooled," it read, striving to sound like it was written by a concerned community member. And this was just one of over two hundred initiatives aimed against the Black Panther Party—and among the tamest. As the FBI initially sought to undermine the party's standing in the community, it, like the MSSC, focused on propaganda and misinformation through pamphlets like this, heckling at events, and then sowing doubt and internal fissures among members and supporters through fake letters and phone calls alleging a variety of ills, from stealing money to sexual impropriety to being in cahoots with the government.

And for a while, public sentiment seemed to be split on the local actions of the Panthers. Some saw them as increasing police presence and violence, especially as police harassment of the new chapters was sometimes met with antagonism by local youth, who might set fire to trash heaps to lure police to an area where they might throw bottles at them. In one instance, Brooklyn police in Crown Heights, the neighborhood next to Bedford-Stuyvesant, were hit with buckshot. The police claimed there was a Black Panther Party button found at the scene, which further justified unwarranted harassment. The people who had moved to escape from the fear and racial tension of the South could imagine what fate might befall them or their children at the hands of an angry, White police force. One could imagine why residents of neighborhoods like Bedford-Stuyvesant and Harlem might blame increased police activity on the actions of this new activist group. And likewise, it wouldn't be a stretch to think of J. Edgar Hoover celebrating this victory.

But that dynamic began to change as the Free Breakfast for Children Programs expanded in scope and popularity around the city in early 1969, followed by their other survival programs. This first sustained survival program showcased the real goals of the Panthers, and community relations and public sentiment both saw stark improvement. These positive daily interactions made the Panthers heroes in the eyes of the children, and many parents as well, and also created a direct line of communication between the community and the Panthers. The more the Panthers supported and interacted with their communities, the more their message of empowerment and revolution was both heard and modeled. They didn't have to wield a gun to have power.

The seemingly benign breakfast program became J. Edgar Hoover's formidable enemy; he saw the inherent power in feeding a daily hot breakfast to poor kids—and how this would undermine his own conservative and racist agenda, so much so that he didn't care who was harmed to stop the Black Panther Party from winning public trust.

On May 15, 1969, he sent an internal memo to "ALL OFFICES" with the subject BLACK NATIONALIST—HATE GROUPS. It read, in part, "The Breakfast for Children Program (BCP) . . . has met with some success and has resulted in considerable favorable publicity for the BPP. . . . And what is more distressing, provides the BPP with a ready audience composed of highly impressionable youths. . . . Consequently the BCP represents the best and most influential activity going for the BPP and, as such, is potentially the greatest threat to efforts by authorities . . . to neutralize the BPP and destroy what it stands for."

8

"WE WON'T BUY NO MORE BEER," Joe Martin encouraged the group of Black tavern owners he assembled. Martin was around the age of Mama Quin's older daughter Carolyn, who had graduated high school a few years earlier, and he was now active in the voting rights efforts around McComb. He had just heard that local officials had rescinded Mama Quin's beer license, for no apparent reason other than to work to drive her out of business. This was just one more example of the economic sanctions levied on the Black community. Mama Quin, while long watched by the MSSC and known to be a local activist and NAACP member, was finally being painted as dangerous in the eyes of local officials.

The gathered local tavern owners—all men—initially agreed with Joe. They would stage a beer boycott. While this would be a hardship for many of them—low-alcohol beer was the only legal alcoholic beverage in Mississippi from post-Prohibition until 1966—Joe convinced them that if officials were able to bully Mama Quin, it would only be a matter of time before they decided to wield their power to undermine someone else who fell afoul of their racist agenda.

So they stopped buying beer and continued the boycott for six weeks. Finally "the White man down there who owned the companies went to his White friends and said, 'Look, you take care of me; I've been taking care of you.' . . . and then Mama Quin had her business back and booming again." This message of solidarity among Black business owners was a signal of power, not just to the White officials, but within their own community: "because their customers were Black; they didn't have to depend on nobody."

Although one attempt to undermine Mama Quin's work was averted through a coordinated community effort, local officials and law enforcement still sought to enact economic sanctions against Mama Quin and other business owners in what ways they could. Even as Black business owners anchored the local activist work, there were always ways to exert pressure. It was backroom dealings that gave the MSSC power. If someone was White and glad-handed the right people, they might be able to join the governor's handpicked commission itself, work with a cooperative White Citizens' Council, or otherwise benefit from this established White supremacist system. And once one was in the system of power, it was relatively easy to use available resources to keep that power central. The MSSC actually agreed to give taxpayer money—money Black people paid—to White Citizens' Councils to work toward upholding segregation and the disenfranchisement of around half of the Mississippi population. And while this was challenged in the courts and questioned even by politically moderate officials, it was still allowed to continue. This money ostensibly went mostly for propaganda campaigns in support of segregation, euphemistically called "public relations," but the lack of oversight meant that it was hard to trace exactly how it was spent by those actively working toward Black oppression.

And this power brokering happened at every level. There were those who were sent on MSSC-paid speaking trips to states around the country to espouse the glories of segregation to a welcoming audience. There were the county registrars who would look at the Black face filling out the poll test and know before he or she read a word that they would decide that person would not pass. Didn't matter what he or she wrote down. Many loan officers at the banks would deny an applicant for their race alone, not needing a justification for their rejection. Others might offer less money or unfavorable terms, putting in jeopardy the Black applicant's dream of owning a home or land or starting a new business, and keeping wealth in the pockets of White landlords and businessmen. Access to financial resources was key in Black wealth building, and this was a tool of oppression used by White supremacy—this was also why some business owners were reluctant to risk something so hard fought.

The FBI would come to town to investigate a crime, such as one of the many times the KKK shot at the home of a Black person—because the Black people were activists, tried to register to vote, or perhaps were too successful or not deferential enough. Was the FBI told by their director not to interrogate any suspects, question the victims for themselves, speak with Black witnesses, or assess the crime scene? Or were they so entrenched in their own narrative—that the local cops were, of course, correct in their assessment that the activists had shot at their own home for publicity reasons—that they neglected to investigate further? Perhaps all of the above.

Certainly employers would fire Black workers for known or suspected activist work, and landlords might kick them out of their homes for the same. There was almost no chance that local officials would stop this eviction—whatever decision the White man made was justified. This is the insidious nature of White supremacy, particularly when it infiltrates every nook and cranny of governmental power. The explicit intention of the action doesn't matter; the outcome is the same.

Within this climate, Aylene Quin understood that to be free, she had to provide for herself. And she did that through her legal businesses—South of the Border, a beauty shop, and later one of the only Black-owned hotels in the area—as well as bootlegging, which then gave her the financial means to continue to expand her businesses and move when necessary. And this financial security—and business diversity—meant that she could afford to support her family and feed the SNCC workers as part of the many ways she supported the voting rights movement.

For an intelligent Black woman who was denied formal education—Aylene only finished the seventh grade, but Jacqueline says she "would be adding something on the adding machine [while her mother] would be doing it in her mind"—she realized her power was in her self-sufficiency, not just to feed her own family but also to help provide for others in her community who were also fighting for freedom.

———————

"Our money was no good there," Curtis Muhammad says, and other SNCC workers have said the same. In the oral histories and personal interviews with local activists and SNCC workers alike, many people mention eating for free at South of the Border. SNCC worker D. Gorton extols, "That was extraordinary food that she gave away free to SNCC. . . . For days we would talk about that because she would cook those beans and those peas and different things for those plate lunches . . . in that incredible tradition in the Deep South" where inexpensive cuts were made richer through the love and labor of the cook.

And not only did she feed the folks coming into the cafe, but also she cooked food for those who were in jail and later brought food to the COFO house. It was this way she modeled generosity with her food, money, and time that gave her influence in the community—and presented an option for folks beyond the White supremacist capitalistic structure within which most Black people were being oppressed. These meals were also a form of mutual aid: she fed those who were working for the movement, often volunteers or those getting paid mere dollars a week by SNCC. How could they do their work if they were always hungry or counting pennies to figure out what food they could afford? What would a community look like, and how much could be accomplished, if instead of money the motivating factor was helping everyone thrive?

Mutual aid, or the concept of local communities providing resources and support for each other, had been an important institution in many southern Black communities since the end of the Civil War and, one could argue, in various ways prior to that. In these formal, informal, and ad hoc mutual-aid and benevolent societies that were often organized through local churches, Black women were seen as important community leaders. These groups provided resources as varied as food for the hungry, personal necessities, financial support, and even land for churches and individuals—and were often a lifeline for victims of White supremacist violence and economic sanctions and provided a safety net for those who wanted to continue to challenge the local racist systems. Black Freemason chapters, which provided meeting space and other support and resources for civil rights work in Mississippi and around the country, were among the formal groups that provided an array of mutual-aid resources. Yet while there was certainly immense food insecurity among a great many Black communities, especially around the South, much of the local mutual aid was informal, like in the Burglund neighborhood where Aylene lived and worked.

Frankye Adams-Johnson, who was active in the movement as a teen and grew up in a small town outside of Jackson, remembers, "In Mississippi, I felt poor but rich, because I never knew what it was to go hungry. I grew up on the land and in the community. People were poor but people had . . . unity. . . . If my neighbor did not have food, we broke bread and shared food." Many Black communities had been practicing this interdependence, in part from necessity, since they were enslaved. There was great benefit in uplifting a community—whether through the church, where much mutual aid was centered, or informally among neighbors. While some of this mutual aid was influenced by African culture—such as the *sousou*, where community members pay in when they can and have access to the funds when in need, as a kind of community bank—much of this interdependence and mutual aid was developed out of more immediate necessity. There is power, of course, in this sharing culture that illustrates socialist qualities at work—power that White leaders sought to stamp out and that Mama Quin sought to wield by feeding those who were hungry. After all, what if a community's needs were met? Then White supremacist leadership would have to find other ways to exert power. And they did.

One outcome of this alternative economy was a proliferation of female leadership within Black communities, a relatively high percentage of female property and business ownership, and a deep integration of mutual aid as an important element to a healthy Black community. This respect for Black female leadership, and the ways in which it works within the Black community and beyond, has long been overlooked and undervalued in the dominant White culture and has only very recently become more broadly recognized and respected.

Aylene Quin was as much a community leader because of her position as a business owner in McComb as for her work organizing mutual aid in the interest of her neighbors. Folks looked up to her, were employed by her—at the restaurant and later at her beauty shop and motel—and saw her as a role model for a different way of community support: one that gave as much as she could. She also frequently served in leadership positions in the community across institutions: as a board member of the PTA and president of the NAACP—positions that asked for much time and energy but didn't pay. But through these positions she knew people and could work to convince them to help whatever cause she—and her larger community—thought was worthy. She was known to do her voter rights canvassing during the day, to help convince the women of the household who would typically be home then, to join a class or agree to try to register. At the same time, she'd be included in conversations of local influential business owners, generally all men.

Yet this community building, done around kitchen tables rather than on the front lines, has been historically underdocumented and unsung. How many people did she convince to join the struggle over a long-simmered dish of black-eyed peas? But it wasn't just this "women's work" of home-cooked meals and sweet potato pie discussions that gave her power. She also found it through work that was typically reserved for men, such as being a leader among the Black business owners. "Men were her friends. . . . [They] treated her as an equal." And while her daughter Jacqueline also believes that her mother was judged by some in her community and in the movement—and by history—for her boot-legging business, she was always proud that her mother did what she needed to provide for the family, especially given the strictures in which she had to succeed. Her daughter's assertion is certainly supported by the scholarship that pervasive stereotypes limited the perceptions of Black women, even within some aspects of Black communities. The local women noted in the movement in Mississippi were painted as selfless and honest-working mother figures—while men could have much more complicated livelihoods and legacies.

———————

Curtis Muhammad walked into South of the Border to pick up Mama Quin for a corn whiskey run. She had summoned him on the phone, asking, "You got time to go down the coast with me?"

"Yeah baby, I'm coming," he said, and headed over. Curtis was only a few years older than Mama Quin's daughter Carolyn, and she knew him from around McComb but also trusted him from his work with SNCC and other local activist groups. And she also knew that he and his buddies souped up cars—Curtis had a 1956 Buick that could go 140 on the backroads. And "we didn't stop for nobody."

Curtis worked for Mama Quin whenever he was in town and she called. They had an understanding that certain things that were, perhaps, extralegal needed to happen if they wanted the means to work toward things that *should* happen. Like voting rights, desegregation, and racial equity.

"She understood the justice question," Curtis says years later. "White boys didn't get busted for corn whiskey, the stills didn't get busted. They didn't bust the producers or the distributors." In fact, there was even a semiofficial black-market tax on illegal liquor, levied by the state tax collector, who checked wholesalers' records coming out of neighboring states where liquor was legal, and billed wholesalers accordingly. The state received much of this tax, and the tax collector was allowed to keep a rather large cut, encouraging his forensic accounting work. But just because tax was paid didn't mean anyone was immune from prosecution. And Black bootleggers, or the large number of Black folks in the community who regularly drank liquor, were particularly susceptible to getting fined should someone need a reason to punish or intimidate them. No matter that plenty of White establishments and individuals alike trafficked and drank liquor with impunity.

"We had a constable, he would let some of the men get the whiskey and bring it to us and would mark an 8 on this bottle," Aylene explained. "He'd come and raid you and if he found other liquor there you had to pay a fine. By the time you pay this fine and you sell your liquor you don't make anything. So you had to study how you get by when everybody else was doing the same thing."

Like the racket that it was, Mama Quin had to pay off some cops to help establish her illegal liquor business—and there were a few officers who were happy to make the extra cash. If her man got word of a raid, he would come out and warn her so she could get rid of the evidence. But despite Aylene's connections, South of the Border was scrutinized, including more than a dozen citations for illegal liquor between the years of 1955 and 1964, all noted in the MSSC files, which certainly points to political retribution. There have been plenty of reports about illegal liquor planted by local police or federal agents in a ploy to falsely arrest or fine members of the Black community. As she said, "I seen where I could make a living and that's what I did. . . . And if I could outsmart the law, I did that." And while these citations certainly had a political agency, as Aylene's daughter Jacqueline says years later, "if they fined my mama for it, it was for real." She laughed and then turned serious. "I was proud of my mama for always providing for us. She did what she had to do."

———————

But even paying off cops meant that Mama Quin had some leverage over certain members of that department who didn't want to lose their pocket money. "She was an anomaly in McComb," explains Mississippi-born SNCC volunteer Freddie Biddle. "The fact is that she owned her own home. She had a business. So in some ways, she was a lot more insulated than a lot of people were. You know, for Black people during those years to own their own home in Mississippi was a real big point. Because it definitely sheltered you from so many of the problems." However, her continued activism made her a target for law enforcement and the Ku Klux Klan, which was growing in numbers again after decades of decline.

So Mama Quin pressed on, raising her four kids as a single parent, feeding folks whether or not they could pay, and making a living through serving food and drink. Her enterprise enabled her to create an extended family among her regulars in a way accessible to her as a woman, and though her gender also made others underestimate her, she used what resources she had to tirelessly fight for voting rights and Black Freedom. "She was just built like that," Jacqueline says decades later. "It was just the way she was: if it wasn't right, it wasn't right. It was just in her DNA." She paused and then added that White people "can't imagine how this is . . . it's what she felt. This is what we still feel today. It's nothing that can be put into words, but you know the injustice of it."

9

MAMA QUIN WAS KNOWN FOR HER LONG-SIMMERED BEANS, macaroni and cheese, gumbo, and chicken and dumplings—all food that she and her family would call soul food, even as this might not fit the dominant culture's narrow definition of this cuisine, or "Down Home Southern Cooking," as food historian Adrian Miller calls Black rural foodways from the 1890s to the present. It was food that wasn't expensive, but skilled cooks like Mama Quin, who learned from her once-enslaved grandmother, could eke the most flavor out of the most modest ingredients.

But to reduce her cooking to the food of poverty, and narrow the possibilities of what is considered soul food, is to misunderstand—and even marginalized, Black food culture is of course not monolithic. In many ways, however, Aylene Quin's family history was somewhat typical. Her grandparents were enslaved and brought their knowledge of farming and cooking to their rural homestead by the time she was young, although they did own their land, which was not the norm.

"We had cattle and we had chickens, we raised practically everything that we used . . . except flour. We had corn and we shucked and shelled all the corn and turn it into meal. We had butter, we had hogs . . . we really had everything we needed to get by, except clothes . . . we had peach arches and plum trees and there was a stream running through this land and we could gather muscadine and grapes and everything," Aylene recalled. "I always wanted to redeem it back." They cooked what they grew and could procure other local products, which had more in common with neighboring Whites than Black people farther across the South. So what makes what she cooked soul food?

The history of what is considered soul food is wrapped up in the history of Black America—which inevitably traces back to generations of enslavement. As Adrian Miller explains, the majority of enslaved people lived on southern plantations where their access to food was highly regulated, giving way to the well-known soul food trinity of pork, cornmeal, and molasses. These were cheap and easy-to-procure ingredients, and often were what was available for sustenance. Sometimes enslaved Black people could grow their own garden, which might have crops like okra, sweet potatoes, collards, beans, and corn—of which Native Americans were sometimes known to have provided guidance on propagating. On larger plantations, enslaved cooks might be tasked with making dishes for the "Big House" that ranged from high-end southern food to faddish European-inspired recipes, resulting in knowledge of these cooking skills and dishes—and an elevation of these dishes as higher class and more desirable in the dominant culture.

Enslaved Black people on smaller farms or in urban environments often ate more shared food with the enslavers, perhaps given the least desirable cuts of meat or the pot likker—the broth left over after stewing collards or other greens—or sometimes eating the same food, especially when living on a less prosperous farm in closer quarters. Aylene was told that her grandfather's father was White and his enslaved mother "lived in a house in the back," and her enslaver "would divide food with her." This was not uncommon, as food was often used as a way to control and even brag to other enslavers. As Miller details, enslavers might pass out rations "with great fanfare" in a show of "bravado" and control. Those who fed their enslaved population poorly might be shamed or at times accused of stoking unrest from hunger. Yet there were also many instances of withholding food to exert power. The point was control—creating both scarcity and plenty, at the enslaver's will.

The Civil War created scarcity for White and Black Southerners alike, with the Union army using food blockades as a military tactic, often to great effect, creating rampant hunger across the South. During much of the war, what food that could be procured and cooked was what was previously considered poverty food. These shared foodways diverged as soon as White Southern leaders regained their economic power after the war. During Reconstruction, Adrian Miller writes, the Freedmen's Bureau provided food rations to the widely impoverished Black and White residents of the South, in addition to helping represent Black people in salary, work, and living negotiations with their new plantation owner "landlords." However, the influence of the Freedmen's Bureau was short lived—Whites in power saw the federal food rations as a way to allow Black workers independence as they negotiated work, and the Whites began a propaganda campaign against food rations, saying that it would create "laziness and freeloading," a false and racist argument that continues to the present day with regard to entitlements. Northern politicians would bow to these demands in their own interest to remain in power, and food rations, among other support, would be discontinued before the end of 1866, clearing the way for landowners to include food as part of sharecroppers' new work agreements. Landlords could, and did, charge exorbitant prices, and they added interest for rations, controlled what food Black sharecroppers had access to, and even prevented Black tenant farmers from growing their own food on the plantation land they worked. The goal was power, of course, but also a move to separate Black and White foodways. Yet, as Miller notes, landowning Black farmers who were able to navigate the White racist system of landownership ate similar foods as landowning Whites: pots of long-simmered beans and stewed greens, hunks of slow-cooked meat, corn bread, maybe apple or peach pie, and milk and butter. It was not unlike what Aylene and her family ate on the farm on which she grew up, nor radically different from what Cleo's grandmother cooked.

And while the majority of Black Americans remained in farming from the late 1800s to the early 1900s, there were, of course, other burgeoning businesses—including restaurants and taverns. Black-owned restaurants in the South generally cooked southern foods common among both Black and White communities: in addition to the typical fare, perhaps also fried chicken or fish, or regional specialties like gumbo. While Aylene's brother had started South of the Border, perhaps as a way to continue to build wealth beyond his farm, it made sense that he would ask his sister to come on board as the chef. Cooking was one of the few

entrepreneurial roles that were socially acceptable for women, as feeding others was considered women's work. Women had long been the
ones cooking for their families and providing the food for holiday or
communal meals, which often happened within the church community,
and these celebratory dishes, like macaroni and cheese and fried chicken,
were popular among paying customers as well. Restaurant menus of
Black-owned establishments came to represent this "Black" cuisine to
Black and White Americans alike. Thus, Adrian Miller explains, southern foodways were "widely similar" among Black and White southerners.
"But soul food, represent[ed] both the food eaten at church meals (where
food and community fed the soul) and also . . . the soul of the Black
community. . . . Soul food was what was served as Black communities
celebrated—it was tied in with joy and self-determination and culture
and was meant to remind the eater of these attributes over the most
humble dish of food, prepared with care." It is perhaps the combination
of well-cooked food—as one SNCC worker says Aylene "could cook her
butt off"—and community that made South of the Border so popular.

Midcentury in the Mississippi Delta, the majority of the Black population were employed on former plantations as sharecroppers or day
laborers, where little had changed since Reconstruction. White people
owned the vast majority of the land—90 percent in Leflore County, in
the Delta—and would give sharecroppers only a small patch of land
near their plantation-owned dwelling, called a truck patch, to grow their
own food and, perhaps, raise a few animals, if they were allowed this
space at all. For most sharecroppers, who were predominantly Black, the
parameters of their work, dictated by the plantation, barely made them
enough money to pay the plantation owner for "rent" for their small
shack and a few other necessities. Their long hours during the growing
and harvest seasons—and sometimes direct rules from the plantation
owner—discouraged them from other work, often including even growing their own food. They rarely had enough money for food outside
of cotton season, and their small truck patch garden was usually not
enough to last them through the winter. Whatever money they had left

from their farmwork often went back to the plantation owner during the lean months, to buy cheap commodity food, often at unfair prices or offered at a high interest credit if cash was not at hand. Plantation owners understood that if they could control the farmworkers' access to food and leave them without a means to leave for better work or pay, they could continue to exploit Black labor. Moreover, if they could deprive Black workers the food of their heritage, they further delegitimized this heritage and the community built around it.

Plantation owners further created a culture of fear by kicking share-croppers out of their homes as one form of economic sanctions if they pushed for better conditions or higher pay or became involved in civil rights work. And if a family loses their home, they lose their garden and immediate community of folks with whom they'd share food and other resources. This history of systemic oppression and deep poverty made it difficult to organize actions in the Delta, particularly around voting.

By the early 1960s an increase in mechanization on plantations meant that fewer farmhands were needed, and more tenant farmers were being forced to move to towns and cities like Greenwood, in the Delta, and travel to the plantation as day laborers, with the number employed dropping each harvest season. Despite the close proximity to rich farmland and generations of knowledge, farmworkers in the Delta were among the most impoverished, and they relied heavily on the federal surplus commodity food program to stave off hunger between growing seasons. Despite, or perhaps because of, this oppression, the city of Greenwood became a home base for activism, led in part by Black residents who had more economic independence. Greenwood was in Leflore County, whose population was two-thirds Black and whose gov-ernment officials were all White, and it housed both a SNCC office and an active NAACP chapter—as well as the state White Citizens' Council headquarters. Historian Greta de Jong notes that these intersecting fac-tors created an even more openly hostile environment perpetrated by the Whites in power, intended in part to push Black people to leave the area, both to mitigate the changing need for labor on the farms and "minimize the threat of [B]lack political power."

In 1962 Whites in this power structure used access to food as a weapon to uphold their supremacy and attempt to punish activists in a battle for power. That fall the Leflore County Board of Supervisors voted to end the county's participation in the federal surplus commodity food program, which had been established during the Great Depression and involved the government's buying surplus food from farmers and distributing it to those in need around the country. This vote was widely seen as a rebuke to the activist work happening in the Delta, where even with community mutual aid, many folks still needed additional provisions to get by. This would be the first instance of a local government explicitly blocking access to food as their own tool to attempt to thwart the local voting rights activism in the South.

While this program was open to Whites as well, almost all of its twenty thousand recipients were from the Black community. Local NAACP officers contacted federal officials to let them know what had transpired, and worked with COFO and SNCC to create a coordinated response to aid those in need. Vera Pigee, a longtime NAACP member and activist, became the de facto leader of the response, coordinating food donations and distribution around the county through the Emergency Welfare and Relief Committee, established with a SNCC representative. COFO, the umbrella group under which SNCC worked alongside other activists, would dub this initiative Food for Freedom, and its goals were to request donations from around the country and also amplify the plight of the Black farmworker, while connecting this to larger political and social goals that these activists were working toward. At the same time, SNCC filed suit against the county alleging that this move was politically motivated and harmful to residents.

While the lawsuit languished in the legal system, Vera and volunteers around the county accepted donations of mostly food but also medical supplies, clothing, and money, to distribute to those most in need. Vera Pigee was long known as a local leader in nearby Clarksdale and around the Delta. Like Mama Quin, she owned her own business—a beauty shop—and used her space for organizing and as a safe place for people to meet, be educated, and decompress. She was known for getting into good trouble—having been arrested for integrating the local bus station and hosting the county's first interracial concert, where her daughter sang on stage with White folk singers. She also acted as a mother figure and activist mentor to the eager group of Youth Council members, while assuring their nervous parents that she would keep them safe. Through analyzing Vera's work, Hamlin coined the term *activist mothering*, which is an apt way of both characterizing and fully appreciating the work of Vera and female activists in similar roles. Building on the relationships she had with so many of her neighbors, Vera created a well-run system of cataloguing needs and ensuring equitable and efficient distribution of the donations that came in for the Food for Freedom program, as they called it, to counteract the Greenwood Food Blockade.

By all accounts, the conditions were horrific in Leflore that winter: White business owners cut wages or even refused to pay them. It was also a particularly cold winter, and many people lived in poorly insulated shacks. Through holes in the floor they could see the dirt ground, and cracks in the walls brought in the cold wind. The Food for Freedom program would soon get national attention—including an article in *Jet* in February 1963—and would garner high-profile supporters, like the comedian Dick Gregory, who sent down an airplane with a huge shipment of supplies. Propaganda articles placed by the MSSC declared that the donations were not needed or were being misused and called them a "food invasion." But widely, news attention reported favorably on what they considered generous donations for needy recipients. Yet while the media's back was turned, local officials did what they could to undermine the donation of food and goods, preferring that their Black neighbors starve and suffer in the name of their racist political agenda.

In one instance, two Black college students from the North drove a large truck full of food and medical supplies to Leflore County, and were almost immediately arrested after they arrived later than local NAACP leader Aaron Henry had anticipated. They were thrown into jail but never charged, so their whereabouts remained unknown. It was standard for arrests to be published in the local paper, a move that often served to intimidate. But holding them illegally without charges meant that no one knew where the two were. It was only after they were able to sneak a note to Mr. Henry more than a week later, through another Black prisoner who was tasked with emptying parking meters, that they were released. They returned to their truck only to find the contents stolen and the food destroyed. And there were other reports of local authorities seeking to stop donations through legal and extralegal means, such as trying to stop and seize shipments of donations and hiring Black agitators to start a fight with volunteers to try to create a reason to arrest them. This was all to keep food and other necessities from impoverished Black families.

Yet while it is these stories of the oppression—the illegal imprisonment and covert destruction of food—that make good storytelling, they also serve to undermine the power of female leaders like Vera Pigee and Aylene Quin and other women like them. Françoise Hamlin has written about Vera Pigee's work in great detail, and there are similarities between her influence and leadership in the Delta and Aylene Quin's in McComb. They were both active in the local NAACP chapter—Vera was particularly influential in leading the youth, who Aylene also supported—and both also "extend[ed] their alliances, loyalties, and memberships to other places," seen in their willingness to work with SNCC on shared goals. Their so-called activist mothering represented effective leadership in the realm of "women's work"—in this case feeding people and making sure they had other needed items, from a warm blanket to basic medical supplies. The importance of this work was often overlooked, in part because it is expected of women to feed and nurture. Ignored was the extreme danger and potential consequences of this kind of activism, in addition to the positive benefit that extended far beyond merely making sure someone had a meal. It was about building a community whose members could support each other to help inure themselves from the economic and other power exerted by the White community. Vera, Aylene, and many other unsung Black women activists "transformed seemingly static stations into weapons of resistance, empowerment," Hamlin explains. "A woman who utilized and expanded the role society and culture assigned her sex in order to organize groups of youths and adults is rarely recognized in the official record." But of course Mama Quin, her nickname reinforcing this role, was also subverting this gendered station through business ownership as a single mother and her bootlegging.

———————

A teenaged Freddie Biddle, whose family owned their home and whose father owned his own house painting business in Greenwood, was among the volunteers who helped organize and distribute food out of the local church. She recognizes now how her family's relative success made them better able to give back to their community, which was something her mother had always insisted on. "Mother had a strong thing . . . that you always had to give things to people. You know, when we outgrew clothes you gave them to people. You always had to make sure that you share what you had with people. My father was active in the NAACP, and he always had this strong thing: if we didn't do anything, nothing was ever going to change."

But, like McComb, many unaffected members of the Black community chose not to become involved. As Freddie recalls, "Now, I have to admit that since I've become an adult, I've recognized that people were really afraid, but when I was in high school, I couldn't understand how come people would not participate. And I realized how much fear that had really set in and the reason why people wouldn't do things. One, you can lose your job. People were not making much money so it wasn't possible to save. So you're talking about somebody fired you and you lost your job. You were basically hand to mouth, from then somebody really had to help you out. And also, physically things can happen to you." Beatings, arrests, harassment, and murder were all very real fears of Black people in the South—particularly activists—and the number who have suffered these fates without justice is more staggering than is generally acknowledged in histories of this time.

———————

By spring 1963 the legal and media pressure had worked—the federal government called on the county to reinstate its program, while national media coverage had told the story of Black oppression at the hands of

White supremacists who wanted to keep them from voting. And that story, as Bob Moses wrote in his "Letter to Northern Supporters" in February 1963, was about the power of food in the larger fight for Black freedom. The Food for Freedom program "served as the immediate catalyst for opening new dimensions in the voter registration movement in Mississippi. . . . The food is identified in the minds of everyone as food for those who want to be free, and the minimum requirement for freedom is identified as registration to vote."

But the unspoken element of this initiative's success—and any of the efforts around the state and elsewhere that aligned food and freedom—was the activist mothers, like Vera Pigee and Mama Quin. It wasn't just providing food for those who are hungry but also engaging them in political and social education, in a conversation about why some folks were made to go hungry and what they could do about it. Through their feeding and their relatively rare role, at this time and place, as outspoken female leaders, they were able to bring more activists into the movement, particularly young people. It didn't take much to activate teens like Freddie Biddle, Carolyn Quin, Jackie Byrd, Brenda Travis, and others, who considered themselves the Emmett Till generation—his body had even come through Greenwood when Freddie was ten. "This is what people lived with, and they knew about people who had gone missing. Fear was based upon something," Freddie says. And activist mothers could, to some degree, help protect and nurture the young activists who were ready to fight for change.

10

VICTORIES LIKE FOOD FOR FREEDOM IN GREENWOOD in 1963 were both rare and short lived and were often punctuated by extreme violence. One example, detailed in the MSSC's own files, is of White supremacists firing into the car of Black activists, including Bob Moses. One passenger was hit, and more than a dozen bullets peppered the car. The MSSC was unconcerned about this attempted murder, and instead insisted that the activists were spreading "incidents whereby they could holler to the skies about discrimination and brutality to the Negroes by White people in Mississippi, including duly qualified police officers." The report notes the facts of the attempted murder in brief but focuses instead on the "agitators" who gave "false statements to the papers" (such as the decidedly true statement that White supremacists had burned down three buildings in retaliation) and "distributing food to what he classified as 'starving Negroes' in Leflore County." The report continues to list people and places in the county that supported these civil rights activities and even notes confiscating donated food. Vera Pigee's beauty salon was on the list.

Voting rights efforts around the state continued to intensify, although the Delta had been briefly forced to direct resources to this necessary work around food justice. But in the wake of the publicity around Food for Freedom, interests and activity soared, led both by local leaders and the continued presence of COFO groups. Likewise there was an increase in retribution.

There were numerous instances of mass arrests of voting rights workers in early 1963. More than once a group of local activists, often supported by SNCC workers, would plan a voter registration drive. Once local officials became aware of it, they might hold an emergency session and pass a new law immediately, arresting workers the following day on charges such as "distributing leaflets without a permit." If the workers dared question why they were being arrested, officers would add "resisting arrest" to their charges. And more often than not, activists suffered violence during these arrests, either by those who were meant to uphold the law or by those who were fully complicit with law enforcement. Other towns began passing similar laws restricting gatherings, protests, or the distribution of leaflets preemptively, all with a goal to stop free speech, protests, and group voter registration efforts. Despite activists' persistence, there were relatively small gains in newly registered voters, and Bob Moses acknowledged that something would have to change for this work to be successful.

Also troubling was the return of the Ku Klux Klan in Mississippi in response to these continued civil rights efforts. While tangible progress was slow, change was in the air—and noticed by those who had a stranglehold on local political influence. Also noted were shifts in thinking among moderate White people who were coming around to civil rights protections, despite their inaction out of fear and privilege. This would prompt White terrorism groups to reactivate.

The last imperial wizard of the KKK, a veterinarian named James Colescott, had dedicated his Klan in 1939 to "mopping up the cesspools of communism in the United States." Perhaps ironically the Klan's affiliation with pro-Hitler groups resulted in Colescott's being remanded to the House Un-American Activities Committee in 1942, where he received a slap on the wrist. During these hearings, committee member Joe Starnes of Alabama tellingly called the KKK "just as American as the

Baptist or Methodist Church, as the Lion's Club or Rotary Club," while another committee member declared that their charge was to "investigate foreign 'isms' and alien organizations" and not, presumably, such "an American institution" as this violent and racist group. However, despite the government's seemingly glowing support of the Ku Klux Klan, the Klan officially disbanded in 1944 primarily over a $685,000 tax bill unpaid for decades, with James Colescott unironically lamenting from his retirement home in Florida, "Maybe the government could make something out of the Klan. I never could."

But by 1960, it wasn't just Bob Moses and Ella Baker who had noticed the sit-ins in Greensboro. So had White supremacists who had initiated a revival of the Klan in various regions of the South. The Anti-Defamation League noted that by the end of 1960 there were between thirty-five thousand and fifty thousand KKK members in the country. In the following years former Klan members populated the White Citizens' Councils in Mississippi—called "a country club Klan"—perpetuating a shared racist agenda and turning a blind eye to illegal actions by former Klan members. But most official reports, including memos by J. Edgar Hoover, note the Klan's official return to Mississippi in late 1963. Prior to 1963 there were plenty of known instances of Klan members from out of state working with in-state vigilantes to commit acts of violence or protest desegregation efforts with guns openly carried, such as the Klan-led riot when James Meredith sought to desegregate Ole Miss in 1962. Unsurprisingly, few were arrested, and those who did see a judge had their charges dismissed.

As organized violence increased around the state, particularly in places where student groups were continuing work, local activists would quietly create safe zones for workers and community members. Despite the edict that SNCC workers couldn't be armed, they were often surrounded by locals who were. Part of the decision by SNCC and CORE (Congress of Racial Equality) to remain officially unarmed stemmed from their stated philosophy of nonviolent resistance to oppression and their concerns about violence; Moses argued that if SNCC workers were known to be armed, they would become even more of a target for White supremacists. It was also strategic, as scholar Akinyele O. Umoja notes, "to maintain the moral standard of nonviolence in order to win support from liberal sentiments in government and the American public." In addition, leaders of both groups believed it was imperative that the federal government provide their protection as well, which they did with very limited commitment.

What was little discussed was that the activists' protection fell to local activists with whom they worked, and they often owned guns for both hunting and protection—a necessity for their collective safety since the federal government was unwilling to intervene. This hypocrisy is striking as we consider how the burden fell on the oppressed to protect themselves from the White establishment—terrorists like the KKK and also government officials who not only failed to protect them but also actively committed acts of physical violence. Even then, "police brutality" was often framed as being committed by a few "bad apples," but the obvious reality was that this threat of violence was systemic. *Every* police officer created fear among locals and activists, because almost none provided protection from terrorism, even as many, but certainly not all, actively took part in beatings and other actions. While commonly taught history does not often highlight the need—and reality—of armed resistance among these activists, this was a regular occurrence and led directly to the stereotypes of armed Black urban dwellers, many of whom were southern transplants and found the same lack of protection and overt terrorism in the city centers where they moved.

Protection by local people was necessary around the state. Amzie Moore had many guns and was known to offer them to visitors by placing one on their nightstand, "in case of emergency," he'd say. There were neighborhoods in many towns with activism where Black snipers kept watch, ensuring that folks outrunning Klansmen or other racists could reach a safe place. Folks like Curtis Muhammad had souped-up cars. He later would be given a gun by another local leader, who explained that he was a Black Freemason—a centuries-old brotherhood that promoted Black financial and personal independence. "It turns out that they had an underground group that had stayed in place since the Underground Railroad," Curtis says. "And they operate the same way in total secrecy. But they protected where we slept; they protected us on the highways." Looking back, Muhammad remembers times when a protector would check in without him or other SNCC workers knowing. "Somebody would always come out, say 'How y'all doing today?' acting like they wasn't nobody. And we didn't know we were being detected. Yeah, but these guys were taking care of business. And I'm not kidding."

Curtis says they acknowledged the Freemasons missed things sometimes, especially with all the volunteers coming through via SNCC and COFO initiatives. "So they started recruiting a few of us that were in the movement. They didn't want to do it, because we were supposed to be nonviolent." Local leader E. W. Steptoe brought Curtis to his place out in the country and asked him if he ever had to defend himself. Curtis told him he had gotten his first gun for his thirteenth birthday for hunting. But he also remembers that he was invited soon thereafter to ride with the men who would sit in the trucks with shotguns to protect their families from the White folks who would drive by and shoot at the houses "whenever something was happening in the news." Emmett Till had just been murdered—he had only been fourteen, a few months older than Curtis. "I felt like a man. Yeah, scared to death. But I did it."

Back in the woods, Curtis and E. W. Steptoe shot a few different guns, until Mr. Steptoe was satisfied that Curtis would be safe. "He gave me a big old long six-inch .38 Special because, he said, 'y'all need some protection among yourselves.' Said you can't tell Bob about this. You don't tell nobody in your organization about this."

But the next time Curtis saw Aylene, "she said, 'You got a gun, don't you?'

I said, 'What you talking about?'

She said, 'You walk different.' She knew everything."

The reality of armed Black resisters in the movement in Mississippi and around the Deep South is rarely acknowledged, despite the fact that White terrorists used the threat of bodily harm—implicit and sanctioned by Whites in positions of governmental power—as a well-known tool for oppression. It was only through the quiet but staunch protection of local Black community members that voting rights efforts could inch forward. And while it is impossible to quantify the number of lives saved by the armed protection by locals, scholars such as Dr. Umoja note that numerous leaders were said to be "targeted for assassination" and infer that the mostly unseen presence of armed guards should rightfully be credited with saving many lives.

Even leaders like Medgar Evers, whose official activist approach was nonviolence, took issue with the stance of SNCC and other groups (like Dr. King's SCLC) on refusing to be armed, understanding the perpetual threat of violence faced by Black people around Mississippi and beyond. A fellow SNCC worker said, as Umoja writes, that he knew Evers carried a gun, adding, "He always talked about how crazy we was, talking about nonviolence."

And so in 1963 civil rights activists in Mississippi began to contemplate their next moves as they waged efforts on multiple fronts: there were the visible voting rights efforts, working as the NAACP wished, within the system of law. And there was direct action, favored by the youth who were gravitating more toward SNCC and their more radical and ambitious agenda based on nonviolent resistance, often to gain attention through the media. At the same time, there was the battle all but invisible except to those on the front lines: the frequent shootings and violence and harassing phone calls that were known by every Black person in the movement but were unacknowledged by local law enforcement and rarely reported accurately by the press. This constant threat of disappearance, of violence, of the system of law turned against you, led to guerrilla warfare waged mainly by the local people, ensuring they and the volunteers were kept safe, homes intact, bellies full.

11

ON MAY 28, 1963, three Black students from Tougaloo College—Anne Moody, Memphis Norman, and Pearlena Lewis—orchestrated a sit-in at a Woolworth's in Jackson. The sit-ins that desegregated the L-shaped stainless steel counters in 1960 in more northern cities didn't crack the staunch segregationists in Mississippi. It was just weeks after the nonviolent student march in Birmingham resulted in thousands of arrests and a violent reaction as police turned high-pressure water hoses and attack dogs on the young people. That march had shocked a nation and also paved the way for desegregation efforts just over the state line in Alabama. Similarly inspired, Black and White Tougaloo students and professors created a plan to have the three students take a seat on the turquoise vinyl-topped stools and pray, while other students staged a diversionary picket line down the street.

Shortly after the three sat down, "a man rushed forward, threw Memphis from his seat, and slapped my face," Anne Moody remembered, before she was thrown against another counter. Memphis, lying on the ground, was being kicked and beaten. The picketers down the street were arrested immediately, and White student Joan Trumpauer Mulholland, whose role was to keep Medgar Evers's office informed, walked to Woolworth's to find that "all hell broke loose." A local high school had been let out for lunch, and White teenagers swelled the jeering crowd, including police officers who were passively observing.

Anne said, "The main weapons were whatever was sitting on the counter . . . vinegar to pepper to sugar to sometimes a fist." Joan and White
Tougaloo professor John Salter both took a seat next to Anne while the
torrents of ketchup and salt and beatings rained down.

The manager waited three hours to finally close the store and disperse the crowd. The Tougaloo students' peaceful demonstration in Jackson became the most violently opposed sit-in of the 1960s, with a mob
of hundreds throwing glasses and ashtrays, spraying condiments, and
verbally and physically abusing the protesters, while law enforcement
stood aside for hours until they arrested the peaceful protesters. This
was just one protest in Jackson alongside a larger NAACP-led boycott
whose goals included the elimination of segregated eating establishments
and water fountains, the hiring of Black workers on the police force
and in other roles, and other demands. With the support of the MSSC,
Mississippi was defying even federal desegregation laws with impunity.

Two weeks later respected leader Medgar Evers was assassinated in Jackson, moments after he pulled into his driveway late one evening after
ensuring the young people he was working with had a safe ride home.
Jackson teenager Frankye Adams-Johnson remembers the "yell coming
out of my mouth, and I sank to the floor, and it just tore me apart"
when she picked up the phone and heard on the other end, "They killed
Medgar, they killed Medgar!" She had seen him hours before, at a meeting with the Youth Council of the NAACP. "For a lot of us who. . . grew
up in single-parent households without a father, he was like that father
figure, that very caring person," she remembers. That someone would
kill him—a person so fundamentally decent and selfless—would forever
change Frankye's involvement in the movement for civil rights and Black
Freedom, and the trajectory of her life. This was the kind of news that
made headlines—and rightfully so—but few outside Mississippi knew
that it was yet another death at the hands of White supremacists, one
of a litany of killed activists, many working modestly at the local level.

Frankye was not alone in changing her perspective on nonviolent
action. Other activists, and in particular young people, were no longer

content to follow the lead of the NAACP, which worked to slowly push changes through the courts. They were ready to act. In Jackson, this created a conflict among the young and eager activists, and the older Black leadership (including influential Black business owners) who wanted an end for direct action. Federal involvement after Mr. Evers's murder reached a pittance of a "compromise" that included promises to hire a handful of Black policemen and crossing guards and hear grievances. Meanwhile, White Citizens' Council members created a fund to bankroll the defense of Mr. Evers's murderer, who was also a known Klan sympathizer.

Conflicting documents put the official rebirth of the Klan in Mississippi at sometime in 1963, with a particular stronghold in southwest Mississippi, which included McComb. With the Klan now an organized local terrorist group, violence against Black people in Mississippi increased, and most known perpetrators were Klansmen or Klan sympathizers. The lure of the Klan in Mississippi was, as historian John Dittmer notes, "a gut feeling that the battle for white supremacy was being lost." This was felt particularly by working-class Whites who were angry that the White Citizens' Councils hadn't done enough to quash voting rights activism. They felt that their economic and social standing would be threatened if the Black community finally received the civil rights that were rightfully theirs. This perspective was only reinforced by the rhetoric of elected officials and the state-sanctioned propaganda of the MSSC.

Evidence shows that while the FBI would officially disavow the Klan by the mid-1960s and even investigated and infiltrated its ranks, there is a long and persistent pattern of the FBI ignoring many violent crimes committed by Klansmen. The FBI greatly understated the presence of the Klan in Mississippi, in one report incorrectly noting that it "numbered no more than a few hundred men" (the House Un-American Activities Committee that notoriously understates the size and threat of right-wing groups would later estimate the number of the Mississippi White Knights at around six thousand), and even the Justice Department couldn't encourage the FBI to act.

A preinauguration memo by a civil rights aide to President Kennedy said, "It is very difficult to get the FBI to move energetically in civil rights cases" and encouraged the incoming attorney general, Robert Kennedy, to use FBI investigation more rigorously, noting that small-time agitators would likely "melt away under any serious FBI investigation of them." Neither Kennedy would become serious about using law enforcement to advance civil rights causes, however, and the relationship between President Kennedy and J. Edgar Hoover would remain strained, with reports that Hoover even skipped early meetings at the White House to flex his power. Eventually, Burke Marshall, head of the Civil Rights Division in the Justice Department, would, under President Kennedy's watch, get the FBI to increase its presence in Mississippi from three agents to 150. However, historians note that the price of getting Hoover to attend more to civil rights issues was that he demanded more autonomy, which would have repercussions for Black activists through the rest of the decade, including the Black Panther Party a few years later. It is hard to understate how different the lives of so many Black Americans would be if the federal government had committed to merely upholding the laws it had passed on civil rights legislation and ensuring the physical safety of its people.

As White terrorism around the state increased in the early to mid-1960s and activists lobbied the Justice Department for protection, members like Burke Marshall and chief lawyer John Doar would find a way to pressure J. Edgar Hoover into taking this terrorism more seriously. One tactic was to play to his hubris and make it so that he couldn't reasonably say no. The Justice Department would give specific requests for investigative work, listing questions to be answered and people to interview, leaving little room for Hoover's team to stop short of a full investigation. John Doar also demonstrated more effective interviewing techniques: for example, he saw that FBI protocol would take local law enforcement at its word, and if agents did interview Black victims or witnesses, they did so in a manner that "scared them out of their pants." Mr. Doar modeled more rigorous and less biased investigation and questioning tactics, which led to more leads to follow up on and took Black victims and witnesses seriously, as they never had been before. But these changes would take years to implement in a way that wasn't reactionary or haphazard.

The aggression would escalate so much that in the summer of 1963 Bob Moses wrote an analysis of the work in Mississippi for SNCC, saying that the unrelenting violence and intimidation condoned and enacted by law enforcement would "force a showdown over the right to vote" similar to school integration. Another report acknowledged the steep price of continued voting rights and desegregation work in Mississippi: activists had every reason to fear both police and White supremacists with little legal recourse and were also likely to be wrongfully arrested and jailed by local officials in retribution for their activism. Without national attention or federal intervention, Moses noted, "the entire white population will continue to be the Klan." If sympathetic White people and liberal politicians continued to stand by without action while these atrocities continued, it would be akin to them donning a hood.

There was no doubt that the MSSC was a state-sanctioned power behind much of the violence, threats, and illegal obstruction. As historians today look back, they describe Mississippi as a "police state." State and local law enforcement benefited from the copious files kept on people whom they deemed a threat: primarily local Black activists and SNCC and other civil rights workers who joined them. The MSSC shared information with local law enforcement and often with local KKK members or other White supremacist vigilantes, and these groups were not mutually exclusive. This intel would detail who was working with whom, where activists lived or were staying, where they were going, what they were doing. An arrest on bogus or inflated charges might spark a call from a police officer to a brother or cousin in the Klan. The MSSC was given implicit freedom to ignore police reports of White violence and intimidation: very commonplace are stories of reports of shooting at people's homes and Black activists receiving harassing and threatening phone calls, happening with increasing ire and frequency. Black people—and especially activists—were arrested more frequently, often beaten at the same time, and accused of the very crimes committed by White supremacists that they might try to report.

Despite this the MSSC was officially disdainful of the Klan's most publicized forms of violence and intimidation, like cross burnings. The governor's office believed that these ostentatious forms of White supremacy were "distasteful" to a more moderate public and brought increased FBI and media scrutiny to the state. The government at all levels approved of White supremacy exerted quietly—in the courthouse, through unfair laws, and behind closed doors. Even better would be getting activist groups to implode through suspicion among members and mistrust by the people they were trying to help—as the COINTELPRO initiative was beginning to utilize to undermine civil rights leaders like Dr. King. But ultimately, by not forcefully eradicating the growth of the KKK and its ensuing violence, the MSSC became complicit in the violent outcomes.

In fall 1963 around forty SNCC workers were working in field offices around the state, organizing the statewide Freedom Ballot. The goal was to create their own version of the state elections to demonstrate that Black Mississippians were interested and engaged in voting, and also to show support for candidates beyond the equally segregationist White candidates who were running for state office. In October an influx of new SNCC volunteers—who were mostly White college students—came to work along with local volunteers to "register" voters for the Freedom Ballot. Along with these White students came increased media attention and FBI presence—and decreased violence. The activists' goal was achieved: even despite ongoing intimidation, more than eighty thousand Black Mississippians cast a ballot, underscoring the obstructionism of the current political system. After the November election, most of these student volunteers returned to their colleges or hometowns.

But Bob Moses noticed something else during this time. He wrote, "That was the first time that I realized that the violence could actually be controlled. Turned on and off. That it wasn't totally random. I realized that somewhere along the line there was someone who . . . could at least send out word for it to stop. And it would. That was a revelation."

As COFO's plans for a major voting rights initiative in Mississippi started to form—during 1964, a presidential election year—Bob Moses considered that perhaps bringing more White students into the state could help keep pressure on White leaders to keep the KKK and other violence at bay. COFO staff met in Greenville near the end of 1963 and debated what a future initiative might look like. Do they bring in more White volunteers or keep the corps mostly Black? Ultimately, leaders, including SNCC chair John Lewis, decided in favor of actively recruiting White students. "Mississippi was deadly, and it was getting worse each day," John Lewis said. "Our people were essentially being slaughtered down there. If White America would not respond to the deaths of our people, the thinking went, maybe it would react to the deaths of its own children." The hope was that their presence would at least create more awareness around Black oppression in Mississippi and elsewhere in the Deep South. So as 1963 turned into 1964, SNCC and COFO began planning their most ambitious project yet.

Despite the tension that caused Bob Moses and SNCC to leave McComb a few years earlier, Mama Quin was among the McComb local leadership who was ready to welcome back SNCC for a massive voter registration drive leading up to the 1964 presidential election. They had been risking everything for what had felt like incremental progress for too long. Now was the time to put it all on the line to push for the rights they knew they deserved—no matter the cost.

12

"WE DIDN'T STOP FOR POLICE, not on back roads. And that was the mistake those three civil rights workers made," Curtis Muhammad said decades later. Locals knew what the SNCC workers didn't. Or maybe the two White SNCC workers who came to Mississippi for Freedom Summer were used to a world where their relative privilege meant they wouldn't be harmed by the police. Perhaps the third member of their team, who was Black and from Mississippi, warned them of the danger, but they assured him they would be fine. Or maybe, like so many others, they didn't feel like they had a choice.

So James Chaney, Michael Schwerner, and Andrew Goodman stopped when they were pulled over by local policeman and Klan member Cecil Price on June 21, 1964. They were on the way back from a trip to visit a bombed church that had also served as a Freedom School site, in a town northeast of Jackson. Price took the three to the local Neshoba County jail while he assembled fellow Klan members and then released the trio. As they drove away, a mob of KKK members ran them down and cornered them in a secluded wooded area, where they shot and killed them. But this fate would go unknown for almost two months. After the initial disappearance, and presumed murder, of the trio—which local law enforcement, the FBI, and even President Johnson inferred might be a publicity stunt by activists—fear became a constant companion among the civil rights workers. They were under COFO orders to travel in groups. But despite local protection, seen and unseen, there would be much more violence before the year was out.

The inklings of Freedom Summer began in January 1964 with Freedom Day in Hattiesburg, where COFO organized a mass voter registration and picket as a show of strength among the local Black community. COFO was the umbrella group that included members of SNCC, CORE, SCLC, and even the NAACP, and was created to bring members of these groups together in a focused initiative while also giving space for local leaders within the movement. Fannie Lou Hamer, one such leader, was a share-cropper's daughter who had worked with her husband on a plantation until she was fired in 1962 for her right-to-vote efforts. She was on hand to help organize with Bob Moses, with media, White pastors, and even the historian Howard Zinn there as witnesses. One hundred fifty people took the poll test and only Bob Moses was arrested, which COFO considered a peaceful success. While retribution from law enforcement did step up after the media left, a blueprint for future Freedom Days was established for other counties.

Three more counties hosted a Freedom Day into the spring, but with media interest waning, law enforcement and the White establishment leadership increased their pressure, arresting dozens for minor infractions and exercising other forms of intimidation. Across Mississippi there was also a noticeable increase in KKK violence, intimidation, and economic and legal retribution, particularly for anyone associated with these voting rights efforts. This made some people more resolute in their efforts and others retreat in self-preservation.

Although COFO hadn't returned yet to McComb before the summer, it wasn't sheltered from the increasing violence and Klan presence. On January 16, South of the Border was shot at while Mama Quin and three others sat inside. The bullets shattered the glass in her front door and were found in the plate glass window next to it. She called the police who "did not say anything and acted like nothing happened." Aylene later heard that the same white Pontiac with four or five White men were seen shooting at places around the neighborhood. "I am active in civil rights and I don't try to hide it and this is the only reason I can see for them doing what they did," she wrote in a notarized affidavit. And then on January 25, likely in response to the first Freedom Day, as many as fifty crosses were burned on activists' front lawns across the state, including in the yard of C. C. Bryant. He carried the cross to the courthouse, showing it to multiple officials including a police sergeant, but no one came to investigate, and no arrests were made. By spring things would further escalate.

On April 29 a firebomb was thrown into C. C. Bryant's barbershop. His neighbors helped him put out the flames, which caused interior damage. Mr. Bryant called the police department and John Doar at the Justice Department, but no arrests were made. US Attorney General Robert Kennedy reported to President Johnson's office that there were more than forty instances of Klan violence in the first few months of 1964, and that he "had every reason" to think it would increase. But little would be done to help keep law and order, despite entreaties by Robert Kennedy, John Doar, and Burke Marshall. The president demurred to Hoover, who insisted it wasn't the FBI's jurisdiction but rather that of local law enforcement.

In early June, Burke Marshall even went to southwest Mississippi, near McComb, and saw for himself the strength of the Klan there. He reported back to Attorney General Kennedy, who told the president that he considered "the situation in Mississippi to be very dangerous" and recommended a much stronger FBI presence. But Attorney General Kennedy's influence in the Oval Office was limited after President Kennedy's assassination the fall before. Burke Marshall would later note that the FBI refused to put resources into the state.

Not long after his June visit, Burke Marshall sent an organized crime unit to investigate the Klan, as a workaround to avoid Hoover. He found that the FBI had twenty officers in the state—mostly from the South—and that they were "doing nothing." While there were no immediate actions taken, historian Dittmer acknowledges that this "may have goaded the FBI into doing something." Ultimately the FBI would delay involvement in the state as long as it could, only acting when pressured by the president or Justice Department. Even then it would drag its feet on investigations and tailor findings toward its own agenda as much as possible.

Bob Moses was so concerned about the safety of the voting rights workers in Mississippi that he insisted that President Johnson ensure the safety of volunteers, requesting a meeting to discuss the dangers. President Johnson's adviser Lee White said the president was too busy, adding, "It is nearly incredible that those people who are voluntarily sticking their head into the lion's mouth would ask for somebody to come down and shoot the lion." But still, while the question of volunteer safety was still being discussed, the groundwork for Freedom Summer was being laid around the state.

COFO had been working on plans for months and had recruited young people, both Black and White, from around the country. Their goal was to start Freedom Schools not just to teach potential voters how to pass the poll test but also to provide political and civic lessons for local people of all ages, in addition to other voting rights work. They understood the power of education in helping people understand the history of the oppressive White power structure—and how to fight against it. Volunteers would embed themselves in the communities in which they were working, usually staying with local families, or sometimes together at what was called a Freedom House or COFO house, whose space was donated by a supportive local. They would eat around a communal table or at local restaurants, teaching at Freedom Schools or going door-to-door to encourage attendance and voting by day, continuing and expanding on the work local people had been doing for more than a decade.

McComb's Freedom House was owned by local supporter Willie Mae Cotton, a friend of Aylene's, and would finally be ready for eight COFO workers in early July 1964. Freddie Biddle and her brother George from Greenwood would be staying there, along with Curtis Hayes Muhammad and five others. One of the two White volunteers at McComb's COFO house was the son of California congressman Don Edwards, who made it no secret that he was going to drop off his son and spend the night in solidarity with the Freedom Summer mission. He had been warned ahead of time by a Justice Department official that his safety was in danger in McComb. The congressman had responded by asking why the federal government hadn't provided any protection for the workers if that was the case and insisted on staying. Apparently the official conveyed the message to local law enforcement: it was quiet before Congressman Edwards left, and the workers continued planning and recruiting for their Freedom School, which would operate in the house.

———

A few nights later the eight COFO volunteers went to sleep in their new Freedom House. The next day was the first day of Freedom School. They would still instruct folks on how to take the onerous poll test and teach the nonviolent resistance that had so inspired students three summers earlier. But this summer's Freedom School would also teach the untold history of Black people in America and around the world to young kids and adults alike: the treachery of slavery and colonialism, and the accomplishments of Black inventors and leaders, so often omitted or whitewashed by the mainstream curriculum. They were excited and giddy to start working with the local people after months of planning.

Deep into the night Curtis Muhammad remembers hearing voices and noises summoning his consciousness, but he was too deep in sleep to fully wake up. The next thing he remembered was fellow volunteers peering down at him, shaking him awake. He could see the night sky— the wall of his bedroom had been blown off by dynamite planted by the Ku Klux Klan.

It was a circus clown who, years later, explained to Curtis why he wasn't killed by the bomb left under his bed. Dynamite blows outward, the clown explained. That's why it tends to be used in slapstick comedy and performances. If placed correctly, you can actually be on top of it and not get seriously hurt, other than experiencing the deafening noise and flying debris. It was a miracle that Curtis had only minor injuries, and another volunteer a concussion. The next day the police and FBI investigated, but, as usual, no arrests were made.

Undaunted, the volunteers held Freedom School on the lawn.

"It's like having the lights turned on after you have lived all your life in a darkened room," one student said of the Freedom Schools set up around the state. They were originally conceived of to serve about one thousand teenagers, with courses like Black History, Black-White Relations, and Mississippi Now. The goal was to counter the biased curriculum mandated by the state, which essentially ignored history considered antithetical to its White supremacist mission, like the entirety of the Civil War. From their previous work in the state, the activists knew that a lot of Mississippi youth were buying bus tickets to Chicago or California as soon as they graduated—if they graduated—in hopes of finding more opportunity. But what they found on the other end of that bus line was often very different from what they imagined. The activists hoped the Freedom Schools might inspire teens to stay in Mississippi and help make their home state a better place, or at least better prepare them for the future.

What the activists found as they opened their schools in the beginning of the summer was interest that far exceeded their expectations. Kids from preschool age to community elders were "all anxious to learn about how to be Free." And their course offerings, while still focused on history and civics, were expanded to other subjects as diverse as typing and foreign languages.

Curtis and other instructors gathered groups on the lawn of the bombed COFO house, sitting in a circle beneath the shade of a tree, and held lessons through the hot summer. Mama Quin or other local women might bring a pot of stew for whoever was hungry, and the White and Black volunteers sat alongside the local students and parents, eating a meal. It was this sharing of a table that so incensed White supremacists. It was both familiar and intimate and demonstrated the common humanity in full display on a Mississippi small-town lawn. As Angela Jill Cooley notes, this flagrant flouting of dominant social norms broke down the racial caste system expectations, including the White supremacists' differentiation of Black and White southern foodways and the belief that if white Women and Black men were to eat together, this would lead to further "intimacies" that would sully the White race.

These scenes of racial unity, undaunted by the bombings, only incensed the KKs and other stark segregationists. The intimidation never stopped. If Mama Quin brought over her rice and beans and macaroni and cheese, making sure the workers had dinner, she risked a fine for "serving food without a license." This interpretation of a law, one that was certainly being enforced unequally, would seemingly make it illegal to have a dinner party. And this was common around the state, targeting women who brought food to feed the hungry, striving to take away that latent power a communal table could wield.

D. Gorton says there was "a constant feeling like something was going to happen." After the three SNCC workers had disappeared in early June, SNCC workers were constantly in fear. There were few moments when those involved in the movement felt safe, able to decompress or recharge, without jumping at each backfire, each sound of screeching tires. South of the Border was one such safe place where people could gather, perhaps talking about the movement but also simply living their lives, and perhaps hear music too. Mama Quin often had blues and rock 'n' roll playing, because, as a SNCC worker recalled, "sometimes when you play the blues it would make you feel kinda better." Maybe they laughed and flirted. Maybe they felt comfortable for a bit.

The stress of Freedom Summer was so great that SNCC built in short mental health breaks, where workers might head to New Orleans for a few days to leave the pressure cooker of fear that was Mississippi. But locals didn't have such an option. A few beers—or something stronger—at Mama Quin's, alongside a bowl of gumbo, would have to do.

That was, until local police decided to take that respite away from the Black community too. Joe Martin recalled, "They would bring dogs and stuff in the cafés and try to sic them on people like that. Harass people just for going out Sunday afternoon or Saturday night, and wasn't doing nothing, just out." Police dogs were trained to only attack if somebody moved, so some of the activists trained in police tactics knew to stay perfectly still, hoping their heart beating out of their chest wouldn't betray them. Others flinched or moved away in fear, dogs biting after the space they just occupied, police straining on their leads. Law enforcement was chipping away at every public place of respite.

Nights in McComb were, perhaps, the most stressful. It would be quiet as many residents stayed inside waiting. They knew there were a number of locals on roofs or in high weeds keeping watch. Perhaps those who were in their beds would fall asleep—they needed it, after all, for the work to be done the next day. Patsy Ruth Butler, who served as secretary of the NAACP with Mama Quin, remembers the elaborate warning system the neighborhoods established, with men with shotguns lying low on roofs across the neighborhood, who would whistle or bird call if they saw a suspicious car. The calls would echo across the neighborhood, one call sparking another and another, the sound of alarm following the car as it traveled down the block. Maybe there'd be a warning shot or more silence. Or the night, heavy with humidity and fear, might explode in the sound of gunfire or boom of dynamite that could be felt in your bones. Gunfire might be returned, or more whistles or yells. Folks nearby would attend to what had been bombed and call the police, not that it helped. It was like being in a war zone.

_____

One steamy day that summer, Mama Quin was behind the counter chatting with SNCC worker Jane Adams. Perhaps they were talking about the most recent house or church bombed in McComb, or reports of another local arrest. It might have been because Jane was anxious as a young White woman in the movement, or maybe Mama Quin demonstrated her fearlessness to folks more frequently as a show of strength and comfort. Mama Quin reached into her ample bosom and pulled out a small pistol and smiled. "And I'm happy on the trigger," she said. Jane saw the metal glint in the sunlight streaming through the narrow windows and then it disappeared back from where it came. It was clear that those in the Black community felt that they had no choice but to protect themselves.

_____

Throughout the summer, Rita Schwerner, wife of one of the three miss-
ing civil rights workers, made public pleas for the FBI to both investigate
and ensure the safety of the volunteers. Under pressure from the Justice
Department, the FBI opened a field office in Jackson, Mississippi, on
July 10, 1964. At a press conference upon its opening, however, J. Edgar
Hoover signaled to the White supremacist leadership that he would not
get in their way. With the Mississippi governor at his side, he declared,
"We most certainly do not and will not give protection to civil rights
workers. . . . Protection is in the hands of local authorities."

On July 26 a car sped down C. C. Bryant's road, slowing just long enough
for a crudely made bomb to be thrown in his yard. C.C.'s son Curtis, who
was on watch at the time, witnessed the incident. While the bomb did
not cause physical damage, the psychological toll was rising. The sheriff
was called, but no arrests were made. He would claim that he interviewed
dozens of suspects and couldn't make a connection to the perpetrator,
telling the local press that he wouldn't be surprised if it "was planned by
the Negroes there in McComb for publicity purposes."

Two days later shots were fired at the Bryants' house. Mr. Bryant
provided a description of the vehicle, but, of course, no arrests were
made. After these acts of violence, the Baertown neighborhood put
together a plan to protect the Bryants' home. Teenagers lay in the tall
grass to keep watch and record details of cars, while armed neighbors
stood watch both day and night. They even dug a tunnel for the family
to escape if they had to. Mrs. Bryant would wear her work coveralls
and C.C.'s railroad hat at night, a gun by her side, watching over her
husband so he could sleep. He and his family would suffer four direct
incidents of violence during 1964, none taken seriously by local police.

The FBI, under pressure from the media and Justice Department, provided more resources to look for the three missing civil rights workers.
Their initial efforts uncovered the bodies of other, most likely murdered,

Black men—one a young teen wearing a COFO T-shirt. Two of them were Henry Dee and Charles Moore, names that are rarely mentioned in reports around the SNCC activists' murder investigation, and none of their disappearances had ever made the news. Curtis Muhammad says that he and others in the movement were the ones who made a Klan member talk, who discovered the location of the bodies of the civil rights workers two months after their disappearance. And eventually this pressure increased federal protections to some degree, including rather quick arrests of the Klan mob who murdered the three once the FBI were forced to pay attention. "They had no choice," Curtis Muhammad says. The national pressure was finally too great to ignore the murder of the White activists.

C.C.'s brother's house was bombed around the same time: another car driving past, a bundle of dynamite thrown from the window. His wife, Ora, was keeping watch, and she fired at the car as soon as the dynamite hit their front yard. It sped away and then turned back around, likely incensed at the returned fire. On their next pass the perpetrators shot twice into the house while Ora woke up her husband. He ran outside with his gun, and they returned with another bomb made of dynamite. "Next time they came round the block he let them have it. The dynamite blew him off the ground still shooting," Ora added when she recounted this instance later that summer. "From that time 'til now I don't sleep at night." Her fate, and that of other local activists, still did not concern the nation.

13

THE COFO WORKERS—A GOOD NUMBER were from around Mississippi, although locals were never assigned close to home for fear of retribution against their family members—continued their work. In addition to engaging in their voter registration and Freedom School efforts, the SNCC volunteers were encouraging local people to take part in the Mississippi Freedom Democratic Party (MFDP) vote. Building on the successful Freedom Vote in fall 1963, activists around the state were organizing their own MFDP delegation to challenge the state's all-White Democratic delegation. The MFDP state convention would be held August 6, 1964, and there they would choose sixty-eight delegates and alternates to travel to the national convention a few weeks later.

To help establish their legitimacy and show that the Black community tried to take part in the established Democratic Party election process, COFO volunteers helped organize local people to make attempts to register to vote and attend some of the 1,884 precinct meetings around the state. Victoria Gray, a movement leader in Hattiesburg and a national delegate, noted that they were undermined at every turn. She said, "White officials played all kinds of games. They would say the precinct meeting was going to be in one place at a certain time. We'd get there, and there would be nobody there. Or we'd get there, and the meeting would be over. Or we'd get there, and they just wouldn't let us in."

Activists believed that this was the moment they had the people power and collective national attention to highlight the vast Black disenfranchisement across the state. While Johnson was a very likely win for the presidential election, there were no Black delegates or candidates for major parties in the state. Furthermore, while President Johnson had promised to continue Kennedy's civil rights legislation, he had been slow to act, and activists worried that he would continue to stall on promised voting protection and other civil rights measures.

At the national convention in Atlantic City, New Jersey, starting August 24, the MFDP made the case that they better represented the will of Mississippians and had been systematically shut out of participation in state and local governance. Their conversations, speeches, and mere presence were intended to show the lack of voting rights in the state to a national audience. And it worked—so much so that President Johnson instructed others to work to minimize their disruption, fearing that the MFDP delegates would anger the Southern Democratic contingent if they began to create a groundswell of support.

Women would play an outsized role in the building and activism of the MFDP, and especially at the convention. Fannie Lou Hamer stood in front of a microphone, and speaking in her southern drawl, she told fellow delegates and the whole country in a nationally televised speech about her quest to register to vote, starting just two years before. She recounted how her employer evicted her and her husband because she went to register, and then the next year how the group of Black Mississippians who later attempted to register again were fined, then arrested; in prison, fellow Black inmates were instructed to beat her and others until they were "exhausted." Hamer said in her speech, "I was in jail when Medgar Evers was murdered. All of this is on account of we want to register, to become first-class citizens. And if the Freedom Democratic Party is not seated now, I question America. Is this America, the land of the free and the home of the brave, where we have to sleep with our telephones off the hooks because our lives be threatened daily, because we want to live as decent human beings, in America?"

The speech was so impassioned that President Johnson manufactured a last-second press conference so that live coverage of the convention would cut away in the middle of it. His plan backfired.

Mrs. Hamer's speech would end up being rebroadcast on various news shows, becoming an eye-opening moment for so many northerners who, despite sporadic media coverage, still had little understanding of the voting oppression in the state.

———————

Hamer's speech and her involvement in the MFDP would help to establish her role as a leader in voter registration efforts and, a few years later, in innovative initiatives centered on food security, which she believed was integral to freedom. Annie Devine and Victoria Gray were both also delegates. Each deserved more credit than history has afforded them, and their work can also be better understood and honored through the lens of scholarship on Black female leaders such as Aylene Quin.

Ultimately the delegates were offered a "compromise" of two non-voting delegates out of their sixty-eight, which they rejected because of its tokenism. Although they returned to Mississippi feeling defeated, their activism at the convention did bring their cause to a national stage, and many historians note that it was needed fodder for the fight for voting rights legislation and was integral in making the 1968 convention the most racially diverse in history.

———————

While so many accounts of this summer focus on the extraordinary efforts of the local activists in McComb and elsewhere around the state, the truth was that only a relatively small percentage of the Black community was engaged in these efforts. Because of the violence and retribution, which many locals believed were brought on by the arrival of SNCC workers, some wanted nothing to do with voter registration because of fear. A number of volunteers reported intimidation from the White establishment, but others reported that they often didn't feel welcome by those whom they had, ostensibly, come to help. A priest who had volunteered for a week remembers people who had been sitting on their porches get up and go inside their stifling houses when they saw him coming. Those who stayed to chat told him, "Well, you know, you all are gonna leave here, but we're still gonna be here when you leave."

Freddie Biddle, who was a young Mississippian from the Delta, says that she felt otherwise. Perhaps because she was local, or female, or had a friendly demeanor, she felt that most people were quite receptive to her entreaties to join the MFDP, come to a mass meeting or Freedom School, or attempt to register to vote. Yet she notes, "I have to admit that some of the mass meetings may have been twenty-five people."

The majority of the Black community was "inactive for one reason or another. They were afraid. They had to make a living. They were intimidated. The majority of people were on the sidelines, but they could be, and this was this was the point of organization: to get them involved. And it was always a minority of people who just believed and laid it on the line," John Dittmer explains. This is the reality in so many movements, at so many inflection moments. Luckily these intrepid activists were enough to make a difference.

Community leaders would meet in secret, in fear of being sitting ducks for an attack or a false arrest. They would devise various ways to arrive—there was a secluded alleyway behind South of the Border that would serve as a private entry or escape route, for example, and they sometimes used passwords to gain entry. Mama Quin hosted one meeting for ten local Black businessmen—she was the lone female elder among them—who were invited to gather to form a movement support committee. That evening, a panel truck from a nearby cleaner pulled up to the back of South of the Border, as if making a delivery. Out snuck the men, many of whom did not openly support the Freedom Summer efforts and did not want to be on the receiving end of the dynamite bombs or White harassment, although they did want to help in some way. A COFO representative was there to help steer the meeting, and perhaps it was he who had brought a poem by sixteen-year-old Freedom School student teacher Joyce Brown, written to the community's adults.

By the end of the meeting, Mama Quin helped get businessmen, representing the core of the McComb Black middle class, on board to support the movement. They each agreed to donate fifty dollars and helped to form a food and housing committee. Word would spread of this community involvement—sanctions and intimidation work only if a culture of fear is evoked and keeps people from participating. This money would become the beginnings of a community center meant to support the continued efforts of Freedom Summer, but more so it demonstrated that some of the most trusted members of the community were willing to take on the White supremacist leadership alongside the other activists. After this, churches began to open their doors to mass meetings, and attendance at these meetings among the community began to grow.

As the hot summer continued, both the KKK and local officials increased their harassment of Mama Quin. Whether or not she had her own bootlegged liquor on the premises—they would just plant evidence if they had to—the police would frequently raid her restaurant to terrorize patrons and impose fines. And finally the KKs harassed her landlord, Clyde Gardner, with whom Mama Quin had a good working relationship. She always paid her rent and took care of the place, and he was among the White people in McComb and around the state who were willing to accept what they saw as an inevitable move toward more equal rights for their Black neighbors.

One night during this summer of 1964, the police raided South of the Border when Aylene wasn't there and arrested the woman on duty for selling illegal liquor. Mr. Gardner went to the jailhouse to bail her out with a check, "but they wouldn't take it from him," Aylene explained. "He told them they was getting mighty darn rotten, and they started picking on him then."

Not long after, Aylene's landlord contacted her and said he was going to have to terminate her lease. "I'm sorry," he added, "The KKs threatened my family." So Mama Quin would have to leave South of the Border later that year.

There are other stories of White moderates who quietly tried to prevent more violence. Some just saw this as good business: people were hesitant to visit McComb—White and Black—and families were leaving and businesses closing. One White family, the Heffners, invited a few activists, including a Black priest, over for dinner one evening in an attempt to help broker peace. On paper, they couldn't have better represented Mississippi pride: their daughter was the reigning Miss Mississippi. An entire book was written about how Mr. Heffner's business was ruined and Mrs. Heffner was terrorized by drive-bys and threatening phone calls, to the point where they stayed in a local hotel and eventually moved under duress that September.

And while this highlights the extremity of the White supremacists— both those in power who refused to help the Heffners and the vigilantes who ran them out of town (and these groups were not, by any means, mutually exclusive)—it is ironic that the same terrorist tactics, and more, were inflicted on so many Black families in town, and fewer had the resources to leave or the freedom to move wherever they wanted (and none had a book written about them). While this kind of terrorism is horrific no matter who the victims are, one might argue that much of this violence could have been stopped if White allies in McComb organized like the Black community did and demanded the same things for them: the right to vote, the ceasing of unfettered violence, and equality under the law.

"Yeah, you don't stop on the highway at night," Curtis said years later. He could have been talking about bootlegging or about the dangers of traveling anywhere while Black in Mississippi that summer. "Aylene knew that about us. She wanted me to drive a car. But I used to scare the shit out of her when we had to run. She said, 'Boy you drive a car! Just like a bat out of hell!' We brought them home with us if they wanted to follow us that far. But I bring her home. I always bring her home."

14

Now that the calendar was about to officially turn to autumn, there was hope that Freedom Summer would finally manifest in actual change. Mama Quin had been spreading herself thin. Not only was she a single mom to two young kids still at home (she had sent her older son away in fear for his safety a few years earlier, and her older daughter was in college), but she had a business to run and was central to activism in McComb. Jacqueline Quin remembers spending a lot of time at the restaurant that summer and into the school year when she was eight. "South of the Border was like a shotgun. And you go in the front, but there was a back door [that led] to the alley back then. She had an area in the back . . . where the kitchen was, they would have meetings in the back there." This was also where Jackie spent most of her time at the restaurant. "I would be there doing my homework, getting my lessons or something like that. And when they see somebody coming . . . like the cops pass or something like that," the person acting as lookout would tell the workers eating, or the folks meeting in the back, and they would have time to escape. "That's what happened to Bob Moses and another young worker . . . They hit that back door and they started running down that alley." Jackie remembers it seemed funny to her then and that she was aware of what was going on that summer but did not understand the gravity of it in the moment. "I didn't keep anything hid from them. They heard me walking the floor at night," Mama Quin said.

Sunday, September 20, 1964, was Jacqueline's ninth birthday, and her mama threw her a birthday party. They had cake, perhaps opened presents, and played games. For one evening Aylene wanted Jacqueline to forget the terror that gripped their town each night. There was a field next to their house from which "two men were supposed to guard my house," Mrs. Quin later said. She added, "They said they were there; Sunday night was their night." Jacqueline would later wonder if there had been a snitch among the network of guards.

Once the last guest had left, perhaps Aylene helped five-year-old Anthony change into his pajamas, and then she tucked Jacqueline into bed with a new toy. Johnnie Lee Wilcher, a good friend of Mama Quin's older daughter Carolyn, was a frequent babysitter and settled in the sitting room in the back of the house so Aylene could attend a movement meeting in Jackson, an hour's drive away. Deviating from her usual routine, she left the house without closing the front curtains or turning off the dining room lights. Visible reminders of the evening's festivities—the half-eaten cake, perhaps decorations taped to the wall or clouds of wrapping paper—were illuminated, visible from the street. The neighborhood was quiet, and Mama Quin's children were sleeping when an unfamiliar car raced down the street. There was a brief moment of quiet followed by screeching tires as the car sped off and then an explosion that shook houses for blocks.

After months of bombings and burnings, the target was Mama Quin. Fourteen sticks of dynamite were thrown toward her front door and tore through the front of her modest ranch house. The front door and walls of the rooms where her children were asleep were blown to pieces, and the ceiling collapsed. Neighbors heard—and felt—the boom, which had become all too familiar to Black residents over the previous few months. Windows shattered in nearby homes, and the people inside them held their breath, waiting for more. The wreckage smoldered. The smoke and dust and the lingering, sickeningly sweet odor of nitroglycerin wafted over the cake that the explosion had plastered on the remaining walls and ceiling.

The bomb had exploded the room around Anthony. Pieces of the ceiling trapped him in his bed, pinning him in place in a cloud of dust and smoke. Neighbors came running, and miraculously Anthony was freed in minutes, with little more than bruises. Jacqueline remembers a neighbor picking her up out of the wreckage and carrying her to his house. She waited there with her brother, dust still clinging in her hair, until her mother could be summoned and race home.

A half hour later across the neighborhood, the empty Society Hill Baptist Church was also bombed. The message of the evening was clear: the KKK, and the local law enforcement that turned a blind eye, wanted an end to the church's voter registration classes and Freedom School, among other civil rights activities. They didn't want Black and White people eating together or Black businesses supporting the movement. It wasn't enough that South of the Border was slated to close.

It had been more than two months since the COFO house was bombed at the beginning of the summer and even longer since Mr. Bryant's barbershop had been targeted. Since those first appeals for protection and justice had been ignored, McComb became ground zero for the escalating violence of White supremacists against Black citizens. Records show that more than twenty homes, businesses, and churches in the Black community were bombed or set on fire, as well as dozens of cases of personal attacks (almost always "unsolved"), yet there were numerous arrests of Black citizens on charges such as loitering and "failure to yield right of way" and "criminal syndicalism." The numerous bombings, caused by various explosives from Molotov cocktails to dynamite, created a greater concentration of unchecked brutality than in any other place in the country. The list was so egregious that local activists kept a document listing the injustices and violences; it would number more than thirty instances over a little more than two months—from bombings like at Mama Quin's, to false arrests and imprisonments, beatings, and intimidation with cars, including police vehicles, surrounding and circling the Freedom House from midnight to dawn one night.

The violence in McComb was not going unnoticed beyond the town, despite law enforcement's seeming lack of will to stop it. J. Oliver Emmerich, the editor of the local newspaper the *McComb Enterprise-Journal*, had echoed propaganda talking points from the MSSC and allowed local White leaders to dictate the paper's point of view for plenty of years. However, 1964 seemed to mark a change toward more open support of the COFO activists. He even called out the FBI for falsely calling the NAACP "the best communist-infiltrated organization in America." Since then, his views slowly had become even more outspoken in defense of the movement, and he continued to highlight the violence against local Black citizens—and law enforcement's indifference toward these crimes. Due in part to the growing awareness thanks to this reporting, the White terrorism in McComb started to gain the attention of a larger audience.

That summer Emmerich called McComb "the bombing capital of the world," and after reading the horrific accounts of months of unfettered terrorism, few disputed that dubious claim. He would later be beaten and have flaming crosses lit on his lawn for his growing support of the movement. But his graphic stories about the crimes committed against local Black community members and activists, published in a newspaper that wasn't only for a Black audience, began to grab the attention of larger news outlets beyond his corner of the state. Could it be true that there were so many bombings and beatings in this small city and its surrounding area? Urban and coastal journalists and readers didn't understand the willful complicity of local law enforcement. It was through his amplification of an important story that others in the state had long sought to squelch that made others pay attention. In the wake of this coverage, *Time* magazine described McComb as "the toughest anti-civil rights community in the toughest anti-civil rights area in the toughest anti-civil rights state in the Union." The racial inequality they observed took on a very different pallor in the bigger, northern cities. The irony was not lost on local citizens that it took the murder of two White men for people to start paying attention to the unfettered White supremacist terrorism in Mississippi, but citizens were hopeful that this increased scrutiny—and even the mounting aggression—meant that change was, finally, on the horizon. And this was a reason people like Aylene Quin didn't back down.

"The typical reaction to [a] bombing was to go inside," local SNCC worker (and current Harvard professor) Marshall Ganz said years later. But that night, after phones rang around McComb, spreading the word that yet another bombing had occurred and that it was Mama Quin's house with her children inside, something changed. "It was a big deal, because there had been bombings in McComb. It was just one after another after another. [But] when they bombed her place, everybody came outside. Wow. It was like you could see the fear shift into anger. You could just see," Mr. Ganz says, it was like folks said, "No, enough of this shit."

Soon neighbors came to stand in front of their homes, some with hunting rifles visible by their sides. Local people from nearby neighborhoods showed up as well. There was urgency, a sense that patience for change had finally worn threadbare. No one was going to protect them—even children were targeted—so they had to protect themselves. Many who were in the local movement slept with guns next to their beds already or had someone keeping watch for a slow-moving car waiting to throw a Molotov cocktail or plant dynamite or send a spray of bullets. And when they discovered it was a house with young children, the house of a woman who gave so generously to the community and the movement, they took to the streets. By the end of the night dozens of Black community members and activists were arrested, most charged with exaggerated or bogus crimes, like "criminal syndicalism"—a new state law that prohibited actions by "subversive" groups.

The New York Times declared the group of "2,000 or 3,000" Black residents "angry," while local leaders put the number at 150. Other accounts note the resulting "riot" and that locals "attacked the patrol car with bricks and bottles when it drove up to the wrecked home of Mrs. Aylene Quin." But the reality was that McComb residents had finally had enough and were sending a message of their own. Groups of local men gathered to patrol the neighborhood, legally carrying guns. Young people armed themselves with sticks or bricks, and many were instantly targeted by police and arrested.

———————

One can only imagine the fear and anger Mama Quin felt as she sped the hour back from Jackson toward her bombed home and terrorized children. When she made it back to her Burglund neighborhood, of course she first went to find her children, traumatized but physically OK, safe in the arms of her community. Perhaps it was only then that she fully took in the scene around her home. There were local men, legally armed, standing together in defiance. There were other groups of younger kids, allegedly throwing bottles or rocks at police cars whose presence was menacing and not comfortable. It was clear they weren't investigating this bombing, nor making any pretense of finding the perpetrators. Rather, their presence seemed to be egging locals into any sort of response that would give the officers reason to arrest them, which they were doing in large numbers. "It was tense," Jacqueline Quin remembers. "A lot of people had congregated outside of our house after the dust had settled. It seemed like everybody in the community was out in front of our house. It could've turned ugly. You know, but it didn't." This in great thanks to her mother's leadership.

After seeing her children, Mama Quin was summoned by law enforcement. They wanted her to defuse the protests. "The night my house was bombed, there coulda been a riot," Mrs. Quin said decades later, "but the police, they asked me to make the people go home." Once again she was asked to make concessions to appease the White power structure.

———————

Malcolm X, while considered too radical by many local and even student activists, had forewarned of that bloody summer in a speech a few months before in April. This year of 1964, he said, "will be America's hottest year; her hottest year yet; a year of much racial violence and much racial bloodshed." This had proven to be true thus far. He continued, "The new generation of black people that have grown up in this country during recent years are already forming the opinion, and it's a just opinion, that if there is to be bleeding, it should be reciprocal—bleeding on both sides." Mama Quin was asked to stop a spontaneous protest that would have perhaps proven Malcolm X's point. They had been beaten, arrested, bombed, intimidated, and oppressed for too long, and local people needed to create change. She held them back that day, but she couldn't—and wouldn't—forever.

———————

The next day Aylene Quin packed her bag. A representative from COFO had called, and with money donated by the National Council of Churches, she, Ora Bryant, and Mattie Dillon—all women whose homes had been bombed that summer—were flying to Washington, D.C., to talk to President Johnson and the national press. They went to tell the president that the local people of Mississippi were done waiting.

15

FRANKYE ADAMS-JOHNSON ENROLLED IN TOUGALOO COLLEGE in the fall of 1964, choosing the school, in part, for the activism of the students. And she immediately joined them, working with SNCC on voter registration at the end of that long hot summer. She became only more engaged in activism over the next few years.

On a brutally hot day, Frankye was arrested with a group of peacefully protesting students and held in the sun for hours. Woozy from the heat, Frankye dropped her notebook and bent down to pick it up. *Crack!* A policeman hit her across the back with a baton. She fell to the ground in agony. This injury would pain her for the rest of her life—an eternal reminder of how little her body was regarded by those who held power. Whatever remained of her devotion to nonviolence after Medgar Evers's assassination a few years prior was gone in that moment. Frankye wanted to make a difference, and she was willing to use whatever tools needed to do so—she now believed nonviolence and quiet direct action would not create the change she wanted to see in the world.

Her mother saw the violence around them in Mississippi, the law enforcement agencies' seeming lack of will to stop it, and her daughter's passion. She was afraid for Frankye—afraid that she was getting too radical and would be arrested or injured again, or worse. And so she sent Frankye to live with her sister in White Plains, New York, just outside New York City. Once there, Frankye would take the short train ride into the city to seek out like-minded people, "longing for this connection to the movement." She joined a group of women, including Amiri Baraka's wife, Amina, who would get together and talk about issues. But, she says, "I was used to being active, doing grassroots organizing, getting up and doing things. . . . This was not the kind of movement I was accustomed to."

And then one day in 1969 Frankye was walking down 125th Street and Seventh Avenue in Harlem, and she saw them in black leather and berets. "I liked the language they were talking. I liked their stand of self-defense, not turn the other cheek." It was a group of Black Panthers. *These were my people*, she thought. Frankye joined them but knew it would be challenging to make the trek into the city to work on the breakfast program or attend PE meetings. So Frankye Adams-Johnson, with her sister, founded the White Plains Black Panther Party chapter just outside the city and started and ran a small Free Breakfast for Children Program there. She remembers being excited that "it was all women who ran the offices." And while it may have started with breakfast, it quickly expanded to other forms of care that did not just physically nourish the body but also improved the health of the neighborhood in other ways. One meal in the morning turned to connecting with mothers around their needs, as well as getting involved in local housing issues, particularly in White Plains, where low-income housing was being razed for new buildings—which was also displacing her sister's house and their community—and speeding gentrification. Frankye would then move into New York City.

Cleo remembers working with Frankye in the Bronx at the breakfast program, the two of them up before dawn. Eventually Frankye was asked by the Panthers to move to Brooklyn, to become the officer of the day in Brownsville, Brooklyn. "It was very hard core in Brownsville," she says. "Nobody wanted to go there." Working in Brownsville, Frankye began to better understand the ways that the civil rights efforts in Mississippi both intersected with and diverged from the experiences of those she was helping in northern cities. "Being Black and poor in Mississippi, there was segregation, and there were many injustices through education, but when it came to our community, as poor as we were, we never went hungry. We never went clothesless," Frankye says. "Even with medical care, our parents and community found a way to make sure that we were healthy. It was quite contrary to what I experienced in terms of being Black and poor in the ghettos of New York." There were rats the size of cats biting children, which the Panthers reported on in their Panther paper—something no one else was covering—and addicted young mothers whose kids had nothing to eat at home. In one story she tells, a "four-year-old child had tried to fix himself something, and it was a really dangerous situation because he could have gotten injured. We were trying to help the children," Frankye says, "but we were also trying to help their parents become better parents."

Word of the Black Panther Party began spreading among Black youth around the country. Here was a group that spoke to Black excellence and pride. Teenagers like Mae Jackson and Janet Cyril had found heroes in the young men, just a few years older than them, who made them believe that revolution was, in fact, possible. After working for SNCC just a few years after Freedom Summer, so much had already changed. While there was some tangible change in the South, the day-to-day lives of so many Black people, especially in the cities, seemed stagnant. Laws had been passed, like the Civil Rights Act, that outlawed segregation and formalized discrimination, but actual change was harder to come by. There were still numerous reports of segregated dining rooms and harassment when these now-illegal institutions were questioned, not to mention continued intimidation and violence. It was becoming clear to some activists that their fight would have to happen beyond the voting booth. The Black Panther Party was a group that seemed to be actually doing something about this. The teens saw the Panthers as leaders who would stand up for the atrocities that were happening to Black people around the country every day. When Dr. Martin Luther King Jr. was assassinated in April 1968, many of those who wanted to work toward change but leaned toward Dr. King's nonviolent approach changed their minds, as Frankye had after Medgar Evers's murder. The Panthers' bold actions and rhetoric for change now seemed appropriate to many. But what did this change, this revolution, look like? If you were to ask Cleo or Frankye, both who came to the Panthers with a desire to work in the community toward better living conditions and health, they would say that revolution was empowering the people—Black people, and everyone who had historically been left behind by White supremacy—to work toward systemic change.

———————

"When people talk about the breakfast program," Cleo says decades later, "they only grab on to a little piece of what we were doing and our connection to the community." Cleo was responding to the fact that the wide contributions of the Black Panther Party—from antihunger work, to housing support, to health care—were often reduced to an almost quaint story of tough young Black brothers and sisters feeding kids breakfast. The reality was that the breakfast program illustrated the power of the Panthers' vision of revolution—and also became the conduit between them and the work they could do in the community. It started with food, but its reach and implications would spread far wider.

Part of what made the survival programs—and especially the Free Breakfast for Children Program—so powerful was that they were modeling a worldview in addition to the direct action they were taking. To have a local group embedded in the community, feeding the hungry, giving advice, advocating for basic human rights, and teaching members the skills to do this for themselves, was creating a world in the likeness of the one they spoke about in the Political Education classes. This was what drew Frankye to the Black Panthers and what made Cleo want to join: this was a group that was not all talk—although they did talk and discuss and debate plenty. They were people of action, driven by community needs and informed by their political and social philosophy. And this was also what Hoover found so dangerous. Socialism redistributed wealth and power—two things he and those who supported him didn't want to give up. If the people discovered they had power, real power, to demand adequate food, safe housing, and health care, they would be empowered to demand even more of what they deserved. This was why the common refrain among Black Panthers and other Black Freedom activists was—and is—*All power to the people*. The only appropriate response is to affirm this truism. *All power to the people*.

This fundamental idea of mutual aid, which is by definition socialist, was important to the Panthers' community building, for they made it clear that they did not come to offer charity. Rather, the Panthers' perspective was that those in the community who could help should help support those in need. The Panthers believed that businesses, many of which were owned by people who lived—and spent their profits—in wealthier neighborhoods, had a particular responsibility to give back to those who supported them. The Panthers visited them to solicit donations to support the breakfast program. Their goal was not just to provide the food needed to feed the children but also to engage community businesses in the social and political issues that made free breakfasts a necessity.

Bill Johnson, known as B.J., who worked out of the Corona, Queens, office, was often tasked with soliciting donations. Like chapter members around the city and country, he and his crew established a weekly schedule of what days they would visit different bodegas and grocery stores around the neighborhood to pick up their promised donations. One day, B.J. arrived at a bodega in the neighborhood on his usual day and was taken aback to see that the person working was a woman he didn't know. He took a moment to explain that he and the others were Black Panthers, there for their weekly donation. The look on her face worried him.

"What does he usually give you?" she asked, eyes narrowed.

"A pound of bacon, two loaves of bread, and two dozen eggs," B.J. told her.

"That's it? The cheap bastard." She shook her head and told them to take twice that amount, adding, "Next time come on Wednesday when I'm working."

Generally, local businesses were forthcoming with regular donations such as bacon, bread, grits, cocoa, eggs, or milk. But occasionally there would be resistance. When shopkeepers, many of whom did not live in the neighborhood, refused to donate to the Free Breakfast Program, the

Panthers might organize a boycott. Party members and neighbors would start a picket line in front of the store, carrying placards that said THIS BUSINESS WON'T FEED HUNGRY KIDS and THEY DON'T CARE ABOUT YOU. Another placard had an arrow and an address for a nearby bodega that *did* support the Free Breakfast Program. Most shoppers stopped at the doorway where Panthers and local mothers, perhaps holding babies or with small kids at their feet, were standing with their signs and then turned around and headed down the block to the next shop. Few dared to break the picket line. Inevitably these resistant owners came around, grudgingly or not, donating a few items a week. To the Panthers, full community involvement was part of their philosophy.

"We never spent a penny or a dime to feed children," Frankye says decades later. "We demanded that the greedies who came in our communities, that they should give back. If you want to be here in this community, then you have to contribute to this community. You can't come in here and rob this community." While some Panthers noted episodes of resistance from business owners, Frankye says that from her experience in Brownsville most businesses "cooperated. Because I think they understood our language, they understood that we were a powerful force in the community." They mobilized the community, so that the community understood that "the people had the power."

In other cities where the Black Panther Party had active chapters, there was similar community empowerment. In Chicago, for example, the local Panther leader, Fred Hampton, a charismatic twenty-one-year-old, was working to found the Rainbow Coalition that would bring together activists from diverse groups to fight for common goals around nutrition, housing, and health care. He was teaching others to also realize the power they would have in numbers. Poor nutrition and access to quality food was not a Black issue—it was one that faced many people, particularly people of color, Indigenous groups, and poor Whites in ignored pockets of poverty around the country. As Mr. Hampton sought to connect these groups, he believed—as did so many others—that their power in numbers could truly help to make a difference. Cleo remembers him as one of the most charismatic leaders she had ever met, on par with Cuban leader Fidel Castro and President Bill Clinton, both of whom she met through her activism work.

And, as Fred Hampton explained it, the breakfast program was modeling what revolutionary change would be like, for doubters and sideliners alike: "The pigs say, 'Well, the Breakfast for Children Program is a socialist program, it's a communist program,' and the women say, 'I don't know if I like communism. I don't know if I like socialism. But I know that the Breakfast for Children Program feeds my kids.'" He argued that it wasn't a charity but a program for advancement, saying, "Any program that's revolutionary is an advancing program. Revolution is change. Honey, if you keep on changing, before you know it . . . they're endorsing it, they're participating in it, and supporting socialism."

Another benefit from the breakfast program was the way it connected the Panthers to the needs of the community and allowed them to find new ways to offer support. It was a direct line to public health and agency. Volunteers would hear about evictions or note who was sick or who said their parents or siblings or neighbors were unwell. They could see the growing problem of drug addiction and the complications of housing security. Cleo in the Bronx and Frankye in Brooklyn, and others around the city, began to note the many issues that plagued the populations they were working with and began to think expansively about how the Black Panther Party could further help. Kids would come in looking tired or unwell, and the Panthers would ask them how they were and what was going on. The kids might tell them that the heat was out in their building or rats kept them up at night or a parent's struggle with addiction was affecting them. The Panthers' relative youth, their existence outside "the system" that so many parents taught them to be distrustful of, all built trust to facilitate this kind of communication.

Because of this, across New York City the Black Panther Party offices became a point of contact within the community. And so often this contact was around food. "As the Black Panther Party worked in communities, that's how the attitudes change to become more positive," Cleo explains. "Because they were just very sweet. . . . Any older person that had a bag and it looked like they couldn't carry their bags up to the fifth floor and Panthers are right there, zoom, right up there to the fifth floor. 'Yes, ma'am. We'll take your bag right up there for you.' And as a result, word of mouth was that, 'Them children are nice. Them children take care of you.'" So as a sign of appreciation, the older person might send down to the office a pot of food, like rice and beans, in thanks. It became a way to bridge demographics—Black and Puerto Rican, older and younger—and an opportunity for connection.

Cleo also began mentoring young people through what she called the Black and Brown Cadre: a group of young people she met through her work in the local high schools whom she would often gather for study groups, PE lessons, and dinners out. But first she had to ask their parents' permission.

"I'm twenty-one, and I'm married to a priest," Cleo would tell them, standing in the doorway of the dim hallways in one of the many tenement buildings. Some parents knew her friendly demeanor and youthful energy from around the neighborhood, but others were perhaps a little skeptical. Yet it certainly helped the mostly Catholic Puerto Rican parents that she was married to a former clergyman. "We're going to have a study group," Cleo assured them.

The teens were always excited: "Please let me go, let me go!"

The parents would almost always let them. And as the group continued to meet, and they never got in any trouble with Cleo, the yeses came a little more easily.

Cleo would invite them to her house, her chairs always arranged in a circle in her living room to facilitate conversation and community.

"OK, everybody sit down. Get your books out." Just a few years older than these kids, Cleo would exude her friendly authority. She always had food and something to drink for the kids—sometimes elaborate food like shrimp Newburg. "I always had a taste for the fancy," she says years later with a laugh. But Cleo also acknowledges that this was to help the young people feel "all grown up" and a part of something larger. "They got to help clean up afterwards. . . . Zayd Shakur was one of the great men of the Black Panther Party and always wanted to wash dishes after having a great meal. He really gave the kids the feeling, like, we are going to be revolutionary! We're going to be like Zayd Shakur; we're going to wash dishes and help women!" It was the same meals Cleo might make for the Black Panther leadership when she had them over to her place for a meeting or just to feed them. And it was an assurance for whoever sat at Cleo's table that they were worthy of these elaborate French dishes—and Cleo was worthy of cooking them. Cleo would often cook her White friends coq au vin, inspired by a dinner date at "this really lovely little French restaurant down in the Lower East Side with my husband." She reflects decades later that this might have been her own way of proving to these women that her early-twenties self "was an internationalist to the core . . . and could not cook only southern chicken and rice." French cuisine was a symbol of sophistication, worldliness at the time—however problematic this effect of White supremacy in food culture may seem now—but it was a tool for Cleo to "fight stereotypes" of Black cooking at the time. But she notes, laughing, that if her Panther girlfriends got together for dinner, they would eat fried chicken, potato salad, greens, and a cake. "They used to tell me don't show up if you don't bring the potato salad," she says, referring to a recipe she learned from her grandmother.

Cleo also would take the cadre out to dinner—next to the Young Lords office, there was an excellent, inexpensive Indian restaurant that Cleo and others loved—for the kind of food they weren't likely to encounter at home. They would "share nice food and talk," Cleo says. "We were always running our mouth" talking about school, or ideas from PE class, or recent news headlines. This culinary diplomacy was integral in Cleo's mentorship of these teens. A well-cooked meal was a window into another culture, not just because of where the food might have originally come from but also because of the culture of eating out— of being welcome in a restaurant, of feeling like it was a space where you belonged. By the end of the 1960s there were still plenty of restaurants in the Deep South, certainly around Mississippi, where, although Black people could not legally have been banned, they nevertheless would not have had a welcome experience. Cleo wanted these boys to never feel hesitation walking in the door. This was part of being a Black Panther or Young Lord—to know that you are worthy.

"They all became very sophisticated adults . . . intellectually and socially sophisticated, much more so than they would have been just to be narrowly focused on their own community," Cleo says, reflecting on the impact of these experiences. "You know, we took them around, let them meet people, let them see that as a member of the Black Panther Party, you get to do things." Many of her Black and Brown Cadre members would go on to do community organizing or become successful in other ways—as attorneys, fighting against apartheid, or advocating for immigrant and undocumented workers.

———————

The Panthers also offered organizing help, resources, and people power for other local activist groups, including the United Bronx Parents, helmed by Evelina Antonetty. Kathy Goldman describes one day when "about a dozen women came to somebody they could trust to complain that the food [in the school cafeteria] was so bad . . . that the kids couldn't eat it. And they were so poor and that meal meant so much to them." Kathy, who worked with United Bronx Parents for years, explains that Evelina realized that these women felt that they could speak with authority on proper nutrition for their children, but they were much less confident speaking up about other aspects of their children's education. Food was a way that Evelina could get these parents engaged. "It was and it wasn't about food," Kathy says decades later. She reflects that her life's activism around food justice "came out of that [moment]. . . . It was those women, Puerto Rican mothers, came to somebody they could trust and began something that's still going on." Evelina was known as the person whom parents could come to if they had questions or issues concerning their children in school. Having these parents before her, wanting to help create change around food, gave Evelina an idea about improving food for kids in the South Bronx while also creating local jobs, but she needed first to get government officials on board. What Evelina and the United Bronx Parents would plan was the same kind of dramatic action that the Panthers preferred.

———————

Evelina López Antonetty was born in the small coastal town of Salinas, Puerto Rico, and moved to the Bronx the year she turned eleven, in 1933. A few years later, at sixteen, she joined the Young Communist League, where she was taught community organizing, discipline, and follow-through. She attended the league's' frequent reading groups, which included rigorous lessons on complex social and political topics, not unlike the Panthers' PE classes, and where all attendees were encouraged to speak their mind confidently. These nontraditional education experiences shaped her life and gave her the skills to engage in community organizing, much as they did for members of SNCC and the Black Panther Party. She would go on to be among the first Latinas hired by local union organizers and would devote herself to parent organizing by the mid-1960s when she had her third child.

In 1969 Evelina Antonetty found that the Puerto Rican and Black parents in the South Bronx, where she lived and organized, didn't often feel confident enough to question the schools around education issues, despite the fact that they recognized the many shortfalls and inequities compared to wealthier districts. But they did feel confident talking about what was healthy for their kids to eat—and were livid about the spoiled milk, turned meat, and dry bread their children were being served for school lunch. Food was a way for them to talk about inequality and get engaged in the larger system that supported this disparity of resources around the city and disproportionately affected Black and Brown families.

United Bronx Parents was a group dedicated to advocating for all aspects of quality education in the Bronx. It had a staff of three, including Evelina, Kathy, and Ellen Lurie. These women came to this work because of the real disparity in New York City schools that, while not technically segregated like those in Mississippi—New York City had its own school integration fight in 1964, in which Kathy Goldman was involved—schools in predominantly Black and Brown neighborhoods were still greatly underfunded.

To address this recent concern of inedible food in Bronx schools, Evelina invited "every elected official from congressman on down" to come to the South Bronx and discuss this issue over lunch, Kathy explains. She had already established herself as a trusted community organizer, so officials agreed. "They thought they were coming to have lunch with us at the headquarters. Instead of that, we put them on a school bus, and took them to the school and said, 'We want to show you what's going on.'"

They brought the officials into the cafeteria and fed them what the children ate for lunch. The South Bronx, and many Black and Brown neighborhoods around the city, received some of the worst food in the whole school system. Cleo remembers the Panthers supporting UBP's work and describes the horrific meals as serving "sour milk, meat with green circles around it, deteriorating food that was sent from other districts up to our district." And they didn't have adequate facilities to prepare food and wash dishes. "Believe it or not, [the cafeteria workers] were buying their own soap and scouring powder."

The officials sat down and were served food not fit to be eaten. They were aghast at what was on their plates. Kathy remembers with a laugh, "If we planned every second of that, it couldn't have been better. One congressman was so appalled" because he saw it from the perspective of federal waste. He exclaimed, "The end of all that money is this kind of crap?" And then an assemblyman got sick and ran out of the room.

Their stunt had the intended effect, and by the end of the lunch they got permission to try their own approach to feeding the kids, on a trial basis. UBP went on to hire a former army cook and a woman who was in charge of food at schools in Puerto Rico to help them think about feeding large groups for less money. "We sat down, talked to them, and kept track of every nickel that was being spent and all the rest. And it was so astonishing to me," Kathy recounts, "that for less money than they were spending, you could really do something good. All you need is a little bit of common sense." Their plan involved buying higher-quality and fresh food and hiring local parents to help prepare it, which would provide needed jobs in the neighborhood. Throughout this fight, Cleo and the Panthers provided support in what ways they could, including sharing people power and other resources, brainstorming ideas for action, and connecting interested members of the community.

Not only did the Panthers support UBP, but also the help was reciprocal. From her previous work with school integration, Kathy had met "a really delightful fellow" who also "happened to be a butcher." So when the Black Panther Party was looking for donations for its Free Breakfast program, Kathy called up her friend Murray. "And I said to him, 'You know, they're gonna need a lot of food; they're going to be feeding so many kids breakfast.' So he became the bacon man. And he just gave a lot of stuff." Kathy often helped transport the donations. "It's really a straight line," she says, about how one fight for justice influences and supports another. "Nothing starts from nothing."

Another striking outcome of the work the Black Panthers were doing was how it led to more community engagement: both more problems to solve and more positive outcomes. The Black Panthers and their partners were getting things done. Just as Cleo saw her students become more successful and engaged through her VISTA program, so did the local schools see the performance and energy of students increase when they had a hot meal to start their day. Attendance was up, and tardiness was down—in great thanks to the Panthers' walking the kids to school each morning—and parents and teachers alike appreciated the homework and reading help. Plus this engagement with the kids over breakfast revealed more ways that the Panthers could help the community.

One example was in Corona, Queens, when breakfast program volunteers discovered that some students needed to do research, but the closest library was in the Jackson Heights neighborhood, which was primarily White at the time. At breakfast, children told the Panthers stories of the White gangs who would terrorize them, so the Panthers began to escort kids. But B.J. remembers that some parents were still wary of the Panthers and would say, "Don't you go get the Panthers to escort you to the library—you just go ahead."

B.J. remembers, "One day a little boy and a little girl chased by the thugs. They ran back to the library for safety and the librarian locked the door. They got beat up right in front of the library. And that's when we sprung into action!" He says the Panthers helped research the appropriate avenue for starting a city library: petitioning the city, finding a builder, and locating an appropriate building. And in 1969, working with and within the Library Action Committee, the Panthers helped found the Langston Hughes Community Library and Cultural Center, which is home to the largest circulating collection of Black heritage books in New York City.

Yasmeen Majid was a member of the Library Action Committee and had joined the Black Panther Party as a New York City Community College student "because I wanted to work in the community" of Corona, Queens, where she lived. She was soon elected to the finance committee, and that would end up changing the direction of her life: she changed her major to accounting and has worked in nonprofit finance her entire career. She remembers how they went "door to door in Corona, to different people's houses just to find out what their needs were so that we could meet those needs." This approach to serving the people made a big impact on her then and has continued to demonstrate how the Panthers' work served Corona.

When Yasmeen's daughter was in elementary school, her teacher found out that Yasmeen was a Panther in the neighborhood. "And so one day, she stopped me. And she said to me, 'You know, I was one of the little kids that used to have breakfast.' I thought that was amazing and that just stuck with me, because she's thinking about the number of children that we've actually fed in the morning, and we looked forward to it."

The success of Yasmeen's daughter's teacher, manifested so many decades later, demonstrated that the goal of the survival programs was empowering people to help make incremental change and to imagine a better, different future. The Panthers did this through this most enduring and consistent nutrition effort but also increasingly took on other aspects of survival, including housing, health care, drug rehab, and other efforts. The Panthers commandeered an all-but-abandoned mobile health truck and took it to neighborhoods like the South Bronx to test folks for sickle cell anemia and diabetes. They distributed bags of groceries to neighborhood families in need and organized clothing and shoe drives. In collaboration with the Young Lords, they took on shared causes like

police reform in their neighborhoods and also acted in solidarity to support causes like the California grape boycott that concerned issues more
central to the Puerto Rican population. And Panthers, led in part by
Afeni Shakur, became engaged in housing initiatives, helping to organize
rent strikes and building takeovers, improving the quality of community
housing, and sometimes putting that housing in the hands of community
members themselves by guiding them through legal action. They heard
from kids and parents about lack of heat or hot water in buildings and
worked to organize tenant unions to demand changes and cooperatives
that could work to legally take over or buy buildings from delinquent
landlords to create cooperatives where they were able to own their apartments and manage the building themselves, using tactics informed by
Cleo's work with VISTA. All of this helped to slowly but surely make
progress toward wealth and asset distribution and against systemic economic sanctions that left so many Black and Brown communities out of
business and home ownership.

Through all of this, women in the Black Panther Party continued to
lead—in New York City and in chapters around the country—despite
the fact that the visible leadership continued to be almost entirely male.
In published books and articles, there has been reflection by numerous
female Panthers about the presence—and absence—of chauvinism in the
Black Panther Party, but Cleo has emphasized that she was only respected
by male members, while Panther Dequi Kioni-Sadiki acknowledges that
the Panthers were "indoctrinated" into the same system of misogyny and
patriarchy as our broader culture. These mixed messages can be seen
across the issues of the Panther paper, which might have images of armed
female Panthers but also include language that "tended to argue for an
assertion of masculine authority," writes Dr. Rhodes. Dequi adds, "Even
when we want to change the world, we got to work on changing ourselves. . . . But in terms of how leadership was organized, women, excuse
my language, did not take no shit." And through its language and uplifting of female leaders, the Panthers as an organization certainly spoke
more directly about goals of gender equality and instituted more female

leaders and spokespeople than many other organizations at the time. Dr.
Tracye Matthews's research confirms Dequi's assertions, to which she
adds, "Female Panthers often tested and stretched the boundaries of the
largely masculinized Party structure. Many of these women held low or
no formal positions of rank. Yet their heroic actions thrust them into
positions of prominence inside and outside the Party."

This "prominence" was often as informal leaders—of projects and
initiatives, like Cleo's Black and Brown Cadre—and women were not
often visible beyond the community in which they served. "I was a nice
little girl. Seriously nice girl. And I'd be over at your house for dinner.
And I'm cooking," Cleo says. But what made her and other women like
her so powerful was not just this personal connection with the people
she served but also the way she would use her platform and organizing
skills to push for change. "I'm gonna stand up and say how many people
there were that were shot in a weekend and had spent seventy-two hours
in the emergency room. I could go to the leadership of the New York
City Hospital Corporation and say that. And people were like, 'That's
our girl. She's talking about stuff.'"

As Dr. Tracye Matthews writes, the "explicitly political and public
function" of the survival programs meant women could take on leadership roles within programs that were an "extension of 'traditional' roles
for women" and that "were the lifeblood of the organization and as such
should be understood more accurately as forms of political leadership."
This is one more voice arguing that the contributions of the Panther
women—and other women whose work had similar social and political repercussions but without formal leadership titles—have long been
unsung.

———

At the end of each day, Panthers were expected to give a report on those
they came in contact with throughout the day, what they did, and any
observations or notes. "People in the community would walk up to you
and thank you," Cleo says. "And the reports became more and more and
more positive, especially in communities like the South Bronx. It didn't
start out initially as being superpositive, but boy, after a year of our work,

and especially the work in the hospitals and housing, and supporting the organizations that are doing education stuff, people will just be walking and say, 'Yeah, I like you people; you're bad!'"

It seemed, to many on the front lines, that the revolution they were fighting for was starting to take hold. But all Black Panthers also knew that they were being watched and undermined by the systems in power, especially the local police and FBI. They just didn't realize to what extent those organizations had infiltrated their ranks.

16

THE NEW YORK CENTRAL OFFICE IN HARLEM had a revelation one day. For weeks, more than a few members noticed a click on the phone line moments after they picked it up. Were their phones being tapped? They decided to do a little experiment: they stopped paying their bill. Surely if the FBI or NYPD wanted to keep listening to their calls, the phone would stay connected. They received notices of disconnection and balance due, but the phone stayed on. They knew every word was being listened to.

But despite this evidence, and the obvious arrests and clashes Panthers around the country had with police, few in the New York chapter truly understood to what extent the government was working against them.

"We didn't pay attention," Cleo said years later. The Panthers were "so naive and so not aware" of the many ways that various government agencies, primarily coordinated by J. Edgar Hoover and his secretive COINTELPRO initiative, were infiltrating, undermining, and committed to destroying the Black Panther Party. As Dequi says, "We were really young and underprepared and didn't know. So many of the people who were in the party spoke about just not really recognizing how fully violent this country would come down. . . . I mean, we talked about J. Edgar Hoover who was poisoning the breakfast that was being fed to children so people would stop going."

In addition to having their phones tapped, many of the Panthers were constantly tailed, and they knew that there were spies among the new recruits. But the Panther attitude was that they would make any infiltrator work just as hard as anyone else. "We said we don't give a damn if you are an infiltrator because we're gonna work the shit out of you," Cleo says. "If you're in the Black Panther Party you're gonna be a hard worker, you're gonna be up at five o'clock in the morning."

So at PE meetings they might call out suspected spies in front of everyone, saying, "'How many papers did you sell today? You didn't sell enough papers! Where's the money—come on!' We wanted to know why you wanted to join the Black Panther Party if you were gonna just lay around," Cleo says. "You gotta work hard to be a Panther."

But as the MSSC and FBI knew, even just knowing that one is being surveilled could be its own deterrent. Many people left the movement when they realized they were being watched and listened to, and there was attrition among the Panthers as well. And of course the FBI hoped to gain intel from these wiretaps and stolen documents, perhaps something they could twist to press charges or find individuals who had gone underground.

In one of the FBI's less sophisticated plots, uniformed workers came into the Harlem office saying that they needed to fix the phone. One story has Panther Ali Bey Hassan yelling at them to "Get the fuck out! You ain't no damn telephone man—you the FBI!"

Mae Jackson tells a similar story about men coming to her apartment and saying that they were there to inspect the phone. Mae's mother said, "There's nothing wrong with the telephone. No, you cannot come in." Mae says the men started "fighting and tussling" with her mother, and neighbors came out into the hallway due to the noise. One young woman yelled, "Call the police!"

Mae's mother said, "'This is the motherfucking police!' And then we threw them on the elevator, pressed the [button] and went back into our apartment." Mae says that the FBI also tracked down her father—whom she had not spoken to in years, and in fact had no idea where he lived—and questioned him about another Black activist.

Frankye Adams-Johnson says the FBI visited her mother not long after she joined the Panthers, and they told her that Frankye was involved with "very dangerous people who kill police." Her mother took her first flight ever to New York from Jackson, and demanded to see Frankye with her own eyes, afraid, once again, for her daughter's life. These stories were far from rare. Many Black Panthers have said that they were surveilled, family members were interrogated, and they were the subject of other FBI spy and interrogation tactics—often well past the years they had spent in the Panthers.

———

The FBI or local police (often using questionable "intelligence" provided by the FBI) were attempting to gain access to or raid Panther pads and individual members' apartments with growing frequency as the party expanded in membership and scope in 1969. And increasingly, party offices around the country were set up for local police raids under false pretenses—often due to reports of illegal weapons, of which few were ever found—so that the police could search party records. They were looking for the names and contact information of people associated with the Panthers and any possible evidence or leverage to use against them. Unlike the MSSC, which collected information with a relatively haphazard effort at undermining activists, the FBI took a more systematic approach.

Chicago's law enforcement, encouraged and aided by the FBI, was particularly bent on destroying the local Black Panther Party chapter. In early 1969 Cook County's new state's attorney, Edward Hanrahan, began an offensive against them, calling the Panthers a "gang" and declaring "war" against them, particularly aware of Chairman Hampton's growing popularity. Hanrahan disparaged the Panthers in numerous press accounts, particularly for their efforts to get community control of local police because of the long history of police brutality in the city. The state's attorney brought bogus charges and steep punishments against Hampton and other Panthers to get them off the streets, and in spring 1969, he used the supposed presence of a fugitive, who would later be found to be an FBI informant, as an excuse to raid and trash the Chicago Panther headquarters. These actions had some of the intended effect:

some Panthers left the organization in fear, and the intel Hanrahan's office gained from the raids was used to intimidate members and supporters in ways that wouldn't be publicly exposed for years.

In New York City, the police and the FBI were both also actively recruiting spies—often without collaboration. Some of these informants were threatened with arrest, bogus charges, or retribution against their family if they didn't agree. Others were police recruits, perhaps new to the area. These spies acted as informants, instigators, and much more. And usually they didn't know who else among the Panthers was also spying, so they might end up reporting on each other's provocative actions or words, these purposefully inflammatory suggestions or statements by infiltrators becoming "proof" of Panther misdeeds or radical thinking. The New York Panthers had also been infiltrated since they were founded, and that intel had continually helped the NYPD and FBI work to destroy the party from the inside, even as they continued to carry out bogus arrests and violence. Bob Bloom, a lawyer who long worked for the Black Panthers, said that they now know that three of the founding members of the Harlem office were police spies, including Gene Roberts, who had been sent undercover before he ever put on a uniform, all the better to ensure he didn't use police lingo and would fit in.

———————

While Hoover and the FBI had a larger agenda to eliminate the Black Panther Party in great part to stop Black, Brown, and poor Americans from joining forces to demand a government that better and more equitably served them, law enforcement was certainly angry at the Party for reasons that also included its direct criticism of police. The party often referred to them as "pigs," a term that the Panthers defined as "an ill-natured beast who has no respect for law and order, a foul traducer who's usually found masquerading as a victim of an unprovoked attack." In an early issue of the Panther paper, Bobby Seale explained they were striving to best represent their critique of "the police and fascist bigots who commit murder, brutalize, and violate people's constitutional rights." *Pig* came out of the term *fascist swine*, and when Huey hit on it, "Eldridge sat down at the typewriter and typed out the definition. He gave it to Huey. Huey said, 'Yeah,'" Bobby Seale recalls. They handed this to Emory Douglas, the Panthers' minister of culture, who was also essential in creating the distinct visuals and striking design of the Panther paper and other communications. "Emory had a drawing of a pig," Bobby Seale writes. "We put it on the front page and wrote under it, SUPPORT YOUR LOCAL POLICE, a Birchite slogan which is also supported by 'white citizen,' white racist, so-called 'patriotic' organizations." Equating the police with pigs was a direct reference to the experience of Black and Brown people who had been actively attacked and oppressed by police officers in the Deep South, urban neighborhoods, and elsewhere. Many police officers, particularly in urban centers like New York City, were particularly offended by the term *pig* and considered the oft-chanted phrase "off the pig" a call for murder and violence. ("It doesn't mean commit murder," Bobby Seale writes; rather, its message is to get rid of the metaphoric slave master.) The true intent of the term *pig*, especially when paired with a pig in a uniform, is directed at the long history of police brutality and the use of the police force to enforce White supremacy, especially through violence and intimidation.

The Panther paper pulled no punches when it came to criticism of law enforcement, government policy, and current events. To counter this megaphone, which had national weekly distribution in the hundreds of thousands, the FBI also battled the Panthers through the media. The FBI preferred to perpetuate the image of a Black Panther as tough, militant, and violent, to play into longtime stereotypes of Black men as dangerous and lawless, despite much evidence to the contrary. And the sound bites on national news or in major newspapers—which by 1969 were regularly covering the Panthers—often reflected these biases. A *Time* magazine article titled "The Panther's Bite" describes the Panthers as "not only militant but also militaristic." Asserting the Black Panthers are in "a state of war" and "devoted to some hard-line Chinese Communist doubletalk," the article accuses them of violent and illegal activities. The article reads like FBI talking points, and was likely cribbed directly from a memo from the bureau, exactly as it intended.

One of the recurrent critiques of the Panthers was that they were communists, as activists in the southern civil rights efforts were also called. Playing on the fears instigated by McCarthy's Red Scare decades earlier, the stigma of communism and socialism was an easy target. It was all too convenient to villainize the Panthers and other activist and progressive groups that were engaged in "socialist" mutual aid and critiqued the failures of capitalism as being anti-American. Likewise, Panthers responded to the propaganda in the mainstream press with more pointed criticism of the capitalist system and the ills of systemic power in their own Panther paper, which became an increasingly widely read and important tool in Political Education, communication of their values, and counternarrative to the FBI- and media-perpetuated mistruths about the Panthers' actions and even headlines about major national and world events like the Vietnam War.

Furthermore, their outward embracing of Chairman Mao's Little Red Book and alignment with Fidel Castro's leadership in Cuba were easily portrayed as particularly anti-American in the wake of recent world wars, the 1959 Cuban Revolution, and the current Vietnam conflict—all of which were ostensibly pitting America against communism. While, as the Panthers note, a more socialist approach was in the best interest of so many in the country when it came to public assistance, socialism was equated with communism in the public imagination, and both were a difficult philosophical sell to a broad national audience and even to the communities they were helping. In part what drew the Panthers to an alternative to capitalism was a desired sense of shared wealth and an assurance of a basic standard of living—what Castro and Mao both preached. But through various means—propaganda and fear and subversive law enforcement through the FBI and House Un-American Activities Committee, among other means—the US government vilified these governing philosophies and taught Americans to do the same. The Panthers recognized this and sought to convey, in part through modeling the community benefits of mutual aid, that a more socialist approach would improve everyone's conditions.

In addition, as Dequi stresses, this also laid bare the priorities of those in power by "exposing the contradictions and inequities in capitalism and how it disparately impacts people's lives. That's what the Black Panther Party did. Because with those survival programs, they showed the people in the community that, 'Yo, we can do this.' So this means that if the government had the will to do it, they could. But they don't have the will because of oppression, racism and White supremacy."

What is taken for granted in these conversations is the historical demonization of socialism and communism as a false antithetical to American capitalism. The Panthers taught—in PE class and elsewhere—that socialism was imaginable within the current democratic structure and involved the government ensuring that everyone received basic care and a decent standard of living. "We fight capitalism with basic socialism," Bobby Seale writes in *Seize the Time*. And, as Cleo notes, "You have to get to socialism before you get to communism." In a pure communist society, "everybody believes in sharing and there's a mutual respect" no matter one's background or interests. But while the Panthers studied communism philosophically, they focused their revolutionary goals in the framework of a class struggle. As Seale explains, "In our view it is a class struggle between the massive proletarian working class and the small minority ruling class. Working-class people of all colors must unite against the exploitative, oppressive ruling class."

Numerous scholars have noted that the American government has relied so heavily on the perpetuation of the myth of the American Dream—that everybody can overcome their situation and gain wealth through hard work—discounting the ways that the government supported and relied on the oppression of many to uphold the success of a few. To ignore the ways that the government invokes socialist principles—such as public schools and infrastructure, for example, which help aid the wealthy—while demonizing additional socialist demands like universal health care and adequate food assistance, which those in power see as too costly or negatively affecting their ability to make money, is working only for the good of these already in power. The Panthers were not shy in talking about the White supremacist power structure—although they often substituted the term *pig*—and challenged people to consider the political and social ramifications of the existing power structure for both people of color and for everyone in the working class.

And while some activists coming out of the violence of Freedom Summer embraced this aggressive rhetoric, seeing it as the next logical step to fight for the revolution they had yet to see happen—despite so many deaths, beatings, and bogus arrests—even for some "left of left" activists, the Panthers' rhetoric and provocative actions were too much to support. Many Panthers did own guns, usually legally and for legitimate concerns of self-defense. Certainly, some were used in extralegal activities. And some of the most provocative and aggressive Party members were drawn to join more because of their anger at the existing system or desire to support Black Freedom through aggressive means than because of a call to support mutual aid. More than one Panther acknowledged that this was a group of young people, and that mistakes were made, in part through their passion or hubris or willingness to give their life for the revolution for which they were fighting. One former SNCC leader says, "I don't like cops, but the last thing I would be doing is standing up in some conversation screaming at [them]. . . . I don't think that's a very intelligent tack."

Regardless of the debate over the Panthers' approach, it is known through now-declassified documents that the FBI considered their influence because of their Breakfast for Children and other survival programs, and their political ideology, to be the FBI's primary reason for seeking "neutralization"—not any specifically noted illegal activity some members may have taken part in. This is not to say that the Panthers were always above the law. But it is to say that an analysis of COINTELPRO documents reveals that the cited threat of the Black Panthers was their legal community organizing, growing political influence, and empowering people.

———

While the FBI certainly fed the propaganda machine to discredit the Panthers, there was also already distrust and misconstruing of the message of Black Freedom through the racist and biased perception of mainstream media and even progressive, White America. Malcolm X, who was assassinated in 1965, allegedly by Nation of Islam members who were angry at his split from them, was among the first Black leaders to reach a national platform for his calls for Black Freedom and revolution beyond Dr. King's broader message for nonviolent resistance. Malcolm X's 1964 speech "The Ballot or the Bullet" outlined his belief that activists needed to expand the freedom struggle from "the level of civil rights to the level of human rights" and encouraged involvement in voter registration and community organizing. But of course this wasn't what the press focused on. Rather they highlighted another phrase from this famous speech: that Black people should use "any means necessary" to defend their rights. The FBI, and anyone who wanted to stoke racial tension, decried this as a call for Black violence, which dovetailed nicely with the Black Panthers' visuals as revolutionary gun toters.

Discussions of Malcolm X's speech often ignore its context of false arrests, death, and violence—much at the hands of, or abetted by, the law enforcement agencies. This speech was given months after elected officials in the Mississippi Delta tried to starve their Black neighbors and in the wake of dozens of crosses set aflame around the South in one evening. Malcolm X saw the same horrific housing Black families were forced to live in that Cleo visited, and had similarly witnessed cops selling heroin out of their cruiser window. He hadn't forgotten the assassination of Medgar Evers the year before. He could all but foresee his own murder less than a year later. It was a natural narrative for the media to accuse Malcolm X of inciting violence, and some of his followers would go on to become Black Panther Party members, including one of his bodyguards from the night he was killed. Even today the media, and government coercion of it, and our own taught biases have done such a thorough job of convincing us of Malcolm X's and the Black Panther Party's militancy that many people can hardly see past that.

Many members of the Black Panther Party, as Malcolm X implied, say that they fully believed they would die in the fight for freedom from oppression, most likely at the hands of law enforcement. In fact, in numerous writings by Black Panthers, and in personal interviews, party members said that they honestly believed that they would be killed for this revolution. But it wouldn't be because they were shooting first.

Hoover was happy with their philosophy: it was relatively easy to show the Panthers as violent extremists when they made headlines with guns slung across their backs.

———————

The inner-city Black communities with strong southern roots had a deep memory of needing to carry guns for protection from Klan and White supremacist violence and knew that carrying a weapon might be the only reason an aggressor might take a more measured approach. But for those who were privileged enough not to think about racial discrimination, gun ownership was the stuff of hoodlums or hunters, and they had little understanding otherwise. The armed Black Panthers directly shone a light on the double standard of who represents patriotism and who gets to define it. Armed White supremacists were defended by government officials as upholding American ideals, which they defined through Black oppression. Black activists who chose to, or were forced to, arm themselves for protection or in a show of equal expression of their rights as citizens were, logically, doing more to uphold American ideals than the KKK or police officers working at the direction of the MSSC. Perhaps the young Panthers knew implicitly that capturing the attention of the media was the only way for the reality of the inequities suffered by Black urban communities to be seen by a wider population.

But the reality was that J. Edgar Hoover and other White leaders were afraid of the way the community responded to the Black Panthers, especially around the survival programs, and how their community organizing was giving voice and power to a long-oppressed group. And increasingly the Free Breakfast for Children Program was the conduit both for connecting to the local community and for demonstrating these community-centric values to a much larger national audience. As Chicago Black Panther Party member Deborah Johnson (who would later be known as Akua Njeri) said, "We know that people didn't have an understanding of socialism or communism and that they might say they're against that. . . . But people basically thought that children had a right to be fed and learn on a full stomach."

This popularity, this proof that socialism worked for the betterment
of the people, was also evidence that the government did not in fact
take care of its people and was in part why the FBI had declared the
Free Breakfast for Children Program the "greatest threat" to national
security. And they attacked the Black Panther Party and the breakfast
program accordingly. Across the country there were reports of local or
federal agents destroying food to try to cripple the program. At times
the FBI disseminated purposely untrue information about the food donations being transported to breakfast sites, saying that there were guns or
drugs hidden among the eggs and grits. Local police would stop these
shipments and confiscate or search the food, or render it inedible in
the process. The night before the first Chicago Breakfast for Children
Program, "the Chicago police broke into the church and mashed up all
the food and urinated on it," knowing that the program broke no law
or posed any perceived threat, other than feeding and empowering Black
and Brown kids. In at least one city, parents were told the food was
infected with venereal diseases; in others, law enforcement harassed party
members during breakfast in front of the children or took their pictures,
ascribing to the MSSC's approach as a way to discourage participation.
Vehicles transporting donated food were stopped and impounded on
bogus charges, and fines were given for illegal distribution of food—all
reminiscent of the MSSC's tactics a few years earlier. The Panthers on
duty that next morning would head out to the local store and use their
own money or ask for donations of more food to feed the kids, never
leaving anyone hungry.

But the FBI campaign focused on much more than just destroying donated
food. Its initiatives were much more thorough and tactical. The once-
classified memos that detail the Black Panthers' "threat" and order law
enforcement response use words like "neutralize" to describe the effort
to ruin the Black Panther Party. In its justification for why this is such
a priority, no real fear of public violence or destruction is ever noted.
Rather, the FBI fears the Black Panthers "gaining respectability" and sees
them as the leaders to inspire a "true black revolution." The real weapon

the Panthers needed was whatever was needed for the survival programs. This was what J. Edgar Hoover was afraid of—a healthy and empowered populace—so it wasn't truly guns that were needed for self-defense, but food, clothing, safe housing, and health care. This all points to Hoover's fearing a loss of political and social power as his impetus for his intensive attack on the Black Panther Party.

To that end, as the community and public perception of the Black Panthers began to improve, the FBI continued to expand its multi-pronged attack to "neutralize" them.

The first segment the FBI targeted in trying to discredit the Black Panthers was their local Black community. In one example a kid's coloring book showing Black people violently attacking police, animals, and other figures was printed and distributed in Black communities in an attempt to discredit the party among local parents. While this was allegedly created by an aspiring Black Panther Party artist and later deemed too violent to be used, there are conflicting reports as to whether the FBI doctored the coloring book from its original form and how and why it was ultimately copied and disseminated. What is known is that the West Coast Panther member who made copies of it was an FBI informant and that the FBI used this as "evidence" that the breakfast program was indoctrinating kids with anti-White and antipolice propaganda.

In New York City and around the country, the FBI also used rumors, propaganda, and fake letters and phone calls to sow mistruth and disinformation. The heads of churches that housed breakfast programs might receive a letter saying that the Panthers took part in sex orgies or appropriated funds. Party members received anonymous letters or phone calls alleging that their partners were cheating on them with fellow Panthers or that other members were informants. One FBI memo directs agents to collect intel on male Panther members' wives and "place discreet pretext phone calls, using a Negro accent, to the spouse suggesting various things concerning her husband." All of this, despite the Panthers' knowledge that the FBI was likely behind much of it, succeeded to sow mistrust and wariness.

The FBI fomented distrust in other ways. It made crude flyers that it left on subway cars and local businesses. In one example, when off-duty police officers attacked a leader of the Brooklyn chapter, stealing his briefcase, they passed along the contents to the FBI. Using the illegally obtained contact information and names from the briefcase, the FBI began a discrediting campaign against some of the members. One tactic was to circulate flyers to area businesses, like the local coffee shop Chock full o'Nuts, warning neighbors of the "danger" of certain Panther leaders, claiming they were police informants. Their tactic worked—these members did come under suspicion by the party, fraying trust and their ability to lead in their neighborhood.

The FBI also feared the Black Panthers' own media machine: the Panther paper, which at its height had a circulation of 250,000 copies a week nationally and was the Panthers' primary source of funding. Articles were written in the Panthers' typical forthright voice, critiquing law enforcement, government action or inaction, and the continued involvement in the Vietnam War, or calling attention to policies that were harmful to Black, Brown, and urban communities. They also called out national news items they believed were falsely covered, and they educated and spread information about their own programs and political beliefs.

Multiple Panthers in charge of receiving and distributing the Panther papers that were shipped weekly from the West Coast via air freight told of the ways law enforcement would stop them from receiving their papers. Bill "B.J." Johnson, a Panther from Corona, Queens, says that more than once a Panther would show up to receive the papers at the airport and find them ruined—the airport agent said that law enforcement had come through, perhaps.

After this happened again, a White man in a business suit turned to B.J. "Just get them insured," he quietly advised. B.J. spoke with the national office, and the next shipment was insured. When those papers, too, were destroyed, the Panthers filed a claim. It happened again, and they filed another claim. Finally the insurance company advised law enforcement to stop ruining each shipment, and they left the papers alone.

Soon thereafter, as interest in the Panther paper grew, Brother B.J. was tasked with finding a new printer in New York City to print the Panther paper locally instead of having it shipped. It was then distributed out of the New York office to various East Coast chapters for sale. A West Coast representative flew out with the original proofs of the paper to work with B.J. to find a new printer. Going through the phone book—"I let my fingers do the walking," B.J. says—they started at *A*, and started calling printers. They spoke with more than one press that was interested until discovering the callers were Panthers.

But then B.J. visited a press in Brooklyn that also printed the *Pennysaver*.

"Yeah, we can do that," the printer said with a heavy Brooklyn accent.

"Do you want to look at the proofs first?" B.J. asked, waiting for an inevitable no.

"All right, sure," the printer said, holding them up to the light. He looked at a few pages and turned back, "What color is your paper?" he asked.

"What color?" B.J. repeated, confused.

"Yeah, what color is your paper?" He nodded his head, indicating B.J.'s envelope of cash.

Then B.J. laughed. "Oh, this paper! Green."

"That's the only color that matters to me," he responded.

B.J. went on to coordinate the printing of the papers there, even eventually assembling and boxing them on-site for their trips to Philly and then D.C. and farther south, and Hartford to Boston and northward. The Panthers' system for distribution was thoughtful and efficient, like most of their organizational efforts. A representative from the closest chapters to New York in various directions would receive all papers from places farther away, with the next-closest chapter doing the same and onward, meaning that no one had to drive farther than a few hours to get full distribution within a day or so.

As FBI scrutiny became more obvious to the Panthers, B.J. asked the printer if he had ever been questioned.

"Sure, they come in here and read it," he said, matter-of-factly. "But I don't let 'em mess with it." It wouldn't be long before B.J. discovered that the printer was run by the mafia, who, it appeared, had its own relationship with the FBI. But he was certainly glad to be shielded from the FBI's ire for once.

———————————

Yet despite this quiet—and not so quiet—FBI offensive against the Panthers, interest in, and the broader media profile of, the Black Panther Party continued to improve. Around the country, other Free Breakfast Programs saw the same positive effect on the relationship with local communities as they did in New York City. By early 1969 nearly every chapter around the country had its own version of the program. And the media began to notice this growing popularity. Mainstream newspapers, television, and radio began to present the Panthers in a more positive light, usually focusing on the Panthers' survival programs—namely, the Breakfast for Children Program. And the Panthers gained high-profile supporters, including musicians and movie stars like Leonard Bernstein's wife Felicia, Jane Fonda, and Harry and Julie Belafonte, who had also supported COFO efforts in the South. These celebrities, too, were watched and sometimes harassed by the FBI. In one more notorious case, the married actress Jean Seberg befriended a Panther, and the FBI allegedly spread a false rumor that she was pregnant with his child. In 1970 Seberg had a miscarriage and mental breakdown, which was widely attributed, at least in part, to the stress of this intimidation. Marlon Brando donated bail money to help free Panthers from politically motivated arrests and spoke out against the police shooting of a young Panther killed by police. "That could have been my son lying there," he said. Brando also had his phone tapped and was surveilled and visited by the FBI, both for his outspoken support of the Panthers and his activism in Native American causes.

"This is what the rich people are supposed to do . . . if they believe in revolution," Cleo says. The Panthers were happy for these allies to raise the party's profile in the media and would gladly "take their money to help keep the struggle going." Maybe this infusion of cash would allow some Panthers to take the weekend off while still "keeping programming afloat" and not relying so heavily on newspaper sales. Yet while this money might give the Panthers a brief respite to relax for an evening and "drink some wine," as Cleo recounts with a laugh, the break would be short lived. In New York City and across the country, Black Panthers were feeding thousands of children a day, organizing tenants to secure safe housing, and working to demand better health care, among other efforts.

But more than supporting the day-to-day "survival" of Black and Brown communities, they were also creating the path to a better future: One where people expected and received both basic human rights and social and economic support from their leaders. One where children were fed and healthy, their communities were respected, and every person understood his or her own power. A future where a small percentage of White men didn't keep a stranglehold on power and money. As Chicago Panther Doc Satchel said, "We do not say the Black Panthers will be overthrowing the government; we heighten the contradictions so the people can decide if they want to change the government." People were starting to see these contradictions, to trust that the Black Panthers and other Black activists like them could lead them toward a different kind of future—one in which their voices and needs were heard and valued.

Cleo could feel that change was coming. And she believed that if she kept working for the people in all the ways she had been from across the dining table or bedside or on the streets, her work—and the work of her Panther sisters and brothers—would, in fact, bring revolution. She just didn't know if she would live to see it.

"They hated us in a particularly virulent way because they thought we were having impact and in fact, we were. . . . Some people want to be like, Panthers are bad, and some of the Panthers were embraced because of their roughness and stuff. But I was embraced because I was a sweet girl. I believed in what I was talking about. I never gave up on my ideas. So when you are an organizer like that . . . the government can't really do anything about you. But kill you."

17

THE MORNING OF WEDNESDAY, APRIL 2, 1969, started like most others for Cleo Silvers. At 5:00 AM she awoke to her alarm, like other Panthers around the city. They'd all soon be traveling a few subway stops or blocks to the churches and community centers that housed their breakfast program to start cooking grits and bacon for the hundreds of schoolkids who came to rely on the Black Panther Party for one hot meal a day, homework help, and a little community and acceptance.

She made herself some tea with milk and sugar and splashed cold water on her face, as quietly as she could in the small apartment she shared with her husband. But before she managed to leave the house, the phone rang.

"Come to the office immediately after breakfast," the voice on the other end told her. She had gotten calls like this before. Usually they were for announcements or a trick to get everyone to check in. There was some chatter about it during the breakfast prep among the members, but through the cooking and cleanup, the songs and homework check, Cleo didn't think much about it. And then she and the breakfast crew made their way from the Bronx to the Harlem office.

By the time Cleo arrived at Adam Clayton Boulevard, the office was full and the mood was tense. Yawning Panthers shuffled their feet while Janet

Cyril and others in leadership appeared anxious. It was soon clear that this was more serious than a check-in.

"Our brothers and sisters were arrested last night."

The gathered Panthers were in "shock, angry. Some people were crying, especially the younger people, the newer people," Cleo remembers. It was hard to know the details: twenty-one Panthers had been indicted, others had been arrested in the early-morning raids and then released. Some were behind bars and would stay there, and there was a publicized manhunt for others. "This is our top leadership of the Harlem branch," Cleo notes decades later. "They were the people who are responsible for the whole branch. Every element of work that's being done in the city was led by one of those thirteen." It was no mystery why these Panthers were targeted. B.J. of the Corona, Queens, chapter remembers getting a call from the officers telling him to "be prepared. . . . We thought we was next."

And then they immediately did what Panthers did best. They began organizing. Folks were tasked with organizing protests in front of the jail where the Panthers were being held and in front of the courthouse where their arraignment would take place later in the day. They connected not just with the other Panther offices in New York, but with their supporters: the students, local celebrities, and "all the Left people in New York City" who had expressed support were called on for action in the hours after the arrests. Within hours, B.J. says, "We got a call from the lawyers to come down to 100 Centre Street [the address of the New York County Criminal Court] because we're going to be protesting, and that's what it was; we started protesting."

That evening there was the first meeting to build the Free the NY 21 Committee, "which included fundraising, very rich people, activists, hippies"—anyone who might be willing to come together to help. By the end of the day, the Panthers grew further incensed when a photo of Joan Bird, a nursing student with no previous arrest record, was released. She "was beaten so, so viciously. You couldn't even recognize her," Cleo recalls. Was this the moment when so many Panthers realized the full extent of the "obsession," as a former FBI agent put it, of Hoover in his quest to destroy the Black Panther Party?

It was a few days before all the rumor and undercover work were sorted, but the core of the truth was known from the beginning: that the NYPD in conjunction with the FBI had dealt the Black Panther Party its biggest blow in their attempt to stop its work in the communities around New York City, and ultimately, the country.

On April 2, it was reported that twenty-one Black Panthers—nineteen men and two women—were indicted on numerous charges. Fourteen were in jail, and seven were still missing. Those arrested were by and large pulled from their beds by heavily armed FBI agents who had uncanny knowledge of the layouts of these apartments. Some were lured out, others violently taken with guns drawn. The stories trickled in all day.

Afeni and Lumumba Shakur had been sleeping, awoken by the breaking down of their apartment door and yells of "Fire!" Within moments their faces were held to the floor, their mattress overturned, their hands pulled painfully tight behind their backs. The officers clearly knew the layout of their home—police in full tactical gear had swarmed them in seconds. When these details surfaced, many Panthers would wonder, *Who was the spy?*

At the same moment, an officer was knocking at the door of Michael Tabor some fifty blocks uptown, saying there was a noise complaint. When Mr. Tabor refused to open the door, suspecting a ruse, the officer kicked it down, put a gun to the Panther's head, and allegedly said, "If you move, I'll blow your brains out." He then set about tearing down posters of Malcolm X and Black Panther Party leaders Huey Newton and Bobby Seale, later declaring them evidence.

Each arresting party of officers brought with them a Black officer, to speak "in the style and timbre of address most soothingly familiar," if necessary, noted a book about the arrests and trial. The officers were all given bulletproof vests and told the Panthers were armed and dangerous. Some officers had sketches of apartments provided by undercover agents who had posed as Panthers, dining with them, attending PE meetings, and sometimes suggesting illegal acts in hopes of planting ideas or manipulating conversations that could be used as evidence.

Dr. Curtis Powell, who earned a PhD in biochemistry and was working as a cancer researcher at Columbia University, was living near the
college with his heavily pregnant wife, Lena, and their two children.
When he heard he was indicted, he turned himself in with Roz Payne,
a White Newsreel photographer present and documenting the moment,
believing that was a way to ensure that he would be taken alive. His wife
went into premature labor and lost the baby soon thereafter.

With the papers initially announcing that twenty-one Black Panthers
were indicted, the Panthers were quickly dubbed the Panther 21. Ultimately thirteen were tried together, and their legal fate affected that of
the entire twenty-one. The morning's arrests were ostensibly in reaction
to alleged planted bombs at Bronx and Manhattan police stations a few
months earlier, on January 17. It was curious that neither bomb had
exploded, each having been made with phony components. Police had
claimed these were the work of the Black Panther Party, but New York
and national chapter leaders had denied involvement.

A judge made himself available after hours on April 1 to approve
a hastily written indictment, noting that the attacks were imminent the
next day and immediate action was needed to prevent the murder of
"many hundreds of people." The raids, proudly touted in a press conference within hours, were coordinated among numerous law enforcement
agencies, including the CIA, FBI, US Marshals, and New York State
Police, who worked together "to take these violent criminals off the
streets," the NYPD spokesman said. Bail was set at $100,000 each—an
exorbitant sum with almost no precedent, even among the most violent
of criminals—and the Panthers were not allowed to meet with their
lawyers that day before the group was shuttled to solitary confinement
at different jails around the city.

Also that morning, congratulations were doled out to the spies and
informants for various agencies, some working without knowledge of the
others, whose information and alleged evidence had led to the indictment and arrests. One officer received his gold badge that morning. Gene
Roberts was uncovered as a spy that morning as well. He had been an
original member in the Harlem office, and among his bona fides was that
he had been Malcolm X's bodyguard the day he was assassinated, in a
coincidence that some assert sheds doubt on the official cause of Malcolm's

murder. Others were supposedly Panthers who had been members for months and years, including men who had been among the very first recruits in the city and had worked the breakfast program and had sold papers. One undercover agent, known to be particularly prone to violent outbursts, had showed off numerous guns to a young and impressionable Jamal Joseph, who was a young teen at the time and recounted this incident in his memoir. Another had been the one who had mentioned bombing locations around New York in meetings, while other Panthers dismissed this suggestion, saying it was not part of their mission. An infiltrator might make provocative statements, like suggesting violence against cops in PE meetings, and another informant would report back about the violent rhetoric, attributing it to the Black Panther Party as a whole. The undercover operation was designed to instigate and encourage this kind of evidence. It was an undercover agent who had suggested bombing police stations, and another had procured the dynamite that was supposed evidence. While the Black Panthers had known that they had been tailed and their phones tapped, they didn't know until that day the extent of the infiltration by various government agencies to take them down.

By the afternoon, those arrested were formally indicted and charged with 156 counts of attempted murder, attempted arson, and conspiracy to blow up subway and police stations, five local department stores, six railroads, and the Bronx-based New York Botanical Garden. But it soon became clear that this was like no other previous intimidation tactic—and would, in fact, end up becoming the largest and most expensive trial to date in New York City. These were young people—mostly in their late teens and early twenties—who truly believed that revolution would come. And few understood to what lengths the government would go to stop them.

By the end of the day, the national Panther office appeared in lockstep with the response of the New York office, decrying these false charges and using this as further evidence that law enforcement was out to destroy them and their community work. Bobby Seale was interviewed on national television, denying knowledge of the alleged bombings and declaring the charges false. In between puffs of a hand-rolled cigarette he said, "I don't know what they're talking about. They're lying. They're trying to destroy the leadership of the Party. You know in the past they've trumped up charges on me, myself, and many others. . . . They're trying to destroy the Black Panther Party. They know the Black Panther Party is a moving force for the revolutionary struggle that's going on for change. The pig power structure is being exposed by Breakfast for Children, free health clinics. If it hadn't been for Huey P. Newton there never would have been no Breakfast for Children. And they know it."

The national and New York offices collaborated on their own strategies to tell their side of the evolving Panther 21 story as well as to raise money for bail and legal representation. A full-page article on the arrests was the lead headline of the week's Panther paper. They printed even more than the two hundred thousand copies they usually did, both anticipating demand and to help raise funds for bail. The goal was to raise enough to bail out Afeni Shakur and Jamal Joseph: Afeni's popularity in the party and among sympathetic supporters would be used to help raise funds for the others, and Jamal was a minor.

Over the next days and weeks, the Panthers would come to discover which of the Panthers they had trusted were informants, and piece together those details with who had suggested bombings or had brought bomb-making materials to meetings. And as soon as details emerged of the arrests, the treatment of those arrested, and the preparation for their subsequent trial, the Panther paper reported what was being ignored in the mainstream press. One such account noted that those in jail continued to be kept in separate facilities around the city, "making it impossible for the lawyers to meet with them to properly prepare a defense. They were kept in solitary confinement with the lights on 24 hours a day without mattresses. The women were allowed four small sheets of toilet tissue a day. All were denied reading matter and adequate recreational facilities. Their relatives were denied full visiting privileges and their lawyers were harassed by jail officials."

Within days the enormity of the cost—financial and otherwise—of bail and legal defense became clear, and propaganda that pitted the East and West Coast offices against each other started to take a toll. Although the Panthers remained committed to freeing their brothers and sisters who were taken as political prisoners, as they characterized these false arrests, in the coming months some began to quietly fear that their defense might ultimately destroy the party just as the FBI had hoped.

───────────

But Cleo and the others didn't know that yet on that early spring day in April. So as afternoon turned to evening, they continued as good foot soldiers do. Some made calls to ask for legal or financial help to support the release of the Panther 21. Others joined organizing meetings or went out to sell the Panther paper, certain to be fielding questions about the arrests. By the time Cleo got to bed, it was late, and she had to force herself to sleep even though she wanted to keep working. But she knew she needed sleep to do the work she had to do. She had to wake up in a few hours to head to the Bronx like she did every morning to help make a few dozen kids breakfast.

18

On September 24, 1964, at 1:10 pm, Lee White, an adviser on civil rights issues to President Johnson, and before him to President Kennedy, ushered Aylene Quin, Ora Bryant, and Mattie Dillon into the Oval Office to meet with the president. It was stunning that he finally acquiesced to seeing anyone involved in the voting rights efforts in Mississippi, particularly after he repeatedly refused to meet with activists fearing for their lives a few months earlier and undermined the Mississippi Democratic Freedom Party at the Democratic National Convention barely a month before. Perhaps he understood what others had felt as well: that the bombing of Mama Quin's house could be the act of terrorism that pushed the Black community into fighting back. As Howard Zinn writes, Black activists had only committed to "nonviolence in the face of terrible measures used against them by private and official forces" because of their belief that the federal government would "disarm and neutralize those who would take away" Black Americans' "constitutional liberties." But in the absence of that protection, as Zinn foretold, this justification for nonviolence would be moot. "Hence," Zinn writes, "there is a renewed debate . . . about nonviolence" as an activist philosophy—especially when violence was so clearly perpetrated against peaceful citizens without repercussions. There was an immediate fear that Black residents of Mississippi would finally fight back.

When the women first arrived in Washington, they were told once again that the president was too busy to meet with them.

"We said we'd stay till the next day," Ora Bryant told the *New Republic*. "They said he would be too busy the next day too, so we told them we'd just stay on till we saw him." President Johnson found a few minutes in his schedule, against the advice of Lee White. The Black community of McComb—long terrorized and never faltering— had seemed to see the bombing of Mama Quin's house as a final line that had been crossed. After that night's bombings, activists and locals young and old for the first time had seemed unafraid. There was even talk of federal officials coming to restore order—a move Mississippi state officials found embarrassing.

In the Oval Office Lee White briefly introduced the women's purpose for the meeting, noting that all of their homes had been bombed amid the monthslong violence in McComb. He added that "some say negroes bomb their own houses to attract attention and gain sympathy . . . and Mrs. Quin said that it was a miracle—that her two children could have got killed . . . or seriously injured."

Mama Quin had no qualms about jumping in to detail the carnage. She detailed the scene she had come home to, the horror of seeing "the ceiling on the bed where the children were sleeping." How would he feel, she seemed to be asking, if he had seen the collapsed walls and roof of his house lying where he had kissed his children goodnight?

"The sheriff said that it was a planted bomb," Aylene Quin continued, expressing her indignation along with her fears. "I worked eleven years to buy a house and then you think I would plant a bomb underneath the house where my two children are sleeping? That's the kind of cooperation we get. We're almost afraid to go back home." The other women murmured in agreement.

Lee White brought up the arrest of, he said, twenty-three people in the unrest during the aftermath of the most recent bombings, during the alleged "riot" that Aylene Quin helped defuse. She countered with a report of the unfair charges against one of her neighbors who was being held on $5,000 bond, implying that it was politically motivated.

Mama Quin insisted that "people were afraid to talk" to law enforcement. President Johnson stayed quiet for most of the meeting, with
Lee White leading the retelling of the story, insisting that the FBI was
attentive to the increasing violence in and around McComb and was
considering opening a branch nearby and hiring additional attorneys, as
Lee explained simply, "because voter registration." He added plaintively,
"They're anxious to do something but to be quite honest they're having
a terrible time trying to figure out what to do that they're not already
doing except possibly stepping it up a little bit." While only an audio
recording survives of this meeting, one can imagine the look on Mama
Quin's face. She knew as well as anyone the FBI's apathy toward keeping
the Black community and voting rights activists safe.

The meeting was over in less than seven minutes, the president
listening but saying very little. As it neared the end, President Johnson
escorted the women to the door, and they had every reason to believe
he was serious when he said he wanted to help. Mama Quin seemed
satisfied that she was able to tell her story and express her outrage,
with the other women from McComb adding to the overall feeling of
fear and anger. Before they left the president assured them he would
do what he could.

Later in the day President Johnson spoke with Lee White on the
phone, angry at how the national news outlet UPI had characterized the
meeting in an article. The president read the article that quoted him as
saying that McComb was "the worst place as far as racial tension and
violence is concerned" and said he promised to make a call regarding
civil rights activists who were jailed.

"I didn't say any of those things, did I?" the president yelled, with
much more emotion than he had expressed at any moment in the meeting with Aylene Quin and the other women from McComb.

"Sure didn't, not a word!" Lee White replied. "That's dishearten-
ing. They didn't hear the same thing I heard." Mr. White asked if the
president wanted him to call UPI to make a correction.

"I sure do," President Johnson replied, saying he wanted the quote
corrected to read: "He listened to their story and wanted to do what
he could to be helpful and talk to the appropriate officials." Lee White
also told the president that the *New York Times* had called to fact-check

their story, and he had told them, "The President listened sympatheti-
cally ... as anyone would, to the stories of these women." President
Johnson then asked Lee White to call the women at SNCC headquarters
and tell them that this "is not the way to be helpful. Nobody quotes
the president." Once again the president and his administration would
offer the women crumbs, unwilling to upset the political machine that
was facilitating violence and murder.

"After we talked to him they asked us not to tell what he had promised
us about giving us more protection in McComb," Ora Bryant told an
overflow crowd at a mass meeting at Saint Paul AME church in McComb
days later. She was an imposing woman, almost as tall as Mama Quin.

"We did though. We was putting pressure on him." She continued, "After that they said it was too dangerous for us to come back
to McComb. We asked them where else did we have to go but home?
So they advised us to try to slip into town. Big as we are!" The crowd
murmured in support.

Aylene Quin also addressed the crowd. A reporter for the *New
Republic* who was covering the event described her as having "the
aplomb of a seasoned public speaker, though this is her first public
appearance." Perhaps in a typical underestimation of leaders like Mama
Quin, this reporter considered this speech her first, despite the countless
times she led NAACP or other meetings, spoke up in numerous organizing or town gatherings, or brought together and motivated groups
of businessmen, activists, or neighbors.

She said to the crowd:

> What started it all was the summer project. I let the civil rights
> workers, white and black alike, eat in my cafe. White man I rent
> from came and he said, "you've really got things in a mess!" I
> looked 'round the cafe and I couldn't see any mess and I told
> him so.
> "What I mean is, you're serving those people," he said.
> "When you're in Rome you got to do like the Romans."

"I'm not in Rome, I'm in McComb," I told the man.

"Why don't you just close up for a couple of months?" he asked me.

"I can't afford to. What about my help? They need their jobs."

"Take a vacation."

"I've had a vacation," I told him.

I stayed open and they bombed my house. White man's putting me out of my cafe at the end of this month because he's afraid they'll bomb that next. When we told the President how they were doing us in McComb he acted like he was about to cry. He walked to the door with us when we left.

But still she didn't let a moment go by when she didn't focus on her ultimate goal: more voting power for her Black community.

"Now I've got one thing to tell you people. Go down and register please! I've gone down to register three times. I haven't passed but I'm going down every month until I do. Talk loud. Don't do it behind closed doors. The Uncle Toms will tell the white folks anyhow. It's too late to start playing children again. We're not going to turn back."

Finally the mass meeting let out. The large crowd was hard to miss in a small town like McComb. Like most mass meetings that summer, there were unlicensed pickup trucks with two-way radios circling the people who were making their way back to their homes in the dark. The crackle of the trucks' two-way radios meant they were likely the "eyes and ears of the Ku Klux Klan," as the *New Republic* reporter noted. Local police cars were also present, but their presence made those leaving the meeting feel more nervous than safe. That night, at least, those in McComb would not be awakened by a bombing.

During those same days immediately after the bombing of Mama Quin's house, Father Earl Neil—the same priest who would go on to start the Free Breakfast for Children Program with the Black Panther Party—came to McComb as part of the Freedom Summer initiative. He had taken vacation time with another Black priest and three White priests to help with voter education efforts, and he was among the many volunteers who would come for just a week or two at a time, staying in local people's homes. The program, sponsored by the Delta Ministry, suggested participants check in with the local FBI office in Jackson, which is where Father Neil flew to before he was to take a train an hour south to McComb.

The FBI took the volunteer's name, address, and next of kin, Father Neil recalls more than fifty years later from his home in South Africa, where he has lived since retiring from working with Desmond Tutu. "And one of the frightening things that they told us was, 'We can't step in and do anything unless something happens to you,'" he says. The FBI wanted a record of who was working with Freedom Summer, ostensibly for communication and safety purposes, but it would later come to light that it would use this information to create files on those the FBI considered radical.

All the volunteers that summer were matched with locals—in part because of a dearth of hotels that allowed Black guests in McComb—and Father Neil was sent to stay with Aylene Quin. When he arrived he saw that the front porch was blown off and the front wall was boarded over. Additional rooms in the back were relatively unscathed, but the gas was turned off, and one could imagine the smell of singed wood and dynamite slowly dissipating over the course of many muggy days.

When asked why he would still stay there, despite the damage, he said that so many homes of those in the movement had been bombed that summer that staying or living in them was common, as there was no place else to go. The feeling was also that the residents wanted to show that they wouldn't be driven from their homes.

Father Neil tells of the extreme fear in McComb during that summer and how many locals were not always welcoming of the help from him and the other clergy members. "Even when you went to their houses, some of them sitting on the porch, and they see you coming, and they turn around and go into the house. And some that you did talk to, they would say . . . 'Once you are gone, and it's going to come down on us.' So there was some successful registration, but there was a lot of resistance out of the fear factor that was in McComb at the time."

Was this understanding of being shunned as an outsider with a specific agenda something that inspired his thinking when he went to work
with Black Panther Party in Oakland a few years later? Decades later
Father Neil notes the lessons he learned in community organizing from
both McComb and Oakland. Activists in both places were "people taking charge of their own destinies, not just waiting for the government
to help them." And he notes the importance of organizers in the community identifying their own needs and issues "to use their reason and
imagination to find solutions and then look and mobilize themselves and
see what energies and resources they have and put them to good effect."

In addition to the canvassing work he did that week, he and the other
priests went to visit a group of more than a dozen young Black men and
boys who were arrested in the protests that erupted after the bombing
of Mama Quin's home. The five priests all donned their clergy collars,
hoping to visit the young men to check on their well-being and perhaps
advocate for the release of those who were underage.

Once the populated trappings of the town gave way to farmland and
fields as Father Neil and the other priests drove toward the county seat
of Magnolia, he remembered the fear still present from the murder of the
three activists at the start of the summer. And that feeling only amplified
once they arrived. He tells, "As we walked down the street to the sheriff's
office, people just disappeared. It was just an eerie silence. People just
disappeared off the street. And I chuckled because when we went into the
sheriff's office, they had two windows where you could ask for information, one for Whites and one for Blacks." To ask the same question they
had to separate and go to two different windows—an act they all found
wryly funny in its absurdity. They were told that the sheriff was out to
lunch, so they returned outside to wait. "And just as people had disappeared, a lot of White men reappeared on the street." Father Neil says
the fear was palpable. The priests quickly decided to leave and clamored
back into the rental car to begin the seven-mile drive back to McComb.

They had barely left town when two cars "full with White men"
began following the priests. They held their guns in full view, pulling

close enough for the fathers to see their firearms as they drove as fast as they dared back toward the relative safety of McComb. Father Neil remembers, "And so we thought about the three that went missing . . . and that were we going to be a part of that? It was a very fearsome situation. We didn't know whether we were going to be dead or alive. And when we got back into McComb, we felt very relieved. We didn't think we'd feel relieved when we got back into McComb," and their bombed-out churches and homes, all symbols of the same kind of hate and open intimidation and a seeming promise that more was to come, "but we were, following that experience."

During that week as well, it seemed that the media and law enforcement began to turn its biased eye back toward the violence in McComb and around the state. The bombing of Mama Quin's home—and the subsequent protests, often represented as riots—made national news, and the Justice Department threatened to send in federal troops and declare martial law if the governor couldn't get his state "under control" and stop the violence. The Justice Department's message was that the state needed to stop ignoring White terrorist violence.

This threat was enough to encourage action, and within days eleven Klan members accused of bombing Mama Quin's home were rather swiftly arrested, and a large quantity of explosives, weapons, and ammunition was seized. This quick action attested to what most in the Black community believed: that law enforcement knew or could easily discern the identities of the Klansmen and their associates who had been bombing and terrorizing Pike County, but it long chose to implicitly grant them permission to continue.

The trial got underway quickly, with the defendants pleading no contest to charges, including attempted arson and bombing, carrying a maximum penalty of death. However, the judge gave them all suspended sentences and released them on probation. Historian John Dittmer writes, "In justifying his leniency, Judge Watkins stated that the men had been 'unduly provoked' by civil rights workers, some of whom 'are people of low morality and unhygienic.' The bombers, on the other hand, were from 'good families.'" That same afternoon, thirteen COFO workers were arrested and jailed for "operating a food-handling establishment without a permit." They had been making and eating food in their own COFO house.

While the bombing of Mama Quin's home was far from the only incident of terrorism or Black resistance around the state, this act of violence—and the community response—seems to represent the moment in Freedom Summer when the local Black community reached its limit: the pain of staying silent was bigger than the risk of fighting back. As Marshall Ganz remembers, "Whether it was because it was her, or whether it was because of the timing, of having been building up a movement, building up more hopefulness, because that's what gets people to act, I don't know. But boy, it was like, day and night . . . because the community was really mobilized."

The SNCC workers who stayed in McComb continued to mobilize the Black community around voter registration, with another group heading to Magnolia to register on October 27, 1964. Marshall Ganz would later detail in a sworn affidavit that as they walked to the back of the building to enter the courthouse to register, their "path was blocked by a large group of Mississippi Highway Patrolmen, Sheriff's Deputies and others who were unidentified."

"What do you want?" asked one of the mob.

"We're Pike County residents, and we're here to register to vote," one of their number—possibly Mama Quin—responded. It would be her fourth to attempt to register. They were told that the circuit clerk's office was closed because court was in session "and that the judge had issued an injunction against groups gathering in the Courtyard." They would have to leave or face arrest.

Then Mama Quin sat down on the pavement and the group refused to leave. Marshall Ganz was grabbed by two patrolmen, one on each arm. After a few steps one of the men grabbed Marshall's right arm and twisted it hard against his back. Marshall noted that at the doorway to the jail cell he "pulled my arm up as tight as it would go and asked, 'Are you going to sit down here?' . . . and heralded me inside across the room into a table and the wall."

"Get in there you son of a bitch," Mr. Ganz was told and was kicked in the buttocks. He spent the night in a cell with no cots or mattresses. The prisoners were segregated—Marshall Ganz is White—and he later learned others were not allowed a phone call.

SNCC worker Mendy Samstein also noted seeing a state investigator abusing local activists, including Mama Quin, whose arm was injured when the officer slammed it in a door. Both Mr. Ganz and Mr. Samstein recounted these abuses to FBI agents soon thereafter, but the agents did nothing.

The next day, Marshall Ganz and others were released "and told to leave the area. This we did not do." They remembered the murdered activists as well and asked to use the phone.

"There are a lot of other phones in town," the jailer replied. The group was finally able to call for transportation and stood near the courthouse waiting, watching a "large and threatening crowd" gather. Mr. Ganz noticed "a leader of the local Ku Klux Klan, standing in the doorway of the Courthouse." He had seen him there the day before as well. Also present were two FBI agents. Mr. Ganz asked if they could stay until the group was picked up to help ensure their safety.

"They replied that they could not protect us," Marshall said, and he replied that he thought that their mere presence could help the group.

"We have a lot of work to do," one agent retorted.

"I don't want there to be more work for you to do in the form of new indigents," Marshall responded. "They said they would take my request under consideration," he noted. That day the group returned to McComb without further incident, but it was clear that despite these feelings of hope, change had not yet arrived.

But hope did keep the movement active during the fall and past President Johnson's reelection, working to keep pressure on him to continue the civil rights progress he had promised. Mama Quin had to close South of the Border not long after the bombing, as her landlord worried about his property and the safety of his family. Mama Quin just continued to serve food out of her home while looking for a new space to open a restaurant, perhaps months later.

SNCC sent thirty-seven teenagers from McComb to New York City at the end of 1964, and on New Year's Day 1965 they visited the Hotel Theresa in Harlem, where they were among the small audience listening to Malcolm X speak. He told them:

> So I myself would go for nonviolence if it was consistent, if it was intelligent, if everybody was going to be nonviolent, and if we were going to be nonviolent all the time. If they make the Ku Klux Klan nonviolent, I'll be nonviolent. If they make the White Citizens' Council nonviolent, I'll be nonviolent. . . . If the leaders of the nonviolent movement can go into the white community and teach nonviolence, good. I'd go along with that. But as long as I see them teaching nonviolence only in the Black community, then we can't go along with that. We believe in equality, and equality means you have to put the same thing over here that you put over there. . . . So I think in 1965—whether you like it, or I like it, or we like it, or they like it, or not—you will see that there is a generation of Black people born in this country who become mature to the point where they feel that they have no more business being asked to take a peaceful approach than anybody else takes, unless everybody's going to take a peaceful approach.

It is easier to look back at the end of 1964 and the beginning of 1965 as a time of change because we know what was to come next. But to those who kept the faith in McComb, against all odds, it must have felt like movement at glacial speed. After the summer of bombings and a lifetime of intimidation, to come so close to justice—only for the terrorists' sentence to be suspended and the same voting intimidation methods to continue—might not have felt like progress at the time. What would come in 1965 might seem inevitable from our vantage point now, but it was a direct result of all of these seemingly small but consequential moments that demonstrated that those in McComb and others like them around the state and country were not going to stop in their fight for voting rights.

19

On June 17, 1965, Mama Quin took her younger children to the state-house in Jackson for a voting rights march. President Johnson had insisted on his intention to pass the Voting Rights Act, but Aylene and many of those who joined her knew better than to take a White man in office at his word. The march was swarming with police officers who were arrest-ing marchers left and right for any infraction.

The family was sitting on steps near the march, Mama Quin holding her homemade sign that read No More Police Brutality We want the right to Register to Vote. Another sign read Unseat Five Illegally Elected Mississippi Congressmen, referring to congressmen who had been elected from districts where Black people were not allowed to vote. Young Anthony was holding an American flag, a symbol, at the time, for integration.

After being denied their demand to see Governor Paul Johnson Jr., the group, which included Dr. June Finer, an official with the Medical Committee for Human Rights who was present to help treat protest-ers' medical needs, sat on the steps of the side entrance of the gover-nor's mansion. Dr. Finer, a thirty-year-old trained medical doctor, had attempted to gain access to those arrested to ensure their health and safety. She had a hefty bag with supplies slung over her shoulder and intended to also get arrested so she would be able to serve the impris-oned activists.

A policeman approached Mama Quin and demanded they move, taking her sign, which she gave up without a fight. Dismayed but unsurprised, she knew the punishment for an adult resisting a police order. But then a second officer next to the first demanded that Anthony give him his flag. He held on tight, his mother shouting, "Anthony, don't let that man take your flag!"

In an interview decades later Anthony remembered that his mother told him not to let go of the flag, not even for a policeman. He said, "I was more afraid of letting go of that flag and suffering her wrath than anything else. The police didn't scare me at all compared to her."

Anthony held on tight as the patrolman, Hughie Kohler, violently wrestled it from the five-year-old, his other hand clutching a nightstick and his face contorted in anger. This moment was caught on film by photographer Matt Herron, who had been documenting civil rights events for years. He would share that image with the country: a White police officer tearing an American flag from the hands of a child, his mother's confiscated poster providing visible commentary on police brutality in the background.

As the *New York Times* reported two days later in an article accompanied by Herron's photo:

> The patrolman tried to wrest the flag from him but the child held on. He was dragged a few feet by the man and then lifted several feet off the ground. Finally the patrolman broke the stick of the flag and thrust the child from him. Anthony fell on the ground and began to cry. He was taken into the paddy wagon.

"The flags were an important symbol in the South," Herron later explained. "An American flag said very simply, 'I would like the laws of the United States to be enforced in Mississippi.' If you had a Confederate flag on your pickup truck, it said, 'We like things the way they are.'"

The jails had been filled and, eager for arrests, the city had already set up the fairgrounds for additional protesters. The Quin family and Dr. Finer were arrested and likely restrained in a cattle stockade.

It had been a mere three months since the "Bloody Sunday" Selma to Mont-gomery March for voting rights had resulted in mass beatings of peaceful protesters by police. On that winter day, the late congressman John Lewis, who was SNCC chairman at the time, helped lead six hundred activists out of Selma across the Edmund Pettus Bridge—named for a Confederate general—toward a wall of state troopers who were told by Alabama gov-ernor George Wallace to "use whatever measures are necessary to prevent a march." Malcolm X borrowed these very words a few months later and received a much different response from mainstream media. The troopers beat the peacefully marching men, women, and children with clubs, spray-ing tear gas to push them back over the bridge while onlookers waving Confederate flags cheered them on. Troopers cracked John Lewis's skull, and officers used extreme force on many other people, causing broken bones, internal bleeding, and other horrific injuries. Print and television journalists documented the brutality for the country to see—the breaking news interrupted a nationally televised movie premiere about the horrors of Nazi Germany to show the US government's sanctioned carnage. The juxtaposition was not lost on many Americans, whose collective outrage finally formed enough of a groundswell to convince Johnson that action had to be taken to protect the rights of Black people in the Deep South.

———————

A week later, on March 15, in a call for comprehensive voting reform in a joint session of Congress, President Johnson finally detailed what members of COFO, the NAACP, and many local activists had been pro-testing against for years: the violence, arrests, literacy tests, poll taxes, misinformation and intimidation, and outright refusal that had kept Black people from registering to vote. And while many consider this march the catalyst that led to the Senate's passage of the Voting Rights Act on May 26, 1965, much less celebrated are the efforts of the local and national activists across Mississippi and elsewhere in the years prior.

The House of Representatives was still debating the Voting Rights Act the day the Quin family marched in Jackson—another protest, another act of defiance. It didn't have the violence of the Selma to Montgomery March, but it was but one more of the many steps that were necessary to convince the Johnson administration and the rest of the country to act to ensure Black voting rights. Much less frequently noted are the many seemingly quieter stories of resistance that lead to an event like the Bloody Sunday march, which is collectively remembered as the tipping point of justice. But these smaller stories did not seem small to those who were living them: the fear of the Black residents of McComb, who felt like they were in the midst of a war, with frequent bombings and true terror, and the many, many beatings and disappearances and murders of people who weren't SNCC activists, whose stories are sometimes briefly chronicled in scholarly accounts and other times are forgotten or left unsaid.

SNCC leader Muriel Tillinghast recalls that "every day somebody in Mississippi was getting killed by somebody . . . for some reason that nobody knew anything about. I was getting . . . lists of people who had disappeared and who died," on a regular basis. We wouldn't have the Voting Rights Act without the work of the many local people and COFO volunteers during Freedom Summer, and we likely wouldn't have had the Selma to Montgomery March without the many smaller acts of defiance and resistance in support of voting rights and civil rights across Mississippi and the Deep South in the years before that. Mama Quin was an integral part of this story, in her corner of the state, and there were many others like Mama Quin who were just as important but whose stories are not yet widely known.

The Voting Rights Act was signed into law on August 6, with Dr. King in attendance. Its provisions included making it illegal to thwart registration and turnout, and it required federal oversight in areas where there was low voter turnout for non-White citizens. While not perfect—there was still lax enforcement and some outright flouting of the law, especially in the South—this law did give voters the legal means to challenge voter disenfranchisement and provided for more federal oversight at particularly contentious polling places.

And in 1965 the Ku Klux Klan would finally be investigated, albeit by the House Un-American Activities Committee. Some COFO activists, even those who had been terrorized by the Klan, spoke out against this, in part because they felt that an investigation by the same group that had also investigated and undermined civil rights leaders would be inherently biased. Furthermore, their opposition was ideological. COFO veterans, who spanned activist groups including SNCC and CORE, thought that calling the KKK "Un-American" was a misnomer—rather, they believed that the KKK represented a particularly American point of view. COFO activists believed that if the government investigated KKK under this umbrella, the government could help claim lack of culpability. One journalistic critique said this was like "having the rat king guard the cheese bin."

Regardless, President Johnson and other government officials spoke out vehemently against the Klan and its reign of terror in the South. And as if to assuage the fears of doubters, the FBI claimed that more than twenty thousand man-hours had been dedicated to investigating the Klan, which many civil rights activists and supporters would claim was done too late. This included investigating eleven people involved in the bombing of Aylene Quin's home and the larger connection to sustained White supremacist terrorism that summer and beyond in and around McComb.

During the trial, with additional details added during HUAC testimony, a fuller picture emerged of the night Aylene Quin's home was bombed. Not long before 11:00 PM, four members of the KKK pulled up in front of her house in a black 1961 Ford. The driver managed the local service station, and the man next to him in the front passenger seat held a 16-gauge shotgun. One man in the back seat lit the long fuse attached to fourteen sticks of dynamite and handed the sizzling bundle to the fourth man, who was given the "honor" of throwing the bomb because it was his first time. He hoisted the bomb from the car window and it landed on Mama Quin's porch. The car sped away while the fuse burned down toward detonation, Jackie and Anthony sleeping feet away.

As for SNCC and workers like Muriel Tillinghast and Jane Adams and Freddie Biddle and Marshall Ganz, some remained in Mississippi working on smaller projects in 1965, including in McComb, where they continued their work with voter registration. They were still welcome at Mama Quin's house—and in fact, Freddie Biddle stayed there during the summer of 1965 while conducting this work. She remembered the group continuing its organizing for voting rights, especially as the Voting Rights Act was signed into law by the end of the summer, allowing the local Black community to feel safer to register in greater numbers.

While projects like the organizing in McComb continued, SNCC leaders were actively thinking about their next steps. At a fall 1964 meeting to discuss their focus and priorities, a shake-up of leadership allowed former Freedom Rider Stokely Carmichael to help shift SNCC priorities toward local politics, to home in on issues that directly affected the daily lives of the Black community while also lessening its reliance on White volunteers or leaders. However, with the organization of the Mississippi Freedom Democratic Party, many in Mississippi were committed to working within the Democratic Party to increase influence on local politics. So Stokely and a handful of other SNCC members saw an opportunity to enact a project that focused on local politics just over the border in Alabama.

The finally realized Selma to Montgomery March happened a few weeks after Bloody Sunday under federal protection and took activists through a large swath of the Alabama countryside in Lowndes County. Mr. Carmichael, who unseated John Lewis for the chairmanship in 1966, and a small SNCC team attended—but he wasn't among the marchers. "We trailed that march," Mr. Carmichael would later explain. "Every time local folks came out, we'd sit and talk with them, get their names, find out where they lived, their address, what church, who their ministers were, like that. So all the information, everything, you'd need to organize, we got."

When they returned to Lowndes County shortly thereafter, they found an eager group of local activists, not unlike what Moses found in McComb four years prior. Barely a month earlier a few dozen locals had arrived at the county courthouse together to register to vote and had been turned away. Undaunted, an even larger group tried again two weeks later.

Stokely and his team set to work organizing, helping to support and empower local leaders and showing their commitment by helping them work on projects other than voting—such as improving and desegregating schools, setting up antipoverty programs, and implementing other initiatives that affected their everyday lives (not unlike some of the Black Panther Party's future survival programs).

Mr. Carmichael and four other SNCC workers canvassed the Black community in the county like SNCC had in Mississippi the summer before. Lowndes was similar to many rural counties in the neighboring state: the county's population was 80 percent Black with more than five thousand eligible Black voters, yet there had not been one Black voter in the twentieth century. Since Reconstruction, there had been a strong spirit of activism in the county, yet White supremacists used murder, violence, and economic sanctions to suppress this activism, all actions that, like in Mississippi, were seemingly sanctioned by law enforcement, earning the county the nickname "Bloody Lowndes."

For months in the first half of 1965, a small team of SNCC workers knocked on doors, handed out pamphlets, organized mass meetings, and encouraged groups to register, while also striving to build on what local activism was already present in the county. As in Mississippi, workers and local activists were targeted by terrorists: their headquarters was shot at, locals lost their homes and jobs in economic sanctions, a SNCC worker who stayed on after the march to Montgomery was murdered, and so on. In their first few months the SNCC workers registered only a handful of new voters. But in August 1965, federal registrars arrived because of the newly signed Voting Rights Act, resulting in about two thousand new voters across the county.

The tone and approach of these SNCC organizers shifted since the shutout of the Black delegates at the Democratic National Convention the previous summer and the local party's refusal to support or recognize Black members. So SNCC researchers did their homework and found that independent parties were allowed at the county level in Alabama—ironically, thanks to a law created to bolster Confederate influence during Reconstruction. If an independent party received enough support, it would be formally recognized at the state level. In organizing an independent political party, which the national SNCC office watched closely, this small group, as scholar Hasan Kwame Jeffries writes in *Bloody Lowndes: Civil Rights and Black Power in Alabama's*

Black Belt, "transform[ed] the county into a laboratory for testing the feasibility of mobilizing local black residents into truly independent political organizations."

As they created their new Lowndes County Freedom Organization, the workers also needed a logo so that illiterate voters would be able to participate. After considering a dove drawn by a SNCC member, they were inspired by a local college's panther logo. This seemed apt because the Alabama Democratic Party's logo was a rooster and "panthers eat roosters," as SNCC workers began to say. The party's slogan became "Pull the lever for the Black Panther and go home!" Their goal was audacious and simple and revolutionary: they intended to take over county elections, voting in Black candidates to serve the mostly Black population. In the fall of 1966 they intended to run Black candidates for every available seat.

This tactic was the next logical step in expanding local influence beyond merely voting for available candidates. As SNCC worker Jane Richardson says, "We realized we could no longer operate within the Democratic Party structure and had to think about independent organizing. After Atlantic City it's very clear that traditional politics is not about morality. It's about power."

Much to their frustration, despite registering thousands and running a full slate of candidates, the Lowndes County Freedom Organization Black Panthers lost every race. Amid charges of voter fraud and intimidation, these losses were painful. But this approach to organizing voters and candidates inspired activists around the nation and also provided a playbook for doing the same elsewhere.

———————

In June 1966 SNCC workers were also involved in another action back in Mississippi: supporting James Meredith's March Against Fear. Mr. Meredith was the first Black student admitted to the University of Mississippi in 1962—the integration of the locally mythical Ole Miss was, for some arch segregationists, the tolling of the bell for segregation across the state. White supremacists revolted, and Klan members came from hours away to riot and intimidate, guns slung across their backs.

Stokely Carmichael, as the newly elected SNCC chairman, stood to address the crowd of more than six hundred, who came to support Meredith's march to encourage Black voting efforts. His leadership signaled a more "revolutionary" stance, where the activists would be more forthright in encouraging Black people to grasp the political power that was, legally, theirs. In internal meetings, fellow SNCC field secretary Willie Ricks had used the term *Black Power*.

"Suppose when I get over there to Mississippi and I'm speaking, I start hollering for 'Black Power'?" Stokely asked James Forman. "Would you back me up? Do you think it would scare people in SNCC?"

James responded, "Sure, try it. Why not? After all, you'd only be shortening the phrase we are always using—Power for poor Black people—Black Power is shorter and means the same thing. Go on, try it."

Stokely Carmichael would first proclaim to the crowd, "We been saying freedom for six years and we ain't got nothin'. What we got to start saying now is Black Power! We want Black Power."

The refrain later echoed again and again at the March Against Fear and many protests afterward. "What do we want?" Stokely would call out. The crowd would yell back, "Black Power!"

James Forman details what he was thinking as the chant became contagious: "Black People wanted power. . . . Only power could change our condition . . . not merely for the vote, not for some vague kind of freedom, not for legal rights, but the basic force in any society. . . . To achieve that power, poor black people had to take power from the racist, exploitative masters of the society, who are white." Mr. Forman remembers raising the cry among "a mass of people who were in front of news cameras." He wanted "black people in all parts of the United States to hear the slogan, to be stirred by it, to adopt it."

Muriel Tillinghast, who was in the crowd that day and had been present at previous SNCC internal meetings and debates, remembers her discomfort with the term—and other activists felt the same way. It wasn't a phrase or stance that they had internally discussed. "By the time this emerged, Carmichael's exhortations didn't actually explain to me sufficiently how this gets to be a next step. And how does this get to be a next and positive step on our behalf as opposed to just sort of putting people on notice that we were very unhappy?" she said decades later.

Stokely Carmichael would go on to better clarify the definition of Black Power, most visibly in a speech that was reprinted in the *New York Times* a few months later, in August 1966, in which he uses food as a metaphor for racism. He says, "Thus the white people coming into the movement cannot relate to the black experience, cannot relate to the word 'black,' cannot relate to the 'nitty gritty,' cannot relate to the experience that brought such a word into existence, cannot relate to chitterlings, hog's head cheese, pig feet, ham-hocks, and cannot relate to slavery, because these things are not a part of their experience." The speech transforms, as Adrian Miller writes, "'soul food' into edible Black Power." This explanation shows the pride in culture, in dishes cooked low and slow, in the "[B]lack religious experience," in which both the soul and body are nourished.

As Black Panther Dequi Kioni-Sadiki says years later, "I think that it was misinterpreted, because . . . the English language is predicated and built on White supremacy. So just everything is viewed—from language, to dress, to food, to music—[through a] a White supremacy lens. So when people say Black Power, what it didn't mean, that they didn't like other people, and that they were going to use their power to oppress other people. It meant that Black people should have the power to determine their own destiny . . . have self-determination and human rights and their dignity. It wasn't a pejorative, but because it was viewed from a White supremacy lens, then it was viewed as something dangerous and something to be avoided. And something that was problematic."

What Carmichael was speaking about is the power of local people: this is what Ella Baker knew in her training of SNCC organizers and what John Dittmer wanted to emphasize so much that he named his detailed monograph of the civil rights movement in the state *Local People*. It was the power of women like Mama Quin—who was a force and who dedicated so many hours to organizing and supporting social and political change, all fed by her restaurant and bootlegging and facilitated by the conversations around the table, whether in a jail cell, her restaurant, or in someone's kitchen. It was the power of local people who wouldn't get the recognition they deserved because they were merely seen as "bridge leaders," as Belinda Robnett notes, whose leadership was not codified by official titles or roles, or because their work fell within the realm of "activist mothering," as Françoise Hamlin writes, of women doing the work that was expected of them, the great social benefits of it being long overlooked. In addition, as has long been the case, as Melissa V. Harris-Perry explores in her book *Sister Citizen*, these roles hold inherent challenges—the "burdens many African American women experience as a result of attempting to fulfill multiple, competing roles that serve the needs of others more than themselves." And considering the intersection of racism and sexism, Black women in particular have had to work harder and for less remuneration to be seen as the leaders of change that they are, especially by those outside of their communities and particularly by the long-standing mostly White and male storytellers and gatekeepers of history and privilege. These experiences and identity markers compound, as Kimberlé Williams Crenshaw, the godmother of intersectionality, explains in her work, because of the "stubborn endurance of the structures of white dominance" that remain in our culture, no matter what laws are passed or enforced.

Other people understood these enduring structures all too well: women who were local organizers and activists around the state—including Vera Pigee and of course Fannie Lou Hamer—and others as well. That was what Stokely Carmichael and Willie Ricks were talking about with Black Power: the power of the Black communities that they saw in action around Mississippi and the Deep South and the ways that these communities had to fend for themselves because the government was, quite literally, trying to starve, imprison, or kill them. To find ways to feed, to house, to protect and empower each other through their own organization and fortitude and persistence, given what hard-fought resources they had, was powerful—and a concept this more radical iteration of SNCC wanted to capture to inspire others who wanted to create change. As SNCC worker, activist, and teacher Marshall Ganz says, "Organizing is not about charity, but justice is working with other people in a way that respects and enhances their agency and my own at the same time."

Huey Newton and Bobby Seale came across a Lowndes County pamphlet in 1966 and were inspired to name their own nascent organization after it. How could they not have heard the term Black Power, which was by then being dissected in news op-eds and spoken of in activist circles around the country? And while there was much to contrast with their tactics and rhetoric, in many ways the Black Panthers picked up where SNCC left off. The Black Panther Party for Self Defense was the dynamism of Stokely Carmichael and the SNCC Lowndes County "experiment" but repackaged for young, Black, urban activists who wanted to be those local people in their own community. They were tired of waiting for other leaders, especially in places where communities were more transient and had less agency. They would bring Black Power beyond the voting booth.

These Black Panthers have, of course, been remembered differently than the seemingly selfless and nonviolent students of Freedom Summer. This was, in part, aided by Hoover's COINTELPRO, which waged propaganda to perpetuate an often wholly fabricated and always mischaracterized narrative of Black Freedom Movement activists. This was also aided and abetted by inherent media bias—still obviously present today—that paints Black self-preservation and assertion of rights as aggression and anti-White. As Malcolm X said, "The [B]lack man in America is the only one who is encouraged to be nonviolent. . . . Never do you find white people encouraging other whites to be nonviolent." Conversely, one can see the more generous depiction of SNCC both at the time and also from history's gaze: SNCC touted nonviolence, despite the fact that armed defense and resistance were necessary to keep so many of the volunteers and local people safer than they would have been without that hidden army. Their goal was to have access to the same system as fellow White citizens. The Black Panther Party, however, refused to hide that resistance, and it ultimately called for a different system beyond—not within—the White power structure status quo.

As African American studies scholar and Professor Eddie Glaude said, "We often tell the story of Black Power and the civil rights movement as if they're wholly separate. When we look at SNCC and we look at the life of John Lewis, we see that many of the people who cried 'Black Power' were some of the same young people who risked their lives nonviolently in the bowels of the South. They confronted the terror of the country, the betrayal of the country, and their anger bubbled over. They sought power as an answer to the moral question."

There were numerous SNCC activists who became Panthers, like Mae Jackson and Frankye Adams-Johnson; they were drawn to the community work or message of Black Power. SNCC, under Stokely Carmichael and H. Rap Brown's leadership, forged a loose alliance with the Panthers, one that was taken note of by the FBI and actively undermined through false letters and news reports intended to disparage one group before the other, among other efforts that did eventually help to dissolve any possible collaboration. There were also others, such as Muriel Tillinghast and John Lewis, for whom the changing SNCC rhetoric and the more revolutionary approach of the Black Panthers were not compatible. Both would go on to have influential careers in activism both within and beyond the government system. Representative John Lewis would spend decades as a congressional leader for Georgia, and Muriel Tillinghast would lead education and advocacy work in New York City and beyond for decades and also be the Green Party candidate for vice president of the United States on the New York State ballot in 1996.

In the years following the passage of the Voting Rights Act, local voting initiatives gave some Black communities more political power. In Mississippi, Black voter turnout increased from 6 percent in 1964 to 59 percent in 1969, and Black candidates continued to run and were eventually elected.

But others also found power beyond the voting booth and organized government. Fannie Lou Hamer, whose speech many credit with helping to personalize the struggle of the MFDP at the 1964 Democratic Convention and with leading to the most integrated convention in history in 1968, found that more direct mutual aid was needed to help immediately change the fates of Black communities in the South. She believed that empowering Black communities through food would be the most effective approach to helping to create positive change. Consequently, she created the Freedom Farm Cooperative, which allowed Black families to work cooperatively owned land, and she started a "pig bank" that provided pigs to families to breed for food and profit. Fannie Lou believed that to eat well, and to eat food stewarded from one's own efforts, was truly freeing. She said, "There's nothing better than get up in the morning and have . . . a huge slice of ham and a couple of biscuits and some butter." After starting with only forty pigs, the pig bank went on to produce thousands of offspring for Mississippi farmers.

Aylene Quin also continued to be a chef and entrepreneur, despite being evicted from South of the Border. She opened another restaurant and then a hotel and continued activism and organizing in McComb: on the school board, through community meetings, and as a trusted and successful businesswoman. Her legacy is the legacy of local people—of how her self-determination could both inspire others and bring their success along with her.

20

IT SEEMED THAT DESPITE THE NEGATIVE PUBLICITY from the Panther 21 arrest, the Panthers were only becoming more respected in the communities in which they worked. "It was word of mouth and the survival programs, but it was show and tell," Dequi Kioni-Sadiki says. "If someone was getting evicted and members of the Panthers . . . went to stop that eviction, that let people know who these people are for real. When your child is hungry, you ain't got no way to feed them. But these young people in the community, who could be doing a whole bunch of other things, are getting up . . . in the morning to collect the food and cook the food, then the people in the community are saying, well, this media can say whatever they want to say about these young people, but that's Miss so-and-so's son, or so-and-so's daughter. And I know that she's helping to feed my child."

The profile of the Black Panther Party in New York City had never been higher among progressives in New York City as well—although their appeal was far from universal. Celebrity supporters showed up at the party's frequent rallies in support of their brothers and sisters who were incarcerated, chanting and marching in front of the jail or courthouse. The party was still working on raising bail for Afeni Shakur and Jamal Joseph and raising money for the defense fund for all of the arrested Panther 21. This was law enforcement's plan—to wreak havoc on finances and redirect resources—and it was working.

The arrested Panthers had originally thought this arrest was just one more instance of the police harassment that had been going on since the party's inception. But it soon became clear that this arrest was different. And the Panther 21 really did not believe that they would be freed for a very long time. So much so that they intended to use their trial to make a statement—Afeni even decided to represent herself—rather than strive for a plea deal. They knew they were not guilty of what they had been accused of, that the arrest was a set up in the ongoing plot to destroy the Panthers and everything they had been working toward: specifically, putting power into the hands of the communities in which they lived and served.

J. Edgar Hoover's ire was fueled by the changing public perception of the Panthers. And this was as much thanks to their new media savvy as their increased focus on survival programs. "Party representatives were increasingly armed with the group's speaker's kit, rather than pistols and rifles" at their public rallies in support of their growing number of political prisoners or at other political events, notes Jane Rhodes. And some media outlets were starting to report on the Black Panther Party with a bit more nuance and objectivity as well. An *Esquire* article asked, Is It Too Late for You to Be Pals with a Black Panther?, complicating the negative media-created narrative by highlighting the Free Breakfast for Children Program, among other party survival program community work. Striving to point out the unfair treatment the Panthers had almost universally received through the press, this article uses an ironic tone to pose the questions "Aren't the Panthers helping to create a better world for black kids? What could be more into the good old American populist tradition than that?"

And it was often the Free Breakfast for Children Program that provided prime evidence—and a new, audience-friendly narrative—to help bolster the profile of the Panthers. Progressive media like Newsreel and the San Francisco Bay Area independent radio station KPFA were key to creating opportunities for broadcasting this story more widely. In one KPFA segment an interviewer asks the kids, "If you didn't come here for breakfast, would you be getting the same kind of good breakfast at home?"

A chorus of "no"s provides the answer. Then a group of girls singing "Where Have All the Flowers Gone" is heard in the background and the interviewers ask the kids what they think about eating breakfast with the Black Panthers.

One boy says, "I just come down here because I be eating but I don't eat enough at home." Another says, "I'm just gonna say it in one word: beautiful."

Joan Kelly, national breakfast coordinator for the Black Panthers, is then interviewed, and she notes that the program has become so popular that it has inspired people around the country to start their own. "In Austin, Texas, is a breakfast program run by two individuals who happen to like the idea, and they get their own donations, and they run it. They just send us reports on how their breakfast is doing or any problems that they may or may not have. . . . They're just people from the Black community. Since the program was started . . . a lot of people are hooked on to the program, and they are implementing it on their own like these two people."

A voice-over later notes, "The United States government has acknowledged reluctantly the fact that not only millions go to bed hungry every night in this country but also . . . countless children are denied even the most basic nutrition needed to help them through a day of school. A lot of poor kids spend class time with their heads on their desks, their minds turned off."

Over the strains of the Beatles' song "Blackbird," we hear Chicago Black Panther Party Minister of Defense Bobby Rush saying, "The pigs have attempted to destroy a breakfast program . . . by telling people that we serve poisoned food and that we teach hate. That we teach communism and guerrilla warfare to the children. And [the police are] using all different types of methods even to the point where they pick up children who leave the breakfast program and ride them around the car and tell them they're going to put them in jail if they come back."

Part of this new narrative was to highlight what had long been true: that women were vitally important in running these Panther

programs, amplifying their behind-the-scenes leadership, in reinforcing their role as caretakers, as activist mothers of a sort. At the same
time, in this otherwise progressive radio segment, we still see the
male Panthers spouting the more pointed political critique that was
so tantalizing for the media to quote—and the female Panthers making the case for the Free Breakfast Program and the need to care for
the children and the community, albeit still with authority. In this
representation, as in real life, the action and the political underpin-
ning were intertwined.

Later in the radio program, Ronald Tyson, the New York City coordinator of the breakfast program, is interviewed. He is asked why the
number of children that the Panthers serve in the city is so low relative
to the "millions [of] Black [people] in Manhattan."

"The power structures run down to the people," he responds, noting
the "misrepresentation" of the Black Panther Party in the media and by
law enforcement and calling out the Panther 21 as an example of this
war against the party. "And through talking to people, I found out that
people think that we're going to kidnap their kids or poison their kids
or rape their daughters and things like that. And, and this is a logical
result from the misinformation they received about the party . . . from
the pig media, pig agents, CIA, FBI, you name it."

The interviewer makes the connection for the listener that the
government-led destruction of the breakfast program was a tool to pro-
mote the downfall of the party no matter the cost to individuals, noting,
"So one-hundred-odd children who participate daily in the breakfast
program are a vital link."

"Right on," Ronald Tyson responds. "Because if there's a functional
link between the people and the People's Party—the Black Panther
Party—then whenever the pigs decide to move on to the party and
move on to breakfast program people say, 'Hey, I don't understand
all that rhetoric about socialism and communism that those Panthers
are talking about, but you keep your hands off that breakfast program.
Please feed my kids in the morning.'"

More recently, some major media outlets have admitted their bias in reporting during this time. In 2016 the *New York Times* even critiqued its own coverage of the Black Panther Party, noting that it covered the party with a mix of "fascination and fear." It acknowledged that later-declassified documents detailed how "the F.B.I. had used the press—particularly the New York news media—to create strife within the party and to convey the impression that it was a volatile group." One FBI memo detailed "an effort to obtain news media publicity highlighting friction between east and west coast BPP leadership personnel," while another noted "distributing copies of a critical article on the BPP which appeared in the *New York Times*." The same analysis of the coverage noted some reporting on the Panthers' survival programs, but "with a tone of skepticism," keeping to the FBI's desired narrative of the breakfast program working to indoctrinate kids or "improv[e] its image."

Also, it was, perhaps ironically, the influence of capitalism that offered the Black Panther Party a bit more balanced coverage from the *New York Times* and other major media outlets by the end of 1969. They found that the Panthers sold papers, and to more young and Black readers. The *Times* also credits its increasing number of Black reporters, "who were able to do much better reporting because they had greater credibility and greater access," says Jane Rhodes.

The Black Panther Party itself evolved its rhetoric as it expanded its survival programs and sought to create alliances with other revolutionary groups. In addition to the New York City chapter's alliance with the Young Lords and Fred Hampton's efforts to create the Rainbow Coalition, the Panthers invited other groups, including many progressive White groups like the Democratic Socialists of America (DSA), to their three-day Conference for a United Front Against Fascism in Oakland in July 1969. In rare Newsreel film footage of the conference, women with Afros, dark glasses, and turtlenecks are chanting and clapping, singing "It's time to pick up the gun! The revolution has come!" prompting the majority White audience to chant back, "Off the Pigs!" Members of numerous groups besides the Panthers then spoke, their rhetoric echoing that of the Panthers regarding fighting the existing power structure and putting power into the hands of community members. The Panthers had broadened their message: Black people were not the only ones oppressed, and change could come by empowering *all* the people.

The Black reporter Earl Caldwell covered the conference in an article for the *New York Times*. The article was titled PANTHERS' MEETING SHIFTS AIMS FROM RACIAL CONFRONTATION TO CLASS STRUGGLE, finally acknowledging what had been the Panthers' political perspective since the beginning, now that Bobby Seale reframed the program as "a class struggle" and the solutions as these "basic socialist programs" to support "people's programs" and the "unity of the people." In a follow-up article less than a week later, Caldwell details how the Panthers have "changed in tone, style, and language," putting away their leather jackets and guns and embracing, in particular, the White radicals who made up the majority of the four thousand attendees of the antifascism conference.

This movement to not just mobilize Black people but also bring disparate groups together was a particular threat to Hoover. As Bob Bloom said, "One of the things Hoover was so upset about was what if these groups got together. So he did everything he could to divide." Hoover had his agents anonymously send articles to dozens of colleges detailing "how bad the Panthers are" and expanded his surveillance to groups working with and covering the Panthers. And Chicago Panther chairman Fred Hampton was actively working to create the Rainbow Coalition, which brought together the Black Panthers, the Young Lords, and the poor, White Young Patriots from a part of the city known as Hillbilly Heaven, and which modeled itself after the Panthers. Under Fred Hampton's leadership, these socialist-leaning groups were beginning to work together for common causes, including a stop to police brutality in their communities and better housing, health care, and access to food. The Black Panther Party "was a threat to the order that existed," Bob Bloom explains about Hoover's obsessive focus on destroying the party. "Anytime you can get people to wake up and see what's happening, that's a threat."

Scholars Dr. Rhodes and Dr. Alondra Nelson point to an evolution in the national Black Panther Party, in both rhetoric and action, over the course of 1969 from presenting a more militant image that used arms and military imagery to assert Black Power and Black determinism to one that focused on social problems, revolution of the "racist, capitalist power structure," and "Power to the People." Nelson also notes how the Panthers' own Political Education was influencing this move toward supporting the people through public health initiatives. She writes, "From these thinkers, whose writings were required reading in the Panthers' political education classes, the Party also received health political tools," in essence coming to the understanding that public health—including nutrition, housing, and medical attention—were necessary as a tool of political and social change. And Dequi Kioni-Sadiki reinforces that this aligns with the Panthers' initial mission: "self-defense didn't have to do with just carrying arms; self-defense had to do with feeding people, providing health care, accompanying mothers to welfare office in best self-defense."

Dequi also challenges us to consider the how and why this history continues to be misrepresented. "It serves a White supremacist lens to disparage and to uphold the Black Panther Party as a beacon of misogyny and patriarchy and sexism and violence against women. Because if they really talked about the merits and the legacy of the Black Panther Party, it would shatter the mythology." And to consider this through the lens of the work of both Robnett and Hamlin, the work of these female leaders would be undervalued in part because the work itself was undervalued by the patriarchal power system and because the "bridge" leadership of women was less visible and acknowledged among existing power structures. And as Harris-Perry notes, even as so many Black women were recognized within their communities as leaders, this can also be limiting and obscure the true value and scope of their work.

Regardless of the motivation, throughout 1969 evidence speaks to a shift in the reported national Panther rhetoric toward an emphasis on "to the people," with a more explicit focus on class issues that affected diverse populations and an alignment with activist groups across color lines. Black lives could matter now that other lives mattered at the same time. Coverage was not universally positive, and it still perpetuated the tropes of the aggressive Black male, and mainstream media still often explicitly or implicitly questioned the motives of these more widely reported survival programs and community-wellness-centered efforts.

———————

Cleo remembers the day when fellow Panthers Zayd Shakur (who would later be killed by police during a confrontation at a politically motivated traffic stop in 1973) and Rashid Johnson visited Cleo at her job at Lincoln Hospital and took her to the Young Lords office not long after the Panther 21 arrests. "I felt like they were carrying me, that actually they had me by both arms," she says. They felt the increasing pressure from law enforcement and didn't want their community work with health care, the Lincoln Hospital detox center, or the ongoing planning for the hospital takeover being interrupted by the chaos that the Panther 21 defense, and the subsequent tension with the national chapter in Oakland, was creating. No one knew what government retribution might come down next and they likely hoped to keep Cleo and this work a bit safer from disruption.

Vicente "Panama" Alba, whom Cleo met when he was fifteen, was part of the inspiration for public health work around drug addiction that Cleo and the Panthers initiated in the Bronx. Cleo first met Panama when she was selling papers in her usual spot, on the corner in front of Lincoln Hospital. She remembers seeing two young heroin addicts sitting on the stoop nodding off. At that time in the late 1960s, one in four people in the South Bronx was a heroin addict.

"Every day they would whistle. 'Oh, you so fine. I love them hot pants. So cute.' Finally, after about a week, I said, 'Why y'all harassing me? You see me out here tryin' to sell these newspapers, and you're harassing me and you're really pissing me off!'"

Cleo pointed down the block where policemen in a marked car were selling drugs to addicts like them—drugs they had confiscated from other addicts and sellers.

"'See this? You see what they're doing to you? They want you to be like a dead person walking around with no feelings. They're trying to destroy you. Why would you want to do drugs? Don't you want to get off the drugs?'"

A coalition of community organizers had already been planning to demand a space for drug rehabilitation in their negotiations at the hospital. And now this initiative took on an even more urgent tone. "It took us a week to detox these two," Cleo remembers. "I held Panama in my arms for three days straight, while he went cold turkey, with the use of only Valium and Librium." He would join the Young Lords soon thereafter and end up devoting his life to community organizing.

The work the Panthers were doing around community health care was truly revolutionary. In addition to their drug rehabilitation efforts and rhetoric around free and quality health care as a fundamental right, they were also, as Cleo notes, recruiting and collaborating with activist doctors and health-care professionals to not only provide services in the moment for people but also implement long-term change. They would have actions where the Panthers and health-care allies would provide both education on and screening for sickle cell anemia, for example, but they also were among the first groups to, as Cleo notes, advocate "to do research, to study, and to fight sickle cell anemia. Nobody was doing anything about sickle cell at that time. It was the Panthers who demanded that research be done."

In addition to events where they would invite the community for free food and health screenings, the Panthers would also, as Cleo describes, do "door-to-door disease screenings for conditions that were preventable, like tuberculosis, diabetes, lead poisoning. We were organized to do things out in the streets, out in the community. We'd knock on doors and take our basic health equipment. We worked in teams—a doctor, a nurse, a community health worker or a volunteer, and somebody to take notes." Cleo details their implementation of what is still considered a revolutionary way to practice medicine: to go to where the people are and provide them with necessary care. And still they were met with skepticism. So they "learned to document everything, so that people didn't think you were nuts when we said, 'This is what we learned about the conditions in this community, on this day, and this is how we were able to help.'"

Members of the Black Panthers and the Young Lords, including Cleo, who now was considered a member of both, also worked to expand their detox program at Lincoln Hospital to address the growing heroin problem they were witnessing in the streets. And in an effort spearheaded by Panther Mutulu Shakur, they were even among the first to treat addiction and other ailments with acupuncture, which was still illegal in New York City at that time and was not found outside the Chinese community.

While the New York Panthers continued their work in the community, the Panther 21 members still behind bars worked to secure their defense against what amounted to legal obstruction. After a few months of holding the Panthers in separate jails because of supposed security risks, the authorities finally housed the men together to allow them to prepare for trial. Afeni and Joan were together in the women's jail. It continued to be a struggle for their lawyers to get information on their case. While they would present the strongest defense they could, still the Panther 21 could not imagine that they would be found innocent, despite the fact that these charges were clearly fabricated. As Jamal Joseph wrote, "We knew we were being railroaded and that we had to make our trial a symbol of resistance." That was the best they thought they could hope for.

Afeni Shakur, too, was convinced that she would be found guilty and, inspired by Fidel Castro's book *History Will Absolve Me,* insisted that she defend herself. Lumumba and others protested, but she said, as Jamal Joseph writes, "Since nobody else was going to do her three hundred years, nobody else could tell her how to defend herself."

And then, after months of the Panther 21 languishing in jail, the party woke to another shock. In the early morning of December 4, 1969, Fred

Hampton was assassinated by police while he lay in bed, having been secretly drugged with Seconal by a spy, his pregnant girlfriend trying to protect him with her own body. Despite State's Attorney Hanrahan's account that the police had responded to Panther gunfire, extensive evidence collected immediately afterward showed more than ninety rounds fired into the apartment and only a single bullet, lodged in the ceiling after being fired by an injured Panther, shot toward them. As in so many other raids, arrests, and killings, the FBI had an inside man. Black Panther chief of security William O'Neal would later be exposed as the informant who gave the FBI, at the agency's request, information about the inhabitants, their legal guns, and a detailed layout of the apartment. He had driven Fred's girlfriend, Deborah, to the apartment where Fred was murdered later that evening, had stayed for dinner, and then left. He had been earning around one hundred dollars a week as an informant for the FBI for over a year.

The Panthers gave tours of the apartment in the freezing Chicago winter days afterward, to show the community the evidence of the bloody raid. People could see for themselves the spray of police bullets all directed inward and the lone Panther-shot bullet, fired from a reclined position, clearly after the Panther keeping watch had been hit. There also remained the blood-soaked mattress where Fred had been lying when he was murdered. One elderly woman remarked during the tour, "This was nothing but a Northern lynching."

21

In January 1970 Felicia and Leonard Bernstein hosted an event at their Upper East Side apartment to help raise money for the bail and the legal defense of the Panther 21. Although the press was not invited, an editorial nonetheless was published in the *New York Times* shortly afterward by an interloper from the society page, who called this event "group therapy plus fund-raising soirée" that "mocked the memory of Martin Luther King Jr." Subsequent critique of this fundraiser and the popularity of "Radical Chic" among celebrities in general, would accuse such celebrities of being White saviors. Decades later Cleo would reflect on the significance of this fundraiser: "They were nowhere near saviors; as a matter of fact, we kind of looked down on them. But we would take their money to help keep the struggle going." And this event raised a great deal of money and helped to raise awareness of law enforcement's targeting of the Panthers.

Author Tom Wolfe also "snuck in," according to Bernstein's daughter Jamie, and went on to "skewer" the event in an article that was published months later in *New York* magazine and later be reprinted in a book. He recounted that the Bernsteins served Roquefort balls rolled in crushed nuts, asparagus tips in mayonnaise dabs, and "meatballs petites au Coq Hardi," all proffered from silver platters by waiters in black-and-white uniforms. Wolfe's takedown was mostly interpreted as satire, mocking wealthy and influential celebrities and socialites like

Otto Preminger and Barbara Walters as attending the event because "Radical Chic" was cool. His focus on the food—which he described in detail—worked to dehumanize the Black Panthers who were present. Robert Bay, who was described as "huge" with an Afro "Fuzzy Fuzzy in scale" was not even named until the Bernsteins' famous guest list was name-checked, and only after he was named was his recent arrest mentioned. Mr. Bay's decision to pick up a Roquefort cheese morsel and "plop it down the gullet" seemed to be questioning whether he should be savoring such a bite—as if these hors d'oeuvres represented a rarified world in which he didn't belong.

This was why Cleo loved to cook coq au vin and lobster and shrimp Newburg and why she would take her Black and Brown Cadre out for Indian food and Italian feasts: because she never wanted them to feel the way that Tom Wolfe described Robert Bay.

Black Panther field marshall Don Cox joined from the West Coast, along with some of the wives of the arrested Panther 21. After an hour of socializing, Mr. Cox read the group the Ten-Point Program and then gave an impassioned speech, striving to rectify the false narrative of the Black Panther Party:

> Some people think that we are racist, because the news media find it useful to create that impression in order to support the power structure, which we have nothing to do with. . . . See, they like for the Black Panther Party to be made to look like a racist organization, because that camouflages the true class nature of the struggle. But they find it harder and harder to keep up that camouflage and are driven to campaigns of harassment and violence to try to eliminate the Black Panther Party.

He detailed the charges against the Panther 21 and highlighted the high bail, calling it "ransom," then continued:

> When a group comes along like the Black Panthers, they want to eliminate that group by any means . . . and so that stand has been embraced by J. Edgar Hoover, who feels that we are the greatest threat to the power structure. They try to create the

impression that we are engaged in criminal activities. What are
these "criminal activities"? We have instituted a breakfast program, to address ourselves to the needs of the community. . . . We
have a program to establish clinics in the black communities and
in other ways also we are addressing ourselves to the needs of the
community . . . see . . . so the people know the power structure
is lying when they say we are engaged in criminal activities.

They raised thousands of dollars at this fundraiser, and attendees—
and those who later heard about the event—went on to organize more
fundraisers. While ostensibly this fundraiser was intended to be completely private and only in support of the party and its political prisoners, subsequent coverage of the evening would continue to add to the
lore of the Panthers. Did Wolfe care about the way he similarly treated
the Panthers as stereotypical caricatures in his attempts to prove his
social criticism? Cleo says it didn't much matter to her and some of the
other Panthers. They would get closer to their fundraising goal.

Some Panthers expressed misgivings about asking rich White people
for help, despite understanding the necessity of doing so. The real work
was in the communities—not at fancy cocktail parties, and the almost
all-male group of Panthers invited didn't reflect the fact that the people
who ran the survival programs and the party in the day-to-day were
mostly women. Perhaps many also felt the irony that they were asking for help from those who most benefited from the very system they
hoped to abolish.

Yet the fundraising worked, and Afeni was released, to the relief
of Cleo and their fellow Panthers. Afeni didn't go back to working the
breakfast program with the others but rather spent her time preparing her own defense for the trial that would start soon and becoming
more interested in Cleo's health initiatives—particularly treating heroin
addicts, as she had seen their numbers increase around the neighborhood and had met so many of her Black sisters jailed for drug-related
offenses.

Years later the FBI declassified documents with the files created on those who attended the Bernstein fundraiser—including more than six hundred pages on the Bernstein family alone, dating from the 1940s, although the association with the Panthers created a flurry of new activity. Among the revelations was that the Jewish Defense League's protests outside of the Bernsteins' apartment against the fundraiser were likely instigated by FBI informants, who sought to create discord among Black and Jewish groups that might work together. And much of the hate mail that would come pouring in after a *New York Times* editorial declared the Panthers "an affront to the majority of black Americans" was written by the FBI. Jamie Bernstein also said her "parents suffered public shame and harsh criticism from their friends" as a result of this press coverage, which would also contribute to her mother's sinking into a deep depression soon thereafter, dying within a few years at the age of fifty-six. Two letters of support she noted among this criticism, however, were from Gloria Steinem, who implored them not to be too upset because "getting the Panthers out of jail is all that matters here," and Jacqueline Onassis, who wrote, "I think it is wonderful what you did for civil liberty." These comments reinforced the different experiences of privilege between the celebrities and Black activists.

When the trial began in earnest a few months later, Afeni Shakur was visibly pregnant with her first child, Lesane Parish Crooks, who would later be renamed Tupac Shakur. Other Panther defendants had party-supplied counsel, but Afeni was still insistent on examining and cross-examining witnesses on her own, even as they were tried together.

At one point, Afeni, wearing a simple frock over her swelling belly, questioned an undercover police officer who had infiltrated the party, highlighting how fabricated and politically motivated these charges were.

"Have you ever seen me commit an illegal act?" she asked the officer, whom she had known as a Panther named Yahweh.

"I don't remember you doing anything different than what you have said," he replied quietly.

"I see," she said, and then ended her questioning and sat back down.

Again and again in the trial, there was little evidence that any of the Panthers had committed the crimes they were accused of. Yet few had faith in a system they had long seen to be corrupt. Cleo and the other Panthers would anxiously wait for reports of the trial, which were collected by the Harlem office and then published in weekly Panther paper summaries and sold around the neighborhood. She said later that while she desperately wanted her fellow Panthers to be freed, she knew that Afeni would rather spend her life in jail than walk away with anything other than a full exoneration.

As the Panthers' work in health care continued, Cleo was particularly proud that in April 1970, Bobby Seale directed all chapters to open health-care clinics—an initiative the New York City chapter had already been long involved in. Around the country, chapters would operate borrowed ambulances and offer free health clinics, with the New York group specifically raising awareness for sickle cell anemia, expanding lead testing, and continuing to offer door-to-door health checks, among other initiatives. They also worked closely with doctors, and Cleo was in charge of their political education. Cleo explains in Alondra Nelson's *Body and Soul*:

> I was responsible for giving political education to the doctor's collective [that] had agreed to work with us . . . [and] they taught us. The doctors taught us to use the equipment. We didn't come up with these ideas about the results of the ingestion of lead poisoning [by] ourselves, the doctors who did the research brought the [information] to us. We broke it down and explained it to the community and acted on it: We did this as a group. We had a doctor, a nurse, and a community person and a Young Lord or a Panther.

This community-centric approach to medical care has proven to be effective, and progressive health care providers are still advocating for its wider implementation.

And then on July 14, 1970, at 5:15 AM, about 150 people "led by members of the Young Lords occupied the old Lincoln Hospital School of Nursing in the Bronx . . . and presented a set of demands that the hospital's administrator called valid," reported the *New York Times*. The group, including Black Panthers, Young Lords, and activist health-care workers, occupied the building for twelve hours after nailing the door shut behind them, while helmeted policemen lined up outside. Cleo had been an active member of the planning committee behind this event, and it was, in fact, where she met and was recruited by the Black Panthers over a year earlier.

Negotiations were tense as the group demanded "no cutback in services or jobs, the quick completion of the new Lincoln Hospital, and a drug addiction and a day care center for patients who have to bring their children to the hospital." The situation was dire, noted Gloria Cruz, health lieutenant for the Young Lords, saying "Lincoln Hospital is only [a] butcher shop that kills patients and frustrates workers from serving these patients. This is because Lincoln exists under a capitalist system that only looks for profit. She added that the hospital had been taken to release its potential for the benefits of both patients and hospital staff. This takeover was not entirely unwelcome—even a new hospital administrator admitted to the *New York Times* that the takeover was "helpful" in the community's quest for change, even while he urged patience. Once again, it would take revolutionary action and a willingness to act, no matter the consequences, to create real change on a timeline that better served the people.

A few months later, in November 1970, Cleo and other Panthers, Young Lords, and allies would perform another five-hour sit-in at the hospital, demanding that the hospital attend to the rising heroin epidemic. Soon after the sit-in, Lincoln Detox opened, staffed in part, as the activists wanted, by former addicts themselves.

Cleo, who was also a member of the patient-worker Think Lincoln Committee and the citywide Health Revolutionary Unity Movement (HRUM), would consider her work in healthcare among her most important achievements during this time with the Panthers and Young Lords. With these groups she was instrumental in writing the patient's bill of rights, a watered-down version of which can be found today in health-care facilities around the country.

Yet despite the New York Panthers' many successes, the rift between the New York and national Panther office deepened in the weeks and months after the Panther 21 arrests, alongside cracks within its national ranks. The national office kicked out the Panther 21, and the New York office felt ostracized. Some of it was financial—as Hoover had intended, the prolonged lawsuit took time, money, and other resources away from the party's core mission. But the FBI also continued to sow discontent. Hoover continued his internal disinformation campaign, using fake letters to pit Huey Newton and Eldridge Cleaver and their respective followers against each other, "saying this one's stealing money, this one's having sex with your girlfriend," as Roz Payne documented. Ultimately the New York chapter fissured from the central Panthers.

On May 12, 1971, after two years of legal proceedings, the jury foreman stood up in the New York City courtroom and said the words "not guilty" 156 times. The Panthers on trial that day were uniformly acquitted on all charges after a mere ninety-minute jury negotiation, ending what had been at that time the longest and largest trial in the city's history. The Panthers were elated and surprised—few had believed that the system would actually work in their favor. But they also knew that while they had won this battle, they would have to keep fighting the larger war: someone was always hungry, others were still in jail, many voices remained unheard.

And while the Panthers had largely believed in a true revolution— in creating a new system outside the existing sociopolitical framework that had long oppressed Black and Brown people—in the previous year Panthers had started to help canvass for the first Black female congresswoman, Shirley Chisholm, who was reelected in 1970. She seemed to understand the problem of hunger, the systemic reasons her constituents had less access to fresh food. The work was never done. Despite the Panthers' goals of revolution, it was becoming clear that their idealism was no match for the pressure from law enforcement—and the reality of such a major undertaking. More Panthers turned their efforts toward changing the system from within. Even West Coast Panther leaders Bobby Seale and Elaine Brown ran for mayor and city council in Oakland in 1973, setting up voting registration tables alongside food giveaways and health-care initiatives at Panther events.

There wasn't a day that the Black Panther Party was and then wasn't—for so many it had been a way of life. But if one were to pinpoint a time that it felt like the party was ending, Yasmeen Majid points to 1971 as the year that she felt it was over in the ways she had known it, when it became more "mainstream" and "part of the status quo." And in 1971 as well, the small federal free breakfast pilot program that had previously served only a few schools around the country was finally considered a priority by Congress, which directed that it be expanded and acknowledged the need to improve nutrition, particularly for low-income families. It would become permanent in 1975, with the Black Panther Party widely considered responsible for pressuring the government to greatly expand this program's reach.

Despite the fact that the New York City chapter was no longer nationally affiliated by this time, in 1972 the Black Panther Party's Ten-Point Program was formally revised to include health care, a change that was influenced by the New York City chapter's work. It was amended to call for the government to "provide, free of charge for the people, health facilities which will not only treat our illnesses, most of which have come about as a result of our oppression, but which will also develop preventative medical programs to guarantee our future survival." Yet while the Panthers brought attention to health care as they did hunger, their call for free and universal health care has, of course, not yet been realized. Nevertheless, their legacy includes contributions such as the patient's bill of rights, expansion of acupuncture as treatment for addiction and other ills, rising awareness and testing for lead poisoning and sickle cell anemia, and other community-focused health care. Not to mention the many tenants, particularly in the Bronx, whose families still own their apartments because of the tenant organizing by Afeni Shakur, Cleo, and other Panthers.

Did J. Edgar Hoover win, with his campaign of lies and intimidation and violence? "They wanted us eliminated," Cleo said decades later. "This whole thing that J. Edgar Hoover was saying is that 'I want it so that any young Black person would rather be dead than be a Black Panther. We want them neutralized.' Totally, because they thought we would have had an impact. . . . And to the degree that we were able to, even with that kind of active attempt to neutralize us, we still had an impact. If you could just imagine if they weren't doing that."

Yes, imagine if the people could truly understand what power they have.

22

On November 8, 2020, vice president–elect Kamala Harris, the daughter of an Indian mother and a Jamaican father, spoke to the nation and gave her thanks to the many women on whose shoulders she stood to be elected to the highest office ever for a woman in the United States of America. She added a special thanks to the "women who fought and sacrificed so much for equality, liberty, and justice for all, including the Black women who are too often overlooked but so often prove that they are the backbone of our democracy."

She quoted Congressman John Lewis as saying, "Democracy is not a state. It is an act," and then added, "It is only as strong as our willingness to fight for it, to guard it and never take it for granted. And protecting our democracy takes struggle. It takes sacrifice. There is joy in it, and there is progress. Because 'We the People' have the power to build a better future. And when our very democracy was on the ballot in this election, with the very soul of America at stake, and the world watching, you ushered in a new day for America."

Does the vice president's accomplishment—this role earned by a woman who identifies as Black and Brown, as elected by millions of votes, including larger percentages of liberal-leaning voters than ever in the Deep South—signal that this fight for representation and power of the people, as Mama Quin and so many more fought for, has been won? The answer is both a reserved yes and a decided not yet.

Women who worked for voting rights during Freedom Summer and some Black Panthers with whom I spoke—whether or not they might personally support Vice President Kamala Harris's specific policies or actions in various elected offices—find pride that their work helped pave the way for there to be a Black woman in the second-highest office in the United States. For it was literally in Vice President Harris's lifetime that this all happened: she was born in the fall of 1964, a few weeks after Mama Quin's home was bombed. She is decidedly not a bridge leader, nor is her work as a mother or woman emphasized in her role, even as the media has emphasized her stepchildren calling her "Momala" and her passion for cooking as a way to relax. It's not her job anymore, but a hobby. A Black woman can be both a mother figure and the vice president, can care for her family in her downtime from helping to lead the free world. How far we've come, these media articles seem to say.

Many of her words wouldn't have sounded too out of place, admittedly with some tweaks, at a mass meeting in Mississippi or a PE class in Harlem. There is a belief in democracy that is truly representative and an acknowledgment of a power of the people. Even some of the Panthers would eventually decide to work within the existing political system, which some would say was their "deradicalization," and certainly not all members would agree with. But in 2021 we still see that off the campaign trail or national stage, ending hunger, halting police brutality, providing universal health care, preventing all barriers to true representation of the population in voting by ending voter suppression and gerrymandering, and addressing systemic racism remain radical ideas. If they weren't, we wouldn't still be fighting for them so many decades later, and those in the fray wouldn't still be called progressive, as if progress wasn't something that we all strive for.

In the past decade or so, liberal White Americans finally seem to have begun to see what so many in the Black community and in these Black-led movements have long been aware of: the power of Black women as leaders—whether in "official" positions of power or in less formal, but equally important, community roles—and as agents in many roles of social and political change. In the last sixty years, the avenues available to Black women have also broadened: while many still use more traditionally feminine approaches to community organizing and consciousness-raising—like feeding people, teaching them, or providing nursing services—there are more and more women than ever before entering politics, leading progressive organizations, and serving as visible leaders of movements.

Many praised Stacey Abrams—who narrowly lost the 2018 bid for governor of formerly deep-red Georgia amid reports of voter suppression across the state—for leading the Democratic tide in her state in 2020 and early 2021. It wasn't an anomaly, and it didn't just happen in that election cycle. Ms. Abrams and others (including many other Black women) worked for years in grassroots community organizing to register voters and get Black communities more politically engaged in local, state, and federal politics—all despite, or perhaps because of, the modern voter suppression that cost her the governor's race and kept so many others from elected office for generations. And modern voter suppression is still a widespread issue, with primarily Republican-led state legislators in Deep South states as the worst perpetrators, although proposed laws to limit voting access could be found around the country in the wake of the 2020 election.

All it takes is a quick glance at the photos of local government officers in various towns and counties across the state to note that Black Mississippians now have more agency at the polls. Mississippi now has more Black elected officials than any state in the nation, as well as the largest Black population per capita. Yet many of these local officers are on boards where Black members remain the minority, and this dilutes their voice. And, looking at the persisting larger issues around political power, there had been, as of 2019, zero Black elected officials at the state level since Reconstruction. This is due largely to an enduring state law that further disenfranchises Black voters: in order to win state office, a candidate must win 50 percent of the vote and also win in a majority of the state's 122 House of Representatives districts. If there is no candidate who does both, the winner will be chosen by the White, conservative-leaning state legislature, ensuring that the White leaders keep the nexus of power close at hand. Mississippi boasted the first Black senator in the nation in 1870 but has not been able to elect another since. The state currently has only one Black representative, while White Republicans have a stronghold on Mississippi congressional politics.

Stacey Abrams has detailed the many ways that governments still disenfranchise mostly Black and Brown voters, who tend to vote Democratic, by purging them from voter lists, moving or eliminating voting sites, passing laws that require onerous forms of identification, and attempting to prosecute Black, Brown, and progressive candidates, who do garner votes despite these efforts, with false claims of voter fraud. Are these (hopefully) last gasps of racist power brokering in part because the White supremacist power structure that has kept a grip on political positions sees the tide beginning to change? Among these leaders of change are many Black women, who vote at the highest rate of any demographic in the United States and who have helped elect more Black and Brown women and men to public office in the past few election cycles despite the fact that there is still much ground to make up. Black votes were the deciding factor to elect Vice President Harris to the White House.

But even broader progressive rhetoric has been claiming that we have been in the last gasps of White supremacy for decades now, as these stories note, and this is why the Black Panthers wanted to create a true revolution—a whole new sociopolitical framework from scratch. And while even the most fervent Panthers would probably say that this is increasingly unlikely, the need for true change still exists.

While my majority-Black neighborhood in Brooklyn began a spontaneous street party on the unseasonably warm and sunny Saturday morning when the Biden-Harris ticket officially passed the 270 electoral college votes needed to secure victory, few believed the fight was over. Rather, many saw this as the beginning of a new struggle to create change for historically disenfranchised communities with a more progressive and friendly administration in the White House. Even SNCC, which focused years of resources on the right to vote, knew that voting was part of a larger revolution intended to help improve the daily lives of Black and oppressed people. It wasn't trying only to enact antiracist laws and policies, but it was also trying to change the foundation of American society and what Isabel Wilkerson describes as our caste system that played out in laws enabling segregation and oppression—and the day-to-day realities of these inequities. As Fannie Lou Hamer and others said, it was also about ending hunger, not just that day but forever. As Cleo Silvers knew, it was also about access to health care and a safe and stable home. As Mama Quin knew, it was about Black and White people sharing a table and what could happen over a hot plate lunch. But it was also about so much more.

What we also see here is that the fight can be, and perhaps needs to be, both within the system and outside of it. Mama Quin and the local people who worked with and beyond SNCC's voting rights efforts are no more or less radical than Cleo Silvers and the Black Panthers who also dared imagine and implement survival programs they wanted to see, accessible to all in their community and beyond. And while not all of the Black Panther Party's efforts became permanent reality, they are often quietly (and increasingly not so quietly) credited with inspiring real policy change. Shirley Chisholm, for example, who in 1968 became the first Black woman elected to Congress, was born in and represented Bedford-Stuyvesant, Brooklyn, and adjacent areas that were hard hit by hunger and poverty in the 1960s and '70s. Some members of the Black Panther Party helped canvass for her, and she was written about in the Panther paper.

When Chisholm first arrived in Congress, southern congressional leaders sought to hobble her efficacy and assigned her to the Agriculture Committee, where they thought she would languish because she represented a decidedly urban district. Within weeks she worked across the aisle with Republican Senator Bob Dole, who told her, "Our farmers have all this extra food; we don't know what to do with it."

As one story recalls, Congresswoman Chisholm thought back to a conversation she had had with a local rabbi whom she had often gone to for advice. He had told her, "This country has so much surplus food, and there are so many hungry people. You can use this gift that God gave you to feed hungry people. Find a creative way to do it." But how could she not have also thought of the popular Free Breakfast for Children Program her Panther supporters had run in her neighborhood? She would go on to help greatly expand the food stamps program (now the Supplemental Nutrition Assistance Program, or SNAP), which would help bolster income for American farmers while also providing food assistance for the hungry. This program was mandated across the country in 1973 and is now known as one of the most efficient entitlement programs, adding more economic activity per dollar than it costs the federal government. Chisholm also advocated for the Special Supplemental Nutrition Program for Women, Infants, and Children (WIC), a program that provides food and milk for pregnant women and their infants, which was signed into law only after the USDA lost a federal lawsuit fighting its implementation. The congresswoman, who would go on to run for president, earning 10 percent of her party's vote in the primary, would become known for championing food security programs for her urban district and for the hungry around the country.

On March 8, 1971, at the same time as Muhammad Ali and Joe Frazier's "Fight of the Century," members of the Citizens' Commission to Investigate the FBI broke into an FBI office in Media, Pennsylvania. Their primary goal was to uncover what they believed was widespread surveillance of anti–Vietnam War and other progressive activists. Of the seven who took part in the break-in, one member, John Raines, was a former Mississippi Freedom Rider, Mississippi Freedom Summer worker, and participant in the march on Selma. All identified as White.

Over one thousand documents were stolen, revealing illegal acts by the FBI to infiltrate and sabotage many liberal-leaning groups, among other revelations, and the group coordinated their dissemination, mailing copies to two members of Congress and three newspapers. The *New York Times* and *Los Angeles Times* both alerted the FBI without publishing, but the *Washington Post*, helmed by Ben Bradlee, who had long been critical of the FBI, decided otherwise.

Betty Medsger was the *Post* reporter who received the documents and broke the story. She notes that the fallout from this revelation was that it "caused people to realize, including the US Congress and journalists, that the FBI was something completely different than what they understood it to be. And they quickly realized that was because everything was secret. The culture at that time in Washington among journalists and government officials was that FBI and intelligence agencies should be free to keep their secrets, free to do whatever they wanted to do. But I think it's safe to say that few people would have assumed they were using that secrecy to do something as outrageous as the cumulative crimes that were revealed eventually in COINTELPRO and other FBI files."

Besides the end of COINTELPRO, this revelation led to further investigations into these crimes by the Church Commission and the strengthening of the Freedom of Information Act (FOIA) in 1974, which Medsger called "the single most important" legacy of this burglary.

Ultimately, many of the stolen documents were declassified by the government. That and the strengthening of FOIA combined to usher in greater transparency of the FBI and Justice Department and brought to light numerous illegal actions that had taken place over the previous decades, many against Black activists. However, much damage had already been done—some people were dead, others were in prison, lives had been derailed, and community programs serving the neediest were destroyed. It would take more than a decade for more documents to be declassified—some requested through FOIA as evidence in what many considered politically motivated criminal cases against Black Panthers and other activists—and especially for many to know the extent of the surveillance.

J. Edgar Hoover died of a heart attack at age seventy-seven, on May 2, 1972, barely a year after the initial document burglary. He was never held accountable for his crimes.

In 1973 in Oakland, Alondra Nelson painted the scene of the Black Panther Party's latest initiative, connecting health and nutrition. In addition to tables for health screening and information, there was information on voter registration and requests for support for Panthers who were running for office. By then the New York Panther chapter was no longer an official part of the Black Panther Party, and many New York

Panthers had already moved on, even as the local chapter still convened, although much diminished in number. Other community organizations, many staffed with former Panthers, had taken on some of the most necessary community initiatives. Cleo had already moved on to working with worker union organizing, eventually in Detroit with former SNCC chairman James Forman. While some community groups continued the breakfast programs, both in New York City and in various places around the country, the last Panther-inspired breakfast continued until the federal government fully fulfilled this role. As Black Panther Yasmeen says, "We didn't have to be recognized for starting the breakfast program or testing for lead or the free clinics or the legal support. It's not like we did it as Panthers, but it was really in service for the people. And if the government took it over, so what? That's what they should have been doing all the time anyway."

As the legacy of the Panthers and other unsung women is increasingly recognized, I also want to acknowledge the Panthers' framework for using food as a tool for political and social change, and in particular as wielded by women, because this was a way they could exhibit power—at home, in their communities, and even politically. We see how Mama Quin was able to find financial freedom through her restaurant, which also allowed her to support voting rights and other civil rights efforts with less fear of retribution. Restaurants were among the few businesses that were accessible to her. Moreover, South of the Border provided a physical space and sustenance to support the movement—and even sent messaging about her beliefs. Merely serving White and Black people side by side was a kind of show-and-tell for the world she wanted to see.

While her political messaging may not have been as pointed as that of the Black Panther Party, gatherings over food allowed for Political Education—both explicit and implicit—and the Panthers also sought to use food to demonstrate a worldview where the government provided necessities for the people, where no one felt excluded from political and social power. The Panthers' breakfast program might have been further reaching than Mama Quin's plate lunch, but offering food was a weapon in the Panthers' and Mama Quin's respective communities and their broader fights all the same.

We might be tempted to look back and see women like Aylene Quin or Cleo Silvers as relics of their time, even as Cleo continues to work in community organizing today, now with a schedule full of Zoom meetings. But this is perhaps the main goal of this book: to highlight the stories of the women—and it is often women—who are overlooked, whose work was much more influential than how power structures and history remember them. There are Mama Quins and Cleo Silverses and Vera Pigees and Frankye Adams-Johnsons and Yasmeen Majids out there today. Many are working in more traditionally feminine roles, which we know are also traditionally undervalued. Many could probably be seen as bridge leaders or activist mothers. They might be setting up "freedges" to feed the most vulnerable during the pandemic or organizing community nursing initiatives. They are organizers with Black Lives Matter efforts and are working for school equity with public school districts or PTAs. Perhaps they'll become a mention, or more, in an article or two, or maybe their efforts will be lost to history, along with so many other women—so many other Black women—whose names I don't know and neither do you.

This book is meant to elevate these women and the women they worked with and women like them whose work hasn't yet been written about. It's meant to elevate "women's work"—feminized activism with food primarily, but also with nursing and mothering and in the home. And it is meant to draw a direct line from the work of Mama Quin to the efforts of those in the survival programs of the Black Panther Party to the outcomes and legacy of their work today. But it is also a call to arms for others to honor the leadership of Black women, to not expect and rely on their tireless work—to do more.

Food is still a tool for political and social change, although I would argue that its use has evolved since it was so often the women who needed to wield its power. In the last year-plus, there have been more hungry people than in decades. I watched—and helped—neighbors mobilize on Slack and social media and through block and neighborhood groups to share resources and organize food collections and drop-offs around my neighborhood of Bedford-Stuyvesant and beyond. Food became a way to connect with others and support the most needy—and was also something that was a critical need for so many. Countless communities came together to provide mutual aid in ways many had never done before—and at least in my community, these initiatives seem here to stay.

What has also changed is the way that food in the media has expanded from highly gendered "women's pages," in the 1960s and earlier, to a media genre all its own. Food and food rhetoric exist both in the digital realms, with influencers and leaders who have clout within the food world and beyond, and at in-person events and actions. The intersection of these digital and in-person spaces is where I see influence and change happening today—with groups like the I-Collective, which effectively uses social media to uplift and amplify Indigenous causes and foodways and communicate its anticolonialism messaging. Its members also use in-person events and activities to organize antiracist food security actions like gleaning commercial fields and establishing local gardens, in a way that recalls the Black Panther Party's use of Political Education and direct action.

Curtis Muhammad told me a story over coffee that winter afternoon in New Orleans so early in my research journey. He said he remembered getting a call at the SNCC office in Atlanta in 1968. It was from a member of the Black Panther Party, asking if some SNCC folks could come out to the Bay Area and give a workshop on community organizing. Panthers knew they wanted to help the people, but they didn't know exactly where to start. "So we went out there and told them what Ella Baker taught us," Curtis says.

What are the lessons here, from the stories of Cleo and Aylene that are so connected despite their separation by about two thousand miles and a handful of years? One is the power of community organizing—to ask the people what they want. Don't go in and assume what the community's priorities are, or that they even want your help. Another is the power of food to help create community among activists and local people.

Despite these lessons, there are also warnings that some of the tactics of COINTELPRO are still being used today. Cleo says that she has
been continually followed since her time in the Black Panthers, with her
family receiving frequent visits over the years by, as they call them, "the
guys in suits." Not long after the New York Panther chapter's influence
waned, "the FBI couldn't figure out where the hell I was because I had
kind of disappeared from New York, [and] they couldn't pinpoint me.
So they went to my mother. In the hospital on her deathbed. She was
dying of lung cancer. And they said, 'Where's your daughter?'

"'We don't know where she is. And if we knew where she was we
wouldn't even tell,' my mother told them. And she died promptly. Now,
I think that they killed my mother. Because why would you come to a
woman that's on her deathbed and harass her? . . . I was told at several
different jobs that I've had—I had a lot of jobs too—that the FBI has
been here to tell us that, to threaten us, that it was you or their funding.
And I had been fired from jobs because they had to make a decision
between keeping their funding or getting rid of me.

"I was poisoned in Philadelphia too. I was organizing to free Mumia
Abu-Jamal, and I was going to participate on the panel as to whether
or not Mumia deserves to be free. And before I got there, we stopped
at a little restaurant for a little breakfast. I waited a long time, everybody else's breakfast was served to them. And we saw two guys go
into the kitchen. And my breakfast didn't come out for like a long,
long, time. When I started to eat the food, I started to throw up, like
almost immediately. Yeah. And they took me to the hospital, and I had
been poisoned." It was only then that they remembered seeing men in
suits, looking just a bit out of place. . . . She never made it to the parole
hearing. Even now in Memphis, where she lives with her husband Ron
Painter, who was also a community organizer, she says she knows she
has been followed and checked up on.

Cleo did make her way back to New York City, where she worked
with food justice—helping to found a community garden and public
orchard—and also worked with another love: jazz music. She never
stopped loving music and dinner parties and getting people together to
share ideas. She worked at the famous jazz club Minton's Playhouse for
a while and helped create a program that brought local musicians into

the new Harlem Whole Foods to play free concerts, hoping to bridge the divide that gentrification was wreaking on her beloved neighborhood, while finding a way for wealthy corporations to support local musicians—to give back to the communities in which they operated and made their money.

In articles and books about COINTELPRO that mention an end to the program, the authors are usually aghast at the abuse of power J. Edgar Hoover exerted. But just as I was researching and writing this book, Black Lives Matter protests reemerged even more strongly after the murder of George Floyd (and many others) at the hands of police officers. In the wake of these new calls to defund the police came reports of unmarked vans basically kidnapping protesters and holding them, apparently without due process. And a Black Lives Matter protest leader, Derrick Ingram in New York City, was ambushed by a large faction of police, a helicopter circling overhead with police dogs waiting in his apartment hallway, all allegedly because he yelled in an officer's ear with a bullhorn. In another era his door might have been smashed in by a battering ram, or he might have been quietly taken away, slapped with resisting arrest or assault charges or worse, and perhaps beaten and sent to languish in prison awaiting trial or even held illegally without charges. This is not to say that none of these things are not still done today. They are. But because of his public stature and technology and social media, Derrick Ingram Zoomed with his lawyer while livestreaming this assault to the public on Instagram. If we know about these apparent abuses of power, what don't we know about?

Yet I asked many of the people I interviewed about what they thought of the Black Lives Matter protests and the candidacy and eventual election of the first Black female vice president. And broadly these lifelong activists felt hopeful: hopeful because they had seen many parallels in the previous few years to what they had fought against and endured in the 1960s and beyond, but also because these protests felt different, moving the needle forward more than it had ever been before. Frankye Adams-Johnson says, "Truly I'm very elated to see another group of young people step in very proudly to . . . hold up freedom."

And I asked them about what they saw as the power of food for political and social change. Dequi Kioni-Sadiki responds, "In African and indigenous cultures around the world, breaking bread together is symbolic of so many different things, mending stuff, building stuff, restoring stuff, you know, just gathering to show love and appreciation and meeting people's needs."

It's not a surprise that food led to the changes we see today. *Nothing comes from nothing*, as Kathy Goldman says, and these women all had a hand in inspiring activists and creating the change we see today.

ACKNOWLEDGMENTS

THIS BOOK WOULD NOT EXIST without the work of the many activists who took the time and labor to speak with me, write down or record their experiences, and of course fight to create change in their communities and beyond. Thank you.

Thank you especially to Cleo Silvers, who was so open to sharing her experiences, ideas, knowledge, and time over the course of more than a year. My goal has always been to share your story so that others can continue your work. To Jacqueline Quin, I appreciate you trusting me to help share your mother's work and legacy. And to the many others who took their time to speak with me: Mrs. Patsy Ruth Butler, Curtis (Hayes) Muhammad, Father Earl Neil, Jacqueline Byrd, Jane Adams, D. Gorton, Freddie Biddle, Marshall Ganz, Judith E. Barlow Roberts, Gladys Bryant Jackson, Curtis Bryant, John Dittmer, Muriel Tillinghast, Kathy Goldman, Bill Jennings, Brother B.J. (West Coast Black Panther Party historian), Frankye Adams-Johnson, Dequi Kioni-Sadiki, Yasmeen Majid, Panama Alba, and Mae Jackson.

While I had hoped to spend much more time in and around McComb and Jackson, Mississippi, I appreciate Hilda Casin for sharing her time and her collection of local Black history artifacts; the helpful Katie Blount and her team at the Mississippi Department of Archives and History; and Jan Hillegas, Dr. Susan Glisson, and Cynthia Palmer, who all supported my research and helped me connect with activists in and around McComb.

Thank you as well to Brother Shep, Brother Bullwhip, and Sekou Odinga of the New York Panthers, who shared their ideas and work through publications, incidental conversations, and larger events that influenced this work.

Additional support was provided by the Culinary Historians of New York, which awarded me a Scholars' Grant that helped facilitate travel, and the New York Foundation for the Arts, which acknowledged me as a finalist.

Thank you, Monika Woods, for believing in me and my work for so long and so tirelessly. Your support and feedback are eternally appreciated.

Thank you to Kara Rota for seeing my vision and helping it come to life! And my appreciation to the thoughtful team at Chicago Review Press, whose championing is beyond par.

Deep gratitude also goes to the various readers who have given so much of their time and energy to helping make this book—and me— better and smarter: Sarah DiGregorio, Luisa Tucker, Lisa Selin Davis, Natasha Zaretsky, Jennifer Hyde, Mark Braley, Courtney Chantellier, Christopher Wall, Jeannie Im, Laura House, Liesl Schwabe, Katherine Dykstra, Laura Allen, Aimee Molloy, and Joan Ross.

And to my family: My mother Lin Liedke, who helped feed and watch kids, read, and of course cheerlead. Rocco and Lu, who are growing up fine despite (and perhaps because of) hearing for a year that *mama's working*. And my husband Steve Mayone for keeping all our ish together and giving me as much time and space as is possible in a small apartment during a pandemic to write. The mornings were early, the days were long, the quiet time too short, but I thank you for your eternal love and support to the last writing of these words and beyond.

NOTES

Chapter 1

The biographical information about Aylene Quin and others in McComb was recreated from mostly primary and some secondary sources. Most of these sources are based on people's memories, and there is sometimes conflicting information or details that don't completely align with known historical facts. I have represented characters, dialogue, place, and scenes based completely on a composite of these histories, and have not invented any details. Note that others may remember moments and details differently; however, I have made every attempt to verify details when possible.

I conducted personal interviews with Jacqueline Quin, Jackie Byrd, Curtis (Hayes) Muhammad, Patsy Ruth Butler, Jane Adams, D. Gorton, Freddie Biddle, Father Earl Neil, Marshall Ganz, Curtis Bryant, John Dittmer, and Judith E. Barlow Roberts, and Gladys Bryant Jackson. Other details came from Aylene Quin's own words, from private interview footage that Jane Adams and D. Gorton conducted and filmed to support their documentary *Race: Mississippi*, and graciously shared with me. All direct quotes by Aylene Quin are from this source, which will be referred to as "Private video interview with Aylene Quin." Accounts noted here of the evening when Aylene Quin's house was bombed have been pieced together and corroborated from interviews with Jacqueline Quin and the video of Aylene Quin. There are more details and sources in a later chapter.

Descriptions of Aylene Quin come as an aggregate of comments made by numerous interviewees and represent an overarching impression of her, of which I found few conflicting perceptions.

The scholarly analysis and framework around Black women activists and leadership in this chapter and throughout includes:

Françoise Hamlin, *Crossroads at Clarksdale: The Black Freedom Struggle in the Mississippi Delta After World War II* (Chapel Hill: University of North Carolina Press, 2014).

Belinda Robnett, *How Long? How Long?: African American Women in the Struggle for Civil Rights* (New York: Oxford University Press, 1997).

Martha S. Jones, *Vanguard: How Black Women Broke Barriers, Won the Vote, and Insisted on Equality for All* (New York: Basic Books, 2020).

Patricia Hill Collins, *Black Feminist Thought* (New York: Routledge, 2000).

Biographical details of Aylene Quin come from "Private video interview with Aylene Quin," with additional information from personal interviews with Jacqueline Quin, a personal interview with John Dittmer, and his book *Local People* (for which he interviewed Aylene Quin), and:

"Aylene Quin," SNCC Digital Gateway, n.d., https://snccdigital.org/people/aylene -quin/.

The photograph of Father Earl Neil was published in "The South Today" themed issue of *Ebony* magazine (August 1971). Further details are from a personal interview with Father Neil.

In this chapter the historic and contextual details about the history of Mississippi in the 1800s are gleaned from the following sources:

Max Grivno, "Antebellum Mississippi," Mississippi History Now, Mississippi Historical Society, July 2015, http://www.mshistorynow.mdah.ms.gov/articles /395/antebellum-mississippi.

Edward Fontaine, "The Confederacy Is Lost," ed. John K. Bettersworth and James W. Silver, Mississippi History Now, Mississippi Historical Society, 2017, http:// www.mshistorynow.mdah.ms.gov/articles/175/index.php?s=extra&id=201.

Jason Phillips, "Reconstruction in Mississippi, 1865–1876," Mississippi History Now, Mississippi Historical Society, May 2006, http://www.mshistorynow .mdah.ms.gov/articles/204/reconstruction-in-mississippi-1865-1876.

"Black Leaders During Reconstruction," *History* (A&E Television Networks, June 24, 2010), https://www.history.com/topics/american-civil-war/black-leaders -during-reconstruction.

Details from Dr. Martha Jones's research and quote: Martha S. Jones, *All Bound Up Together: The Woman Question in African American Public Culture, 1830–1900* (Chapel Hill: University of North Carolina Press, 2007).

"slave society did not mirror": Martha S. Jones, *All Bound Up Together: The Woman Question in African American Public Culture, 1830–1900* (Chapel Hill: University of North Carolina Press, 2007), 123.

"Spiritual guides": Jones, *All Bound Up Together*, 180.

Details from scholarship by Patricia Hill Collins come from: Patricia Hill Collins, *Black Feminist Thought* (New York: Routledge, 2000).

Drs. Jones and Collins (and others) have both written about Black female stereotypes and Maria W. Stewart in the context noted here.

Isabel Wilkerson's *Caste: The Origins of Our Discontent* (New York: Random House, 2020) provided essential perspective and scholarship.

Details about voting laws and suppression come from:

"Race and Voting," Constitutional Rights Foundation, n.d., https://www.crf-usa .org/brown-v-board-50th-anniversary/race-and-voting.html.

"Mississippi Jim Crow Laws: Mississippi Close," Bringing History Home, 2005, http://www.bringinghistoryhome.org/assets/bringinghistoryhome/3rd -grade/unit-2/activity-5/3_Mississippi_JimCrow.pdf.

"Mississippi Voter Application and Literacy Test ~ 1950s," Civil Rights Movement Archive, n.d., https://www.crmvet.org/info/ms-littest55.pdf.

The history of McComb was taken from the following sources with additional details supported by my own observations and personal interviews with people from McComb, including Jacqueline Quin, Curtis Muhammad, Jackie Byrd, Judith Barlow Roberts, and Gladys Bryant Jackson.

Trent Brown, introduction to *So the Heffners Left McComb*, by Hodding Carter (Jackson: University Press of Mississippi, 2016), xv.

Hodding Carter, *So the Heffners Left McComb* (Jackson: University Press of Mississippi, 2016).

"Blues Locations—Mississippi—McComb," Earlyblues.org and the text of physical markers placed around the town of McComb.

Details about activism in the Mississippi Delta are from:

Bobby J. Smith, "Food and the Mississippi Civil Rights Movement: Re-Reading the 1962–1963 Greenwood Food Blockade," *Food, Culture & Society* 23, no. 3

(April 9, 2020): 382–98, https://doi.org/https://doi.org/10.1080/15528014.202
0.1741066.

Hamlin, *Crossroads at Clarksdale.*

The history of the MSSC comes from:

Sarah Rowe-Sims, "The Mississippi State Sovereignty Commission: An Agency
History," Mississippi History Now, Mississippi Historical Society, September 2002, http://www.mshistorynow.mdah.ms.gov/articles/243/index
.php?s=articles&id=243.

Jane Rhodes, *Framing the Black Panthers: The Spectacular Rise of a Black Power
Icon* (Champaign: University of Illinois Press, 2017).

Chapter 2

The opening scene of the sit-in and related historic details and insights around it
were re-created from:

Layla Eplett, "Eating Jim Crow," *Scientific American* (March 29, 2016), https://blogs
.scientificamerican.com/food-matters/eating-jim-crow/?fbclid=IwAR2hKC
_PWMuUvqLQTglaWkajuo9nFDTA_FSWH2D-qb7hmJ2FhHYG6GOG74E.

Grace Elizabeth Hale, *Making Whiteness: The Culture of Segregation in the South,
1890–1940* (New York: Vintage, 1999).

Angela Jill Cooley, *To Live and Dine in Dixie: The Evolution of Food Culture in the
Jim Crow South* (Athens: University of Georgia Press, 2015).

Miles Wolff, *Lunch at the 5 and 10* (Chicago: Ivan R. Dee Publishers, 1990).

Details about the lives and actions of Ella Baker and Robert Parris Moses are
from the following sources, and from a personal interview with Curtis Muhammad.

Curtis Muhammad described the scene, and the dialogue is his—admittedly,
secondhand—recounting. Further background information about the initial
SNCC meetings is corroborated by the following sources, as are biographical,
motivational, and other details.

Laura Visser-Maessen, *Robert Parris Moses: A Life in Civil Rights and Leadership
at the Grassroots* (Chapel Hill: University of North Carolina Press, 2016).

Joanne Grant, *Ella Baker: Freedom Bound* (Hoboken, New Jersey: John Wiley,
1998).

Robert F. Smith, Henry Louis Gates, Dyllan McGee, and Deon Taylor, *Ella Baker—
"The Mother of the Civil Rights Movement," YouTube* (Black History in Two
Minutes, 2020), https://www.youtube.com/watch?v=McneFCdHUn0.

Robert Moses, interview by Clayborne Carson, Harvard University, March 29, 1982, Civil Rights Movement Archive, n.d., https://www.crmvet.org/nars /820329_moses_carson.pdf.

The history of SNCC is discussed at great length in Clayborne Carson's book, but some of his specifics slightly contradict my interpretation of the recollection from others in written and oral histories. I have strived to represent individuals' recollections as such—as opposed to documented fact—in this narrative in regard to dates and the actions of organizations, and I have left details a bit more vague where there was some conflicting nuance of detail.

The history of policing comes from Sally E. Hadden, *Slave Patrols: Law and Violence in Virginia and the Carolinas* (Cambridge, MA: Harvard University Press, 2001). Quotes are from pages 4 and 12, chronologically.

Details about C. C. Bryant's life and work come from personal and academic research by his granddaughter, his oral history recorded by the National Visionary Leadership Project, and personal interviews and correspondence with his daughter Gladys Bryant Jackson, son Curtis Bryant, and granddaughter Judith Barlow Roberts. Additional scholarly perspective on the role of barber shops comes from Quincy T. Mills, *Cutting Along the Color Line: Black Barbers and Barber Shops in America* (Philadelphia: University of Pennsylvania Press, 2013).

Judith E. Barlow Roberts, "C. C. Bryant: A Race Man Is What They Called Him" (PhD dissertation, 2012), https://egrove.olemiss.edu/etd/248.
"C. C. Bryant: National Visionary," National Visionary Leadership Project, http://www.visionaryproject.org/bryantcc/.
"*eager to join the movement*": Robnett, *How Long? How Long?*, 16.

The statistic about school funding comes from the document "The Struggle for Voting Rights in Mississippi—the Early Years" as published by the Civil Rights Movement Veterans website: https://www.crmvet.org/info/voter_ms.pdf. A note on this source: it is maintained by veterans of the civil rights movement and relies heavily, but not solely, on lived experience and personal memory. Not all details here can be corroborated.

Details of Bob Moses's first visit to McComb are recounted in numerous places, including Dittmer's *Local People*, Visser-Maessen's *Robert Parris Moses: A Life in Civil Rights and Leadership at the Grassroots*, "Private video interview with Aylene Quin," and personal interview with Curtis Muhammad. These statistics about registered voters can be found in multiple places as well. Also referenced are details from the Civil Rights Veterans archive, including details from the document "Civil Rights Movement History 1961" (https://www.crmvet.org/tim/timhis61.htm).

Additional details about Robert Moses's work in McComb come from his oral history transcript on the Civil Rights Veterans archive, including Doc Owens's quoted description and his comments on working with local people:

Robert Moses, interview by Clayborne Carson.

"*for failing to act forcefully*": This quote and additional details on SNCC and the Freedom Rides come from: Clayborne Carson, *In Struggle: SNCC and the Black Awakening of the 1960s* (Cambridge, MA: Harvard University Press, 1995), e-book.

The letter from Mr. Bryant to Medgar Evers is quoted from: Roberts, "C. C. Bryant: A Race Man Is What They Called Him."

Details of Brenda Travis's story come from her own memoir, including quotes attributed to her. She also added details about life in McComb, Mrs. Quin, Mr. Bryant, Mr. Moses, Ms. Baker, and others mentioned here and in chapter 3.

Brenda Travis, John Obee, Robert Parris Moses, and J. Randall O'Brien, *Mississippi's Exiled Daughter: How My Civil Rights Baptism Under Fire Shaped My Life* (Montgomery, AL: NewSouth Books, 2018), e-book.

The quote from D. Gorton is from a personal interview.

The history of, and documents from, the Mississippi State Sovereignty Commission primarily come from the MSSC's own website (https://da.mdah.ms.gov/sovcom/). Documents noted as being written by MSSC members or official correspondence are all from their publicly available archive, searchable in various ways. At times research from other sources led me back to the MSSC to verify and expand on this writing. Other scholarly and expert perspectives or details to color or frame this story come from sources noted in the text. I have noted scholars' specific ideas in the text when applicable and strived not to claim their analysis for my own.

Mississippi State Sovereignty Commission, "Letter from A. L. Hopkins to Aubrey Bell," SCR ID # 1-71-0-1-1-1-1, April 19, 1963, Mississippi Department of Archives and History, https://da.mdah.ms.gov/sovcom/result.php?image=images/png/cd01/004876.png&otherstuff=171011114756|.

Details on Aubrey Bell and additional research on the MSSC come from:

Yasuhiro Katagiri, *The Mississippi State Sovereignty Commission: Civil Rights and States' Rights* (Jackson: University Press of Mississippi, 2001).

Chapter 3

Details about what life was like for the teens in McComb come from personal interviews with Jackie Byrd, Jacqueline Quin, Gladys Bryant Jackson, Curtis Bryant, and Judith Barlow Roberts, and Brenda Travis's memoir. All quotations attributed to Brenda Travis throughout this chapter, and scenes in which she is present, are from:

Brenda Travis, John Obee, Robert Parris Moses, and J. Randall O'Brien, *Mississippi's Exiled Daughter: How My Civil Rights Baptism Under Fire Shaped My Life* (Montgomery, AL: NewSouth Books, 2018), e-book.

Details on the media's representation of Black people and their experiences are from Rhodes, *Framing the Black Panthers*.

Details about Herbert Lee's murder and E. H. Hurst's trial are widely available and corroborated. One source is John Dittmer's *Local People*, and this is also referenced in Brenda Travis's memoir.

Details on the day of the walkout and its aftermath are from Brenda Travis's memoir, personal interviews with Jacqueline Quin, Jackie Byrd, and Curtis Muhammad, "Private video interview with Aylene Quin," and other reported works noted below:

David Ray, "Brave Times at Burglund High," *Jackson Free Press*, February 19, 2014, https://t.jacksonfreepress.com/news/2014/feb/19/brave-times-burglund -high/.

The driver then jumped out: David Ray, "Brave Times at Burglund High."

Robert Zellner, *The Wrong Side of Murder Creek* (Montgomery, AL: New South Books, 2008).

Judith E. Barlow Roberts, "C. C. Bryant: A Race Man Is What They Called Him."

An oral history with Charles Jones from the SNCC Legacy Project: https://www .sncclegacyproject.org/about/in-memoriam/jean-wiley/104-joseph-charles -jones.

Faith Holsaert, "Copy of Bob Moses Letter from Magnolia Jail, 1961," Duke Digital Collections (Duke University Libraries), accessed January 31, 2021, https:// repository.duke.edu/dc/holsaertfaith/fhpst02028.

The details on what Bob Moses and the men jailed with him ate, sang, said, and did are primarily from the following archived letter written by Bob Moses: https:// repository.duke.edu/dc/holsaertfaith/fhpst02028.

"because strategies of nurturing": Hamlin, *Crossroads at Clarksdale*, 67.

I also want to note that it may seem dehumanizing to reduce the treachery of White supremacy into a sentence or brief summary at times in this recounting, but to detail every arrest, intimidation, and physical assault perpetrated by White terrorists would be impossible within the scope of this book. I have strived to represent this terrorism as thoroughly and compassionately as possible.

Chapter 4

This chapter is based on extensive personal interviews with Cleo Silvers.
  For further reading about community organizing:

Terry Mizrahi, "Community Organizing Principles and Practice Guidelines," in *Social Workers' Desk Reference*, ed. Kevin Corcoran and Albert R. Roberts, 3rd ed. (Oxford: Oxford University Press, 2015), 894–906.

Chapter 5

Sources used to recount and analyze the start of the Black Panther Party:

Donna Murch, *Living for the City: Migration, Education, and the Rise of the Black Panther Party inOakland, California* (Chapel Hill: University of North Carolina Press, 2010).

Roz Payne, *What We Want, What We Believe: The Black Panther Party Library* (Newsreel Films/AK Press, 2006), DVD.

Bobby Seale, *Seize the Time: The Story of the Black Panther Party and Huey P. Newton* (New York: Random House, 1970).

Huey P. Newton, *To Die for the People: The Writings of Huey P. Newton*, ed. Toni Morrison (New York: Random House, 1972), e-book.

Sekou Odinga, Dhoruba Bin Wahad, Shaba Om, and Jamal Joseph, *Look for Me in the Whirlwind: From the Panther 21 to 21st-Century Revolutions* (Oakland, CA: PM Press, 2017).

Hasan Kwame Jeffries, *Bloody Lowndes: Civil Rights and Black Power in Alabama's Black Belt* (New York: New York University Press), 2009.

Paul Alkebulan, *Survival Pending Revolution: The History of the Black Panther Party* (Tuscaloosa: University of Alabama Press, 2012).

Stephen Shames and Bobby Seale, *Power to the People: The World of the Black Panthers* (New York: Abrams, 2016), e-book.

Personal Interview with Brother BJ, West Coast Panther historian.

"largely ignorant": This quote and media analysis on Black Panther Party coverage come from Rhodes, *Framing the Black Panthers*.

Details on the history of the FBI and the start of COINTELPRO are from the following sources, including the FBI's own website (https://vault.fbi.gov):

In addition to the history and analysis from *Agents of Repression* by Ward Churchill and Jim Vander Wall, the following quotes are also attributed to this source:

"brilliant public relations gimmick": Ward Churchill and Jim Vander Wall, *Agents of Repression: The FBI's Secret Wars Against the Black Panther Party and the American Indian Movement* (Boston: South End Press, 1988), 2.

"exclusive and privileged information": Churchill and Vander Wall, 4.

"sympathetic . . . with . . . totalitarian, fascist, communist, or subversive": Churchill and Vander Wall, 32.

"We would not knowingly employ a Communist": Churchill and Vander Wall, 35.

"goose-stepping bundsman": Churchill and Vander Wall, 4.

"According to Churchill and Vander Wall": Churchill and Vander Wall, 36.

Howard Zinn, *A People's History of the United States* (New York: Harper Perennial, 2015).

Specific documents cited from the FBI vault include:

Department of Justice, "Excised Report of the Department of Justice Task Force to Review the FBI Martin Luther King, Jr., Security and Assassination Investigations," January 11, 1977, file 100-106670, section 103, Federal Bureau of Investigation, https://vault.fbi.gov/.

I also used documents from the Tamiment Archives at New York University that are not digitized, including details from the memo by Special Agent Francis Haberek.

Details about the start of the New York chapter of the Panthers and the first Panther events in New York City come from personal interviews with Cleo Silvers, Mae Jackson, and the following sources:

Odinga, Wahad, Om, and Joseph, *Look for Me in the Whirlwind.*

Autodidact 17, "New York Black Panther Party Celebrates 50th Anniversary," *Amsterdam News*, August 16, 2018, http://amsterdamnews.com/news/2018/aug/16/new-york-black-panther-party-celebrates-50th-anniv/.

Details and specifics from the Panther event at the Fillmore are from interviews and the following source:

Dan Sullivan, "Black Panther Benefit Is Held in East Village; 3 Theater Troupes Perform—LeRoi Jones Speaks to 2,600 at Program to Raise Funds for 7 Jailed Members," *New York Times*, May 21, 1968.

"There's nothing wrong in this country": Jon Meacham, "What the Tumultuous Year 1968 Can Teach Us About Today," *New York Times*, October 24, 2020, https://www.nytimes.com/2020/10/24/books/review/what-the-year -1968-can-teach-us-about-todays-divisions-jon-meacham.html.

Details about and analysis of and by the *New York Times* on their coverage of the Black Panther Party:

Giovanni Russonello, "Fascination and Fear: Covering the Black Panthers," *New York Times*, October 15, 2016, https://www.nytimes.com/2016/10/16/us/black -panthers-50-years.html.

"Fascists also carry guns": M. Potorti, "'Feeding the Revolution': The Black Panther Party, Hunger, and Community Survival," *Journal of African American Studies* 21 (2017): 85–110, https://doi.org/10.1007/s12111-017-9345-9.

fit them "into narrow, unidimensional frames": Rhodes, *Framing the Black Panthers*.

Chapter 6

These scenes are re-created from personal interviews with Cleo Silvers.

Malcolm X's speech excerpt is from his speech "The Ballot or the Bullet."

Afeni Shakur, whom Cleo thought of: Odinga, Wahad, Om, and Joseph, *Look for Me in the Whirlwind*, 455–463.

"Being a Panther is about serving the people, mind, body, and soul": Jamal Joseph, *Panther Baby: A Life of Rebellion & Reinvention* (Chapel Hill, NC: Algonquin Books, 2012), 61.

Chapter 7

Scenes are re-created from personal interviews with Cleo Silvers and Father Earl Neil.

"That's some one-dimension thinking, man": Shames and Seale, *Power to the People*.

"We recognize that in order to bring": Huey P. Newton, *To Die for the People*.

"refashion[ing] African-influenced conceptions": Collins, *Black Feminist Thought*, 10.

Details from the referenced FBI memos are from copies of declassified memos from New York University's Tamiment archives, with the exception of the following:

The FBI memo beginning "Consequently the BCP represents the best and most influential activity going for the BPP" is often reproduced and found in many publications about the Black Panther Party and its survival programs.

Additional sources that provided background and context include:

Alkebulan, *Survival Pending Revolution.*

Nik Heynen, "Bending the Bars of Empire from Every Ghetto for Survival: The Black Panther Party's Radical Antihunger Politics of Social Reproduction and Scale," *Annals of the Association of American Geographers* 99, no. 2 (May 1, 2009): 406–422, https://doi.org/https://doi.org/10.1080/00045600802683767.

Payne, *What We Want, What We Believe.*

Chapter 8

The details of the boycott are from a transcript of an oral history with Joe Martin, conducted by the University of Southern Mississippi Center for Oral History and Cultural Heritage, (http://crdl.usg.edu/export/html/usm/coh/crdl_usm_coh_mus-ohmartin.html?Welcome).

This chapter is further informed by details from "Private video interview with Aylene Quin" and personal interviews with Jacqueline Quin, Curtis Muhammad, D. Gorton, Frankye Adams-Johnson, and Freddie Biddle.

Sources that provided further background details include:

Katagiri, *Mississippi State Sovereignty Commission.*

Ashley Elkins, "Bill Minor: 'Black Market' Tax Mirrors Prohibition," *Daily Journal*, March 31, 2005, https://www.djournal.com/opinion/bill-minor-black-market-tax-mirrors-prohibition/article_c09458d5-b576-5605-b298-f845cd80f091.html.

Lynne Olson, *Freedom's Daughters: The Unsung Heroines of the Civil Rights Movement from 1830 to 1970* (New York: Scribner, 2002).

Chapter 9

In addition to a personal interview with Freddie Biddle and "Private video interview with Aylene Quin," the following sources were used:

Adrian Miller, *Soul Food: The Surprising Story of an American Cuisine, One Plate at a Time* (Chapel Hill: University of North Carolina Press, 2013).
"With great fanfare": Miller, *Soul Food*, 22.

The discussion about soul food references and draws from:

Miller, *Soul Food*, chapter 3 (29–48).

Details about life and activism in the Mississippi Delta are drawn from the following sources:

Greta De Jong, "Staying in Place: Black Migration, the Civil Rights Movement, and the War on Poverty in the Rural South" *Journal of African American History* 90 (4): 387–409, doi:10.1086/JAAHv90n4p387.
Bobby J. Smith II, "Food and the Mississippi Civil Rights Movement: Re-reading the 1962–1963 Greenwood Food Blockade," *Food, Culture & Society* 23 (3): 382–938, doi: 10.1080/15528014.2020.1741066.
Hamlin, *Crossroads at Clarksdale*.

Chapter 10

One example, detailed in the MSSC's own files: Mississippi State Sovereignty Commission, "Leflore County," SCR ID # 2-45-1-65-2-1-1, March 6, 1963, Mississippi Department of Archives and History, http://da.mdah.ms.gov /sovcom/result.php?image=images/png/cd02/010562.png&otherstuff =24516521110332|.

Other background sources on civil rights efforts around Mississippi in 1963 and early 1964 include:

Greta de Jong, "Staying in Place."
John Dittmer, *Local People: The Struggle for Civil Rights in Mississippi* (Urbana: University of Illinois Press, 1995).
Visser-Maessen, *Robert Parris Moses*.

Details on the history of the KKK are sourced from:

Michael Newton, *Ku Klux Klan in Mississippi: A History* (Jefferson, NC: McFarland, 2010), http://docshare04.docshare.tips/files/25560/255602616.pdf.
"mopping up the cesspools": Newton, *Ku Klux Klan in Mississippi*, 100.
"just as American": Newton, *Ku Klux Klan in Mississippi*, 101.
"Maybe the government": Newton, *Ku Klux Klan in Mississippi*, 101.

Details on the FBI's knowledge of Klan activity are from:

Dittmer, *Local People*, 237–39.

"*to maintain the moral standard*": Akinyele O. Umoja, "1964: The Beginning of the End of Nonviolence in the Mississippi Freedom Movement," *Radical History Review* (2003): 201–226.

"*He always talked about how crazy*": Akinyele Omowale Umoja, *We Will Shoot Back: Armed Resistance in the Mississippi Freedom Movement* (New York: New York University Press, 2013), 50.

In addition to personal interviews with Curtis Muhammad and "Private video interview with Aylene Quin," the following sources were used as background information.

"Civil Rights Movement History Mississippi Freedom Summer Events," Civil Rights Movement Archive, n.d., https://www.crmvet.org/tim/tim64b.htm#1964fs.

Dittmer, *Local People*.

Chapter 11

Details on the sit-in are sourced from:

Anne Moody, *Coming of Age in Mississippi* (New York: Bantam Dell, 1968).

"Counter Histories: Jackson, Mississippi," Southern Foodways, https://www.zinned project.org/news/tdih/jackson-woolworth-sit-in/#:~:text=On%20May%20 28%2C%201963%2C%20students,sat%20there%20for%20three%20hours.

Personal interview with Frankye Adams-Johnson.

"*a gut feeling that the battle*": Dittmer, *Local People*, 217.

"*numbered no more than a few hundred men*": This and statistics from the rest of the paragraph are from Newton, *Ku Klux Klan in Mississippi*, 128.

"*It is very difficult to get the FBI to move energetically in civil rights cases*": This and details through the end of the paragraph are from Victor S. Navasky, *Kennedy Justice* (New York: Open Road Media, 2013), e-book.

"*scared them out of their pants*": Navasky, *Kennedy Justice*.

"*the entire white population will continue to be the Klan*": David Cunningham, *The Civil Rights Movement in Mississippi* (Jackson: University Press of Mississippi, 2013), 194.

"*That was the first time that I realized that the violence*": "Civil Rights Movement History Mississippi Freedom Summer Events," Civil Rights Movement Archive, n.d., https://www.crmvet.org/tim/tim64b.htm.

"*Mississippi was deadly, and it was getting worse each day*": John Lewis, *Walking with the Wind* (New York: Simon & Schuster, 2015), 230.

Further background information from:

Dittmer, *Local People*.

"Civil Rights Movement History: 1964 Jan-June." Civil Rights Movement Archive, n.d., https://www.crmvet.org/tim/timhis64.htm#1964allen.

Cunningham, *Civil Rights Movement in Mississippi*, 194.

Navasky, *Kennedy Justice*.

Harold Titus, *Harold Titus's Blog* (blog), Goodreads, February 9, 2020, https://www .goodreads.com/author/show/5390145.Harold_Titus/blog/tag/john-doar.

Archived document: Investigation of Dynamite Bombings of Negro Homes in McComb, MS, report by Virgil Downing, June 24, 1964 (from Barlow Roberts).

Barlow Roberts, "C. C. Bryant."

Umoja, *We Will Shoot Back*.

Umoja, "1964: The Beginning of the End."

Harold Titus, "Civil Rights Events—Mississippi 1961–1962—Bob Moses, Voter Registration, and McComb," *Harold Titus's Blog* (blog), Goodreads, February 9, 2020, https://www.goodreads.com/author/show/5390145.Harold_Titus /blog/tag/john-doar.

Newton, *Ku Klux Klan in Mississippi*.

Carter, *So the Heffners Left McComb*.

Chapter 12

In addition to personal interviews with Curtis Muhammad, D. Gorton, Patsy Ruth Butler, Jane Adams, Curtis Bryant, and "Private video interview with Aylene Quin," sources used for background information include the following:

Barlow Roberts, "C. C. Bryant."

Dittmer, *Local People*.

Wayne King, "McComb, Miss., Absorbing Changes Born of Bombs and Burning Crosses," *New York Times*, April 2, 1978, https://www.nytimes.com/1978/04/02 /archives/mccomb-miss-absorbing-changes-born-of-bombs-and-burning -crosses.html#:~:text=Wave%20of%20Bombings,%2C%20capital%20of%20 the%20world.%E2%80%9D

"*the situation in Mississippi to be very dangerous*": This and the following details of the FBI assessment of the danger in Mississippi are from Dittmer, *Local People*, 238.

"It's like having the lights": William Sturkey, "'I Want to Become a Part of History':
Freedom Summer, Freedom Schools, and the *Freedom News*," *Journal of African American History* 95, no. 3-4 (Summer-Fall 2010): 348-368.

"all anxious to learn about how to be Free": "Freedom Schools in Mississippi, 1964," http://www.educationanddemocracy.org/FSCfiles/B_16_FSchools InMSFusco.htm.

"They would bring dogs and stuff": Oral history with Joe Martin, University of Southern Mississippi Center for Oral History and Cultural Heritage, http://crdl.usg.edu/export/html/usm/coh/crdl_usm_coh_mus-ohmartin .html?Welcome.

"We most certainly do not": Umoja, "1964: The Beginning of the End."

"Next time they came round the block": "White Man Ain't Never Going to Let Us Vote," *New Republic*, October 24, 1964.

Chapter 13

In addition to personal interviews with Freddie Biddle, John Dittmer, Earl Neil, Curtis Muhammad, Jacqueline Quin, and "Private video interview with Aylene Quin," sources used include the following.

Background details on the MFDP convention are drawn, in part, from these digital archives:

"MFDP Holds Convention," SNCC Digital Gateway, n.d., https://snccdigital.org /events/mfdp-holds-state-convention/.

"MFDP Challenge to the Democratic Convention," Civil Rights Movement Archive, n.d., https://www.crmvet.org/info/mfdp_atlantic.pdf.

"Building the Mississippi Freedom Democratic Party," SNCC Digital Gateway, n.d., https://snccdigital.org/events/building-the-mfdp/.

Carter, *So the Heffners Left McComb*.

Dittmer, *Local People*.

Chapter 14

In addition to personal interviews with Curtis Muhammad, Jacqueline Quin, Marshall Ganz, and "Private video interview with Aylene Quin," sources used include the following:

"the toughest anti-civil rights community": Wayne King, "McComb, Miss., Absorbing Changes Born of Bombs and Burning Crosses," *New York Times*, April 2, 1978,

https://www.nytimes.com/1978/04/02/archives/mccomb-miss-absorbing -changes-born-of-bombs-and-burning-crosses.html#:~:text=Wave%20 of%20Bombings,%2C%20capital%20of%20the%20world.%E2%80%9D.

"will be America's hottest year; her hottest year yet": Malcolm X, "The Black Revolution" (speech, April 8, 1964).

Details of the bombing and aftermath are also drawn from "Two Bombings Anger Mississippi Crowd," *New York Times*, September 22, 1964, https://www .nytimes.com/1964/09/22/archives/2-bombings-anger-mississippi-crowd.html.

Dittmer, *Local People*.

Harold Titus, "Civil Rights Events—Mississippi 1961–1962—Bob Moses, Voter Registration, and McComb."

Chapter 15

In addition to personal interviews with Frankye Adams-Johnson, Cleo Silvers, Bill Johnson, Kathy Goldman, Yasmeen Majid, and Dequi Kioni Sediki, the following sources were used:

"The pigs say, 'well the Breakfast for Children Program'": This and details about Fred Hampton are sourced from Jeffrey Haas, *The Assassination of Fred Hampton: How the FBI and the Chicago Police Murdered a Black Panther* (Chicago: Chicago Review Press, 2019).

Background information on United Bronx Parents and Evelina Antonetty is sourced from a personal interview with Kathy Goldman and Lana Dee Povitz, *Stirrings: How Activist New Yorkers Ignited a Movement for Food Justice* (Chapel Hill: University of North Carolina Press, 2019).

"tended to argue for an assertion": Rhodes, *Framing the Black Panthers*.

"Female Panthers often tested and stretched": Tracye Matthews, "'No One Ever Asks What a Man's Role in the Revolution Is': Gender and the Politics of the Black Panther Party, 1966–1971," in *The Black Panther Party [Reconsidered]*, ed. Charles E. Jones (Baltimore: Black Classic Press, 1998), 167–304.

"explicitly political and public function": Matthews, "'No One Ever Asks What a Man's Role in the Revolution Is,'" 167–304.

Other sources that provided background context and details include:

Barbara Molony and Jennifer Nelson, *Women's Activism and "Second Wave" Feminism* (London: Bloomsbury Academic, 2017), https://www.bloomsbury collections.com/book/womens-activism-and-second-wave-feminism/.

Lucy Burns, "Free Breakfast with the Black Panthers," *Witness History*, BBC, September 18, 2019, https://www.bbc.co.uk/programmes/w3csyx4p.

"Frankye Adams Johnson Oral History Interview Conducted by Emilye Crosby in Jackson, Mississippi, 2015, December 06" (Library of Congress, 2015), https://www.loc.gov/item/2016655414/.

Mary Potorti, "Feed the Revolution: The Black Panther Party, Hunger, and Community Survival." Journal of African American Studies 21, no. 1 (March 2017).

Haas, *Assassination of Fred Hampton.*

Payne, *What We Want, What We Believe.*

Chapter 16

In addition to personal interviews with Cleo Silvers, Dequi Kioni Sediki, Mae Jackson, Frankye Adams-Johnson, and Bill Johnson, the following sources were used.

Details on the investigations of Chicago-based Black Panther Party members are sourced from Haas, *Assassination of Fred Hampton.*

Details on the investigations of New York City– and West Coast–based Black Panther Party members along with quotes from Bob Bloom are sourced from:

Payne, *What We Want, What We Believe.*

Churchill and Vander Wall, *Agents of Repression.*

The party often referred to them as "pigs": "Seizing the Narrative: How the Panthers Invented 'Pigs,'" *The Cahokian*, July 25, 2015, http://thecahokian.blogspot.com/2015/07/seizing-narrative-how-panthers-invented.html.

"not only militant but also militaristic": "Extremists: The Panthers' Bite," *Time*, September 20, 1968, 29, http://content.time.com/time/subscriber/article/0,33009,838736,00.html.

"We fight capitalism with basic socialism": Seale, *Seize the Time.*

"In our view it is a class struggle between": Seale, *Seize the Time.*

"I don't like cops, but": personal interview.

"We know that people didn't have": Donna Murch, *Living for the City*, 175–176.

"the Chicago police broke into the church": Nik Heynen, "Bending the Bars of Empire from Every Ghetto for Survival: The Black Panther Party's Radical Antihunger Politics of Social Reproduction and Scale," *Annals of the Association of American Geographers* 99, no. 2 (May 1, 2009): 406–422, https://doi.org/https://doi.org/10.1080/00045600802683767.

Details about the coloring book propaganda are sourced from Ann-Derrick Gaillot, "When Is a Children's Coloring Book Really an FBI Conspiracy?" *The Outline*, February 7, 2018, https://theoutline.com/post/3321/black-panther -coloring-book-fbi-conspiracy.

Other details about FBI tactics are from archived documents sourced from the Tamiment Archives at New York University.

As Chicago Panther Doc Satchel said: Haas, *Assassination of Fred Hampton*. Details from and about FBI memos were all from the Tamiment Archive within NYU Library system: TAM 612 - box 20, 21 7 PE.036, Box: 14, 15.

Other sources that provided background and context in this chapter include: Odinga, Wahad, Om, and Joseph, *Look for Me in the Whirlwind*. Murch, *Living for the City*. Churchill and Vander Wall, *Agents of Repression*.

Chapter 17

In addition to personal interviews with Cleo Silvers, the following sources were used.

Details about the arrests are sourced from:

Murray Kempton, *The Briar Patch: The Trial of the Panther 21* (Cambridge, MA: Da Capo Press, 1997).
Odinga, Wahad, Om, and Joseph, *Look for Me in the Whirlwind*.
Jamal Joseph, *Panther Baby: A Life of Rebellion and Reinvention* (Chapel Hill, NC: Algonquin Books, 2012).

Note that at times this recounting conflicts with interviews and other personal accounts. I have strived to not repeat details that were likely in conflict or written with bias, but perhaps inadvertently did so.

"I don't know what they're talking about": *Bobby Seale Discusses Arrest of the New York 21 w Tupac Mom*, 1969, https://www.youtube.com/watch?v=G5PEQp7k_WE.

Chapter 18

In addition to personal interviews with Father Earl Neil, Marshall Ganz, and "Private video interview with Aylene Quin," the following sources were used:

"nonviolence in the face of terrible measures": Howard Zinn, quoted in Jon Meacham, *His Truth Is Marching On: John Lewis and the Power of Hope* (New York: Random House, 2020), e-book.

"*We said we'd stay till the next day*": "White Man Ain't Never Going to Let Us Vote," *New Republic*, October 24, 1964.

The dialogue from the Oval Office scenes is sourced from an archive of White House recordings.

Jan Jarboe Russell, *Lady Bird: A Biography of Mrs. Johnson* (New York: Scribner, 2016).

"*After we talked to him they asked us not to tell*": "White Man Ain't Never Going to Let Us Vote."

"*In justifying his leniency*": Dittmer, *Local People*, 311.

The details and dialogue of the event on October 27, 1964, are taken from an affidavit written by Marshall Ganz immediately after the event: "Affidavit of Marshall Ganz, October 27, 1964," Civil Rights Movement Archive, n.d., https://www.crmvet.org/nars/aff/641027_sncc_mcc_marshallganz_affidavit.pdf.

"*So I myself would go for nonviolence*": Malcolm X, "Malcolm X's Speech to Civil Rights Workers from Mississippi (Jan. 1, 1965)," https://www.icit-digital .org/articles/malcolm-x-s-speech-to-civil-rights-workers-from-mississippi -jan-1-1965.

Additional sources used for context and background include:

Thomas Rozwadowski, "On the Right Side of History," *Charleton College Voice*, Spring 2016, https://apps.carleton.edu/voice/?story_id=1422145&issue_id=1420001.
"Mendy Samstein," SNCC Digital Gateway, n.d., e/.

Chapter 19

In addition to personal interviews with Jacqueline Quin, Muriel Tillinghast, Dequi Kioni Sediki, Marshall Ganz, and "Private video interview with Aylene Quin," the following sources were used.

Details and dialogue about the June 17, 1965, event are sourced from the following:

"Matt Herron and Dorie Ladner Remember the Mississippi Freedom Movement," Teaching for Change, September 7, 2014, https://www.teachingforchange.org /matt-herron-dorie-ladner-event.
"We Shall Not Be Moved," *We Shall Not Be Moved* (blog), n.d., https://blog.not bemoved.com/post/92529841456/this-light-of-ours-activist-photographers -in-the/embed.

"This Light of Ours: Activist Photographers in the Civil Rights Movement," *We Shall Not Be Moved* (blog), n.d. https://blog.notbemoved.com/post/92529841456 /this-light-of-ours-activist-photographers-in-the/embed.

"The '60s at 50," *The '60s at 50* (blog), June 29, 2015, http://the60sat50.blogspot. com/2015/06/.

"Tuesday, June 29, 1965: 'Murder in Mississippi,'" *The '60s at 50* (blog), June 29, 2015, http://the60sat50.blogspot.com/2015/06/.

Paul L. Montgomery, "103 More Pickets Held in Jackson; March Fails to Materialize—Arrests Reach 856," *New York Times*, June 19, 1965, https://www .nytimes.com/1965/06/19/archives/103-more-pickets-held-in-jackson-march -fails-to-materialize-arrests.html.

Alex Selwyn-Holmes, "Mississippi, Matt Herron," Iconic Photos, June 25, 2011, https://iconicphotos.wordpress.com/2011/06/25/mississippi-matt-herron/.

Constance Hale, "Mississippi Eyes," *Princeton Alumni Weekly*, June 4, 2014, https://paw.princeton.edu/article/mississippi-eyes.

"*use whatever measures are necessary*": "Wallace Orders troopers to Stop Negro Marchers," UPI Archives, March 6, 1965, https://www.upi.com/Archives/1965 /03/06/Wallace-orders-troopers-to-stop-Negro-marchers/2541162885347/

Details about the KKK and the House Committee on Un-American Activities are sourced from:

Dittmer, *Local People*.

George Lewis, "'An Amorphous Code': The Ku Klux Klan and Un-Americanism, 1915–1965," special issue, *Journal of American Studies* 47, no. 4 (November 2013): 971–992.

"*We trailed that march*": This and other quotes and details telling the story of SNCC in Lowndes County are sourced from:

Benjamin Hedin, "From Selma to Black Power," *Atlantic*, March 6, 2015, https:// www.theatlantic.com/national/archive/2015/03/from-selma-to-black-power /386989/.

Hasan Kwame Jeffries, "Lowndes County and the Voting Rights Act," Zinn Education Project (Rethinking Schools and Teaching for Change, n.d.), https://www .zinnedproject.org/materials/lowndes-county-and-the-voting-rights-act/.

Jeffries, *Bloody Lowndes*.

The details on the June 1966 "March Against Fear" scenes are sourced from personal interviews and:

James Forman, *The Making of Black Revolutionaries* (Seattle: University of Washington Press, 1997).

"*Suppose when I get over there to Mississippi*": This and subsequent quotes within the scene come from Forman, *Making of Black Revolutionaries*, 456–457.

"*Thus the white people coming into the movement*": Miller, *Soul Food*, 45.

"*burdens many African American women*": Melissa V. Harris-Perry, *Sister Citizen* (New Haven, CT: Yale University Press, 2011).

"*stubborn endurance of the structures*": Kimberlé Williams Crenshaw, quoted in Jane Coaston, "The Intersectionality Wars," *Vox*, May 28, 2019.

See also:

Kimberlé Williams Crenshaw, "Demarginalizing the Intersection of Race and Sex: A Black Feminist Critique of Antidiscrimination Doctrine, Feminist Theory and Antiracist Politics," *University of Chicago Legal Forum* 1989, no. 1, https://chicago unbound.uchicago.edu/cgi/viewcontent.cgi?article=1052&context=uclf.

"*The [B]lack man in America is the only one*": Malcolm X, "The Ballot or the Bullet" (speech).

"*We often tell the story of Black Power*": Eddie Glaude, interview, *Democracy Now!*, July 27, 2020, https://www.democracynow.org/2020/7/27/eddie_glaude _john_lewis.

Statistics about the Voting Rights Act and its impact are sourced from:

"Voting Rights Act of 1965," History.com, November 9, 2009, https://www.history .com/topics/black-history/voting-rights-act.

"Mississippi State Profile 2018," Ballotpedia, n.d., https://ballotpedia.org /Mississippi_state_profile_2018.

"*There's nothing better than get up*": Fannie Lou Hamer, quoted in Maegan Parker Brooks, *A Voice That Could Stir an Army: Fannie Lou Hamer and the Rhetoric of the Black Freedom Movement* (Jackson: University Press of Mississippi, 2014), e-book.

I owe a great debt to the scholarship on and insight into the roles of women during this time by the Black female scholars cited here and elsewhere. And even as we increasingly value these roles through a more progressive retelling of history, Melissa V. Harris-Perry, author of *Sister Citizen*, and others also note how even the perception of the strong or selfless Black woman can be just as limiting. I wish I had the room to more fully explore these nuances, but do read the sources noted, referenced in the chapter and elsewhere in these endnotes, and in the reading list at the front of the book.

Chapter 20

In addition to personal interviews with Cleo Silvers, Dequi Kioni Sediki, Panama Alba, the following sources were used:

"*Party representatives were increasingly*": Rhodes, *Framing the Black Panthers,* e-book.

"Is It Too Late for You to Be Pals with a Black Panther?," *Esquire,* November 1, 1970.

KPFA radio documentary details are sourced from the following:

Revolution for Breakfast, KPFA, August 14, 1970, https://www.pacificaradio archives.org/recording/bb2540.

"*fascination and fear*": Russonello, "Fascination and Fear: Covering the Black Panthers."

"*who were able to do much better*": Rhodes, *Framing of the Black Panthers.*

Details on the Conference for a United Front Against Fascism are sourced from:

Payne, *What We Want, What We Believe.*

The Black reporter Earl Caldwell: This paragraph references the following:

Earl Caldwell, "Panthers' Meeting Shifts Aims from Racial Confrontation to Class Struggle," *New York Times,* July 22, 1969, https://www.nytimes .com/1969/07/22/archives/panthers-meeting-shifts-aims-from-racial -confrontation-to-class.html.

Earl Caldwell, "They Are Not the Same Organization," *New York Times,* July 27, 1969, https://timesmachine.nytimes.com/timesmachine/1969/07/27/89356043 .html?pageNumber=143.

This movement to not just mobilize Black people": The quotes and details in this paragraph are sourced from Payne, *What We Want, What We Believe.*

"*From these thinkers, whose writings*": Alondra Nelson, *Body and Soul: The Black Panther Party and the Fight Against Medical Discrimination* (Minneapolis: University of Minnesota Press, 2011), 73.

"*We knew we were being railroaded*": Joseph, *Panther Baby,* 118.

"*Since nobody else was going*": Joseph, *Panther Baby,* 119.

Details of Fred Hampton's murder are sourced from Haas, *Assassination of Fred Hampton.*

Additional sources used for background research and context include:

Odinga, Wahad, Om, and Joseph, *Look for Me in the Whirlwind.*

Nelson, *Body and Soul.*

Alondra Nelson, "'Genuine Struggle and Care': An Interview With Cleo Silvers," *American Journal of Public Health* 106, no. 10 (October 2016): 1744–1748, https://www.ncbi.nlm.nih.gov/pmc/articles/PMC5024401/.

"The Black Panther Party Stands for Health," *Public Health Now*, February 23, 2016, https://www.publichealth.columbia.edu/public-health-now/news /black-panther-party-stands-health.

"Lincoln Detox Center—Interview with Vicente 'Panama' Alba," Montreal Counter-Information, n.d., https://mtlcounterinfo.org/lincoln-detox-center-interview -with-vicente-panama-alba/.

Chapter 21

In addition to personal interviews with Cleo Silvers and Yasmeen Majid, the following sources were used:

"group therapy plus fund-raising soirée" and quotes from Jamie Bernstein are sourced from: Chisholm, Kate. "The Panther 21 Fundraiser and 'Radical Chic,'" LeonardBernstein.com., accessed April 20, 2021, https://leonardbern stein.com/about/humanitarian/radical-chic-flap.

Quotes from Tom Wolfe and details of the party, including the speech by Don Cox, are sourced from: Tom Wolfe, "Radical Chic: That Party at Lenny's," *New York*, June 8, 1970, https://nymag.com/news/features/46170/.

Additional sources used to describe the Bernstein event and its aftermath include:

"When Leonard Bernstein partied with the Black Panthers," BBC, March 29, 2018, https://www.bbc.co.uk/programmes/articles/3dWyNLc1rMqSnXytbgwhjnh /when-leonard-bernstein-partied-with-the-black-panthers.

Lanre Bakare, "How Hollywood Feted the Black Power Movement—and Fell Foul of the FBI," *Guardian*, December 5, 2019, https://www.theguardian .com/film/2019/dec/05/how-hollywood-feted-the-black-power-movement -and-fell-foul-of-the-fbi.

Additional sources used for background, context, and details on the Panther 21 trials and immediate aftermath include:

Joseph, *Panther Baby*.

Odinga, Wahad, Om, and Joseph, *Look for Me in the Whirlwind*.

Edith Evans Asbury, "Black Panther Party Members Freed After Being Cleared of Charges," *New York Times*, May 14, 1971, https://www.nytimes.com/1971/05/14

/archives/black-panther-party-members-freed-after-being-cleared-of
-charges-13.html.

Murray Kempton, *The Briar Patch: The Trial of the Panther 21* (Cambridge, MA:
Da Capo Press, 1997).

Churchill and Vander Wall, *Agents of Repression*.

Payne, *What We Want, What We Believe*.

"*I was responsible for giving political education*": Nelson, *Body and Soul*, 87.

Details and quotes about the Lincoln Hospital takeover on July 14, 1970, are
sourced from the following:

Alfonso A. Narvaez, "Young Lords Seize Lincoln Hospital Building," *New York
Times*, July 15, 1970, https://www.nytimes.com/1970/07/15/archives/young
-lords-seize-lincoln-hospital-building-offices-are-held-for-12.html.

Josiah Omotosho, "Young Lords Recall 1970 Hospital Takeover," *Bronx Journal*,
September 29, 2015, http://bronxjournal.com/?p=18769.

Chapter 22

In addition to personal interviews with Jacqueline Quin, Cleo Silvers, Yasmeen
Majid, Curtis Muhammad, Frankye Adams-Johnson, Dequi Kioni Sediki, and
Kathy Goldman, the following sources were used.

Do read Stacey Abrams's books, both of which deal with voter suppression
and her leadership in Georgia and around the country: *Our Time Is Now* (New
York: Henry Holt, 2020) and *Lead from the Outside* (New York: Henry Holt, 2018).

The details around Shirley Chisholm's role on the Agriculture Committee
were sourced from the following and corroborated elsewhere:

Dovid Zaklikowski, "Turning Disappointment Into Food for the Hungry," Chabad
.org, accessed April 21, 2021, https://www.chabad.org/therebbe/article_cdo
/aid/558041/jewish/Turning-Disappointment-Into-Food-for-the-Hungry.htm.

The details about the Citizens' Commission break-in on March 8, 1971, are
sourced from Churchill and Vander Wall, *Agents of Repression*.

"*caused people to realize, including the U.S. Congress*": Liam Know, "Remembering the Burglary That Broke COINTELPRO," Muckrock.com, March 8, 2019,
https://www.muckrock.com/news/archives/2019/mar/08/fbi-media
-anniversary/.

The scene of the Panthers in 1973 is sourced from Nelson, *Body and Soul*.

INDEX